1000

HOUSEKEEPING

HINTS

1000 HOUSEKEEPING HINTS

Jean McGlone
Daphne Metland

CONTENTS

First published in 1984 by
Octopus Books Limited
This edition published 1985 by
Octopus Books Limited
59 Grosvenor Street
London W1

ISBN 0 7064 2426 3

Printed and bound in Great Britain
by Collins Glasgow

Illustrations by Mike Miller and Stan North.

1. About the House

QUICK TIPS FOR EVERYDAY JOBS

Bath cleaner and a cloth left in the bathroom, combined with your favourite method of bribery, nagging or persuasion will train the family to clean the bath and wash the basin immediately after use.

Bubble bath is a good investment for children as it saves having to clean the bath afterwards. It also cleans the children with the minimum of fuss.

A cleaning caddy or tray containing polish brushes and cloths can be carried around the house as you clean, and will keep everything to hand. The whole caddy can then be put away in a cupboard after use.

A clutter box is well worth having if there are children in the house. Choose a large cardboard box and stand it under the stairs or in the hall. After a quick daily tidy up, put all the books, gloves, shoes and miscellaneous family debris into it. When cries of 'Mum where's my book/hat/shoe laces' start, you can direct everyone to the clutter box. Anything remaining in the box at the end of the week or month can be sent to the local Oxfam shop or jumble sale. This threat is usually sufficient to clear the box instantly.

Cobwebs can be removed using a duster tied on to a soft broom.

Curtains can be easily dusted using the vacuum cleaner attachment. This is worth doing regularly as dust and dirt left in the fibre for long periods will rot it, with the result that the curtains fall to pieces when washed.

Doormats save a great deal of work as the worst of mud and dust is walked off before the main carpets are reached. Use in porches as well as inside front and back doors.

Dust a room starting from the higher surfaces and work downwards. An old-fashioned feather duster or its modern synthetic equivalent is useful for light fittings and high shelves. Dust after vacuuming.

Finish vacuuming upstairs, then leave the cleaner tucked away on the landing, ready to start vacuuming upstairs the next time. Next time, leave it downstairs and work in the opposite order. This saves carrying the cleaner around needlessly.

Food mixers, processors and other kitchen equipment can be quickly cleaned of food splashes and greasy marks with a little cream cleanser on a damp cloth.

A multipurpose spray cleaner that can be used on wood, glass and plastic is a real timesaver when in a hurry, as almost all the hard surfaces in a room can be polished at once.

A polishing mit can be made from an old woollen sock. Wash and wear like a glove when dusting and polishing.

Saucepans are much easier to clean if they are filled with warm water and a little washing-up liquid as soon as they are emptied. Very dirty pans can be soaked overnight in a little biological washing powder. Wash and rinse, then boil up some fresh water to remove all traces of detergent.

Sheets that have been allowed to become completely dry are hard to iron. If you have an electric blanket, put the sheets on the bed creased, and turn the blanket on for about half an hour. This will get rid of all the creases with little effort. Only do this with a completely dry sheet, and cover it with the quilt or blankets to keep the warmth in. Alternatively, fold and stack the sheets in a pile in the airing cupboard. The weight of the sheets will do most of the ironing for you, on the underneath sheets at least.

Sofas and chairs collect all sorts of dust, dirt and often small toys and loose coins. It is worth checking under cushions if you are short of small change, but also remember to remove cushions and vacuum underneath regularly to extend the life of the chairs and prevent sharp objects tearing the cushions.

Tablecloths made of linen look good but do need a lot of washing and ironing. For family use, a thick PVC tablecloth makes a practical alternative as it can be wiped over after each meal. PVC can be bought by the yard and is available in a wide range of designs. Cut to shape using pinking shears.

Washing up that cannot be tackled at once is best stacked in a bowl and covered with warm water, with a little washing-up liquid added. This prevents food particles drying on.

Wastepaper bins can be lined with a circle of wallpaper or folded newspaper to make them quick to empty. This also protects the bin and reduces the need to clean it.

Wear an apron with large pockets when cleaning, so that all the odds and ends you discover as you go around the house can be picked up immediately, to be sorted out later.

Spring Cleaning

Our grandmothers and great grandmothers tackled spring cleaning with great enthusiasm, turning out whole rooms, changing curtains, washing walls and taking down chandeliers, so that each piece could be washed and buffed up before rehanging. We rarely spring clean on this scale now, partly because our homes are smaller and simpler but also because we no longer have to cope with the by-products of open fires and gas lighting. When the sharp spring sunlight shone through Victorian windows it was possibly the first time for many months that the room had been lit well enough to show up the cobwebs and dust in the corners. Nowadays, however, our homes are probably much cleaner all year round than most homes were at the turn of the century, despite the small armies of housemaids who scrubbed and polished from dawn to dusk.

Nevertheless, there are still cleaning jobs we only tackle occasionally and we do sometimes need to clean a whole room, especially when moving house or in preparation for all over redecoration.

It is important to work to some kind of order, and not to clear several rooms in the initial flurry of energy only to find all the clearing up is waiting to be done late into the evening.

As a start, it is worth trying to offload children and pets while spring cleaning, or choose a warm day when they can be banished to the garden. Very small children love helping, which is fine for general cleaning jobs, but extra care is needed when working with ladders, strong cleaners and buckets of hot soapy water. Also, once the average three-year-old has been persuaded that it is in order to swill water on the walls and floors while spring cleaning, he does tend to carry on doing it! Pets can be equally disastrous, so try to find a like-minded friend who will look after your children and pets while you spring clean, and on whom you can descend for a hot lunch and a welcome rest! Offer to do the same for her while she spring cleans.

BATHROOMS

This room is usually cleaned regularly but the effects of the steamy atmosphere on paintwork and windows, plus the general wear and tear produced by the average family all trying to use the bathroom at once, mean that it does require a good spring clean.

Bathmats can be made from various materials.

* If made of sealed cork they just need to be wiped with a damp cloth.
* If they are unsealed cork, seal them yourself, otherwise wipe with a damp cloth.
* Small plastic mats can be washed in the sink in soapy water. Large ones will need to be cleaned outside with soapy water and a stiff brush.
* Fabric bathmats can usually be washed: follow the care label instructions.

Baths were traditionally made in vitreous enamel.

* This can be cleaned with a good cream cleanser. Avoid harsh powder cleaners, as they cause fine scratching on the surface.
* In hard water areas there is often a build-up of hard water deposits around the plughole, the overflow and the taps. Dripping taps can also stain the bath. There are proprietary cleaners that will remove these stains, available from hardware shops, but do use and store these with care, as they are very strong solutions. Follow the manufacturer's instructions carefully and store them out of the reach of children.
* If these stains are not too ingrained, try dipping a cut lemon in salt and working this into the stained area, leave to stand for a couple of minutes, then rinse well. Do not leave for longer, as the acidic effects may damage the enamel. Repeat this procedure if necessary several times, rinsing well in between.
* Deposits around taps can be cleaned with an old toothbrush dipped in cream cleanser.

* Gold-plated taps should only ever be cleaned with warm water and a soft cloth.

Plastic or acrylic baths and basins have been introduced over recent years and these need a different cleaning system.
* For day-to-day cleaning wipe with washing-up liquid on a cloth.
* Resistant stains can be rubbed with half a lemon, then rinsed well.
* Light scratches and dull areas can be improved with a little silver polish. Rub in, then buff up.
* Don't forget to clean the outside of the basin and the side of the bath, as well as washing soap dishes and containers.

Bidets are made of ceramic.
* Wipe daily with a mild detergent or soapy solution. Use this treatment on the taps as well.
* More stubborn marks can be removed with a smooth cream cleaner.
* Never use a powder cleaner on ceramic ware as it is abrasive and may damage the surface.

Blinds and curtains should be removed if possible and washed or dusted down before replacing (see pages 39 and 48).
* Plastic hooks may need washing.
* Pull-cords on blinds benefit from dusting down to ensure they run smoothly.
* A little petroleum jelly smeared on exposed metal ends of blinds will help protect them from the effects of steam.

Flooring needs to be treated according to type.
* Sealed cork tiles, vinyl and lino can all be mopped lightly with floor cleaner.
* Waxed cork tiles and wood floors need a liquid solvent-based polish.
* Loose rugs can be lifted and shaken outside.
* Recently, special carpeting for bathrooms and kitchens has been introduced. To look after it, follow the instructions supplied with the carpet.
* Avoid putting natural jute-backed carpet in the bathroom as the backing can be affected by damp.

Light fittings do need occasional dusting.

* Make sure the fitment is switched off and the bulb is cool. Remove with dry hands, dust and, if necessary, wipe with a well wrung out cloth. Wipe dry and replace the bulb. Dust around the fitting, with a feather duster or dusting cloth.
* Murphy's Law dictates that the more difficult the light fitting is to reach, the more often the bulb will need replacing, so while cleaning the fitment, it may well be worth replacing the light bulb.

Medicine chests need regular sorting out.

* Old medicines, whether bottles or pills, should be returned to the chemist. It is not always safe to flush them down the toilet.
* Never use up old medicines, or give prescribed medicines to anyone else.
* Wipe out the cupboard with a damp cloth and general purpose cream cleanser. Check that the locking system is still child-proof before re-using.

Mirrors can be cleaned with a damp cloth and a little washing-up liquid, a strong vinegar solution (see page 33), or any good window cleaner.

* Remove hairspray with methylated spirit on cotton wool.
* Prevent steaming up by rubbing with a little neat washing-up liquid, or use an antimisting product.

Paintwork can be washed down using washing-up liquid and warm water.

* Do not use washing powders as these may affect the appearance of the paintwork.
* Dust picture rails, ledges and door panelling before washing, to prevent the dust sticking to the wet woodwork.
* On really dirty walls, work from the bottom upwards to avoid streaky lines running through the dirt, as these are very difficult to remove. Use two buckets, one with soapy water and one with rinsing water. Wet the cloth or sponge in the soapy water, clean a small area, then rinse the cloth in the other bucket. Repeat on the next small area. This avoids putting dirt back on the wall. Rinse, following the same procedure. On lightly soiled walls, this is not so important and the wall can be washed from top to bottom.

* Protect carpets and flooring with old sheets or newspaper before you begin.

* Very dirty paintwork can be washed with a weak sugar soap solution, available from DIY stores and hardware shops. Make up in half strength following the directions on the packet, and use as for soapy water.
* Try using a squeeze mop for large areas.

Potplants benefit from the occasional soak, so while spring cleaning the bathroom remove all the plants to the kitchen sink and stand them in an inch or so of water.

* Clean dust from the leaves with a damp cloth or use a leaf-shine product and check if any plants need repotting.

Shower curtains can sometimes develop dark spots of mildew.

* Wash with a mild bleach or antiseptic solution, using 2 teaspoons of solution to ½ litre (1 pint) water, and wipe dry. Avoid this problem by pulling the curtain across after use to allow air to circulate and dry the curtain.
* The shower head can sometimes be cleaned as well. Modern plastic shower heads can often be removed and taken to pieces. Ensure both water and power are turned off first, then remove the shower head and wash the plastic rings in warm water and vinegar (use about one tablespoon of vinegar to ½ litre (1 pint) water.
* For a build-up of hard water deposit on chrome showerheads use a cut lemon, as described on page 12.
* Scrub the pieces with an old toothbrush to remove hard water deposits, which sometimes slow down the water flow. Dry the pieces and put them back together again.

Shower trays should be wiped daily with a mild detergent or warm soapy water. For stubborn marks use a very smooth cream cleaner.

Sponges, the real ones, sometimes become quite slimy.

* Wash them in a weak vinegar solution (see page 33) and allow them to dry naturally, outside if possible.

Tiles can be wiped over with a cream cleanser and a damp cloth, then rinse off. In hard water areas, tiles often show water splashes even when completely clean. This is particularly noticeable on dark shiny colours.

* Rinse the tiles with warm water and vinegar, in equal amounts, then wipe dry and buff up.
* If the grouting becomes blackened with mildew, this can be cleaned using an old toothbrush and a half household bleach, half water solution. Take care though; protect the bath and basin with polythene or thick pads of newspaper and your

hands with rubber gloves. Stand well back as you do this to prevent the solution splashing you. Work with the window open on small areas at a time, rinsing as you go.

* Better still, cure the problem that is causing the mildew. Adequate ventilation is very important in a bathroom: fit a ventilator or a fan in the window if possible, or train the family to open the window for a short period after having a bath or shower, until the steam has cleared.

Washbasins are made of ceramic.

* Wipe down daily with a mild soap solution, rinse and dry.
* Use the same soap solution on the taps.
* Stronger cleaners should be used only if necessary and then only sparingly. Never use abrasive powder cleaners which may damage the surface.

Wastebins need regular emptying and should be lined with a bin liner or circle of wallpaper.

* Wicker bins can be washed out-of-doors with warm soapy water and salt, then scrubbed lightly with a brush. Wipe round and allow to dry naturally.
* Plastic bins can be washed in warm soapy water to which a little disinfectant has been added.
* Do not use metal bins in the bathroom as they will rust.

WC pans need frequent cleaning.

* Clean the pan with a soft brush and a recommended cleanser.
* Pay particular attention to cleaning under the rim.
* Don't use harsh cleansers which may damage the glaze.
* Wash the seat, handle or chain and surrounding areas with warm soapy water and disinfectant.
* Wash the toilet brush in hot water and disinfectant.
* Hygiene is particularly important with children in the house, as toddlers are usually fascinated with the toilet and will happily try to sail boats in it or even post small items like alarm clocks to see what happens to them!

Windows may need dusting, then washing.

* Use a strong vinegar solution (see page 33) using warm water on the glass, then buff up with crumpled newspaper. Or use a window cleaner. (See also 'Paintwork'.)

BEDROOMS

Bedheads may well need cleaning.

* Upholstered ones can generally be vacuumed and shampooed with upholstery shampoo.
* Brass bedsteads can be cleaned with a brass cleaner. If very tarnished, clean with a lemon dipped in salt, or a paste of vinegar, flour and salt in equal quantities. Both these mixtures must be washed off and the brass rinsed to prevent it affecting the metal but they are worth trying, as they are cheap and effective.
* Cane bedheads can be vacuumed and cleaned with a general purpose spray cleaner.

Beds, when moved away from the wall, generally reveal what looks like a year or two's dust lurking underneath.

* It is worthwhile pushing the vacuum cleaner attachment under the bed whenever possible to remove this before it builds up.
* With beds that have storage drawers or that come down to the floor this is not possible, and indeed it seems illogical that dust can collect underneath but it does, so move the bed out once a year and clean the carpet underneath thoroughly.

Blankets for the once-a-year spring clean can generally be washed.

* Choose a good warm day. If the blanket will fit in the washing machine, the job is much easier, but if it will not, consider taking it to the local launderette, where the washing machines are usually larger.
* Hand washing usually has to be done in the bath; soak first in cold water to remove as much dirt as possible, then wash in warm soapy water. Rinse several times to remove the suds, then drain the water off for an hour or so. Fold the blanket in the bath, squeezing while folding to press out as much water as possible. Place in a large washing up bowl, or an old baby bath to carry downstairs. Hang, still folded, on an airer in the garden and only hang on the line once partly dry. This will mean it is much lighter to handle and prevent too much stretching.
* If machine washing, use a wool programme with a very short spin as many blankets will lose their shape if spun for long

periods. Check the washcare label on any blanket before treating.
* Dry cleaning is another option, but do not use coin-operated dry cleaning machines as the fumes remaining in the blanket are noxious. Send to a specialist cleaner instead.

Duvets make bedmaking much easier and quicker. They should always be used with covers, as the duvet itself should not be cleaned unless absolutely necessary.
* Synthetic fillings can be washed, by hand or by machine.
* Feather and down-filled duvets cannot be washed and need to be sent to a specialist cleaner.
* In either case the filling is not improved by cleaning and it is best to avoid if possible. Instead use a cover, and deal with any spills and splashes as quickly as possible. Push the filling away from the affected area, hold it back with a large elastic band and treat the outer case.

Mattresses should be turned regularly, except graduated foam mattresses which need no turning.
* On old beds, where the springs are not enclosed, stains sometimes appear on the underside of the mattress, so an old blanket, or even a layer of thick paper between the springs and the mattress is a good idea.

Pillows whether filled with foam or feather, can be washed, but drying takes such a long time (especially the feathers) that it is best avoided.
* Always cover with a pillow case and treat spills and stains quickly. Push the filling away from the affected area and hold it back with an elastic band. Then spot treat the case as necessary.
* If washing is really necessary, use soap suds in the bath and squeeze the pillow lightly. Rinse well and, if possible, spin dry for a short period. If not, drain well on a folded towel, then hang out to dry. Turn the pillow over and round several times while drying to move the filling around. Only use again when completely dry. This could take several days.
* Never dry clean pillows in a coin-operated machine, as the fumes from dry cleaning fluids remain in the filling and are dangerous. Some specialist cleaners will treat pillows.

* If the covering to a pillow is badly damaged, either fit a new cover on top, or tack the new cover on to the end of the old one. Sew almost all the way round, then cut the end of the old cover, so that the filling can simply be shaken into the new case. Unpick the tacking and sew up neatly.

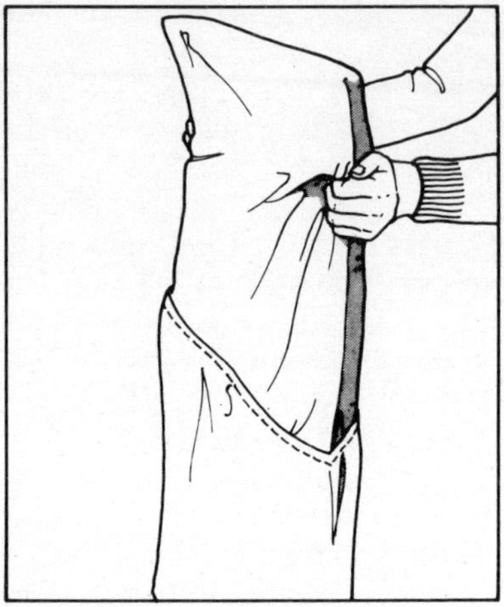

GENERAL ROOMS

Carpets generally remain looking good for most of the year, despite the constant daily wear they usually get.

* If spring sunshine gleaming on the carpet makes it look dull, try vacuuming first, then wring a cloth out in vinegar and warm water and wipe the carpet over with this. Sometimes this will remove a fine greasy layer on the carpet and brighten the colours.
* If this fails and shampooing is necessary, do a test patch first to make sure that the dye will not run. Apply a little foam shampoo on a hidden corner, work in with a brush and cover with a piece of white cloth. If the cloth picks up the colour of the carpet, abandon plans to shampoo it and either learn to love it as it is or call in a professional. If not, go ahead and use a foam shampoo. Spread it thinly and evenly over the carpet with a mop. Allow to dry, then vacuum off. Beware of over-wetting the carpet, which will cause shrinkage and protect the legs of furniture with little 'socks' made of cling film or paper. Treat existing stains before shampooing. (See A-Z Carpets, pages 35 to 37).
* Hot water extraction cleaning, sometimes incorrectly described as steam cleaning, is another alternative, both for carpets and upholstery. This can be done by a company or the cleaner can be hired by the day or week. It is often worthwhile

teaming up with several friends to hire one for a week and share the cost. The only problem is that they generally work so well you decide to clean the whole house and end up still cleaning at midnight because your neighbour is using it the next day! They are quite large heavy machines into which you put water and a cleaning agent. You then use them rather like a vacuum cleaner. They spray the hot water into the carpet, then suck it, and an amazing amount of dirt, out. You need a fine day, as there seems to be a great deal of moisture around, so doors and windows need to be opened. Keep the nozzle moving evenly and steadily. Beware of overwetting your carpets! This is very easy to do with a water extraction machine and can cause pile distortion, colour dilution and mildew with all the consequent possibilities of odour and rotting, especially where there are solid floors. Remember, too, that one method of cleaning may not suit all the carpets or upholstery in your house. Different fabrics require different treatments. Always do a test piece first on a hidden area of carpet or fabric, or on a spare piece, and if in any doubt, call in the professionals. Make sure any carpet cleaning firm you call in is a member of the Carpet Cleaners Association; the CCA ensures that customers can trust its members to carry out cleaning to a high consistent standard and to provide fair trading practices. They will use the cleaning method best suited to your carpets and will recognize any potential problems and will act accordingly.

Curtains Almost all benefit from occasional vacuuming to remove dust.

* Use the dusting attachment and concentrate on the folds at the top. If possible, take the curtains down and remove the hooks or rings. Unpleat the tops by pulling the tapes through (provided you have not cut the ends off), then air for an hour or so out on the line. This will help remove dust as well.
* It is possible to wash glass fibre curtains if you are careful. Wash them in a bath of warm soapy water, taking care not to fold or crush them. Wear rubber gloves as the little fibres can irritate the skin. Rinse well and lay them over parallel lines without folding, or put a few plastic hooks back in the tapes and hang by these on a line. Rehang at the window while still slightly damp and pull gently into shape. Do not iron.

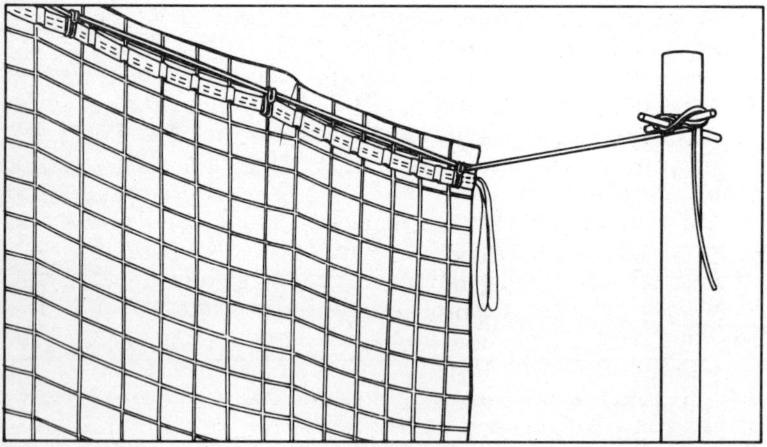

* Many types of curtains can be washed by hand or machine. Many fabrics shrink when washed, so allowance should be

made for this when buying curtains. Take the hem down before washing to aid removal of the hemline.
* Mark hook positions with nail varnish before washing.
* For hand washing, soak the curtains first in cold water to remove dust and dirt, then wash in warm soapy water, rinse well and hang out to dry.
* After ironing, rehang the curtains and re-pin for the new hem position.
* Wash plastic hooks and wipe plastic curtain tracks using warm soapy water. Dry, then polish with a silicone polish to encourage the curtains to pull smoothly.
* Rub metal tracks lightly with a little metal polish.
* Very large curtains and curtains made from cotton velvet, and other pile fabrics, wools, and some man-made fabrics should all be dry-cleaned. If in doubt, contact a specialist cleaner. (See also 'Net curtains'.)

Floorboards with an old seal can be renovated.
* Use a fine grade steel wool dipped in white spirit. Keep a window open and ensure any naked flames are extinguished. Work in small areas, mopping as you go. Allow to dry before applying a new coat of seal. Do not use wire wool on hardwood as it may cause iron staining.

Furniture is thankfully reasonably easy to look after.
* Natural wood needs regular dusting and polishing with furniture polish to keep it in good condition.
* Old stripped wood generally benefits from a light application of good wax polish or cabinet makers' polish.
* Finger marks on waxed furniture can be removed by wiping with a cloth wrung out in a mixture of 2 tablespoons of vinegar to ½ litre (1 pint) of warm water.
* French polished wood can simply be cleaned with a spray polish.
* Plastic furniture can be wiped with a damp cloth and often cleaned with a general purpose spray.

Net curtains often become very dirty at the window and it is not until they are taken down and washed that you realize how dirty they had become!
* Wash in plenty of warm soapy water, so that they can be

gently moved around. The bath is often the best place as a small bowl may cause the nets to become creased.

* Curtains that have become dingy may well respond to a nylon whitener sold specially for nets. Make sure you rinse and drain them well.
* One old-fashioned remedy for making fine nets look crisper is to dip the freshly-washed nets in a solution of 1 tablespoon of sugar and ½ litre (1 pint) of water. Hang the nets at the window while still slightly damp to allow the creases to drop and so avoid ironing.

Radiators are awkward to clean behind. Try padding the end of a garden bamboo cane, then tying an old sock over this. You should be able to reach the difficult parts with this.

Upholstery can usually be cleaned at home.

* Leather sofas and chairs can be kept supple by using the recommended polish occasionally. Some have special finishes, so keep and follow the makers' instructions. (See also 'Leather' on page 42).
* All sofas and chairs benefit from occasional vacuuming or thorough brushing. Remove all cushions and clean underneath, then vacuum and brush the arms and back of the sofa. Dust and dirt can penetrate the fibres and eventually rot them, so this regular cleaning is well worth while.
* Most fabrics can be shampooed, although some such as cotton velvet, chenilles, tapestry, silk and wool are best left to the professionals.
* Acrylic velvet and many other sofa coverings can be cleaned using the foam only from upholstery shampoo. This is available in a liquid form that needs mixing with water, or in an aerosol can with a brush attachment. It makes the whole job much easier and is worth the extra expense. Treat any existing stains first, and always do a spot check on a small piece of the fabric at the back. Apply the foam, on a small brush or using the can, wipe it over the fabric, allow to dry thoroughly, then vacuum off.
* Loose covers can be removed and washed or cleaned as appropriate. If washing, replace them while still just damp to make sure they fit well. (See also Hot Water Extraction Cleaning under 'Carpets'.)

HALL

The hall takes a great deal of wear throughout the year, with people trekking in and out constantly. Since it is the first room visitors see, it needs to look warm and welcoming, but by the end of a winter of muddy Wellingtons, damp coats, umbrellas and dirty pram and pushchair wheels, it can be much in need of a quick spring clean.

Carpets need a good brush or vacuum.
* Often corners behind doors or under tables are forgotten, so remove any furniture and use a stiff brush or the vacuum cleaner attachment to clean any neglected areas.
* Mats can be lifted and shaken outside.
* The hall carpet is one that may be improved by shampooing. (See also page 20.)

Dusting should be done from the top down, using a dry cloth and, if necessary, a broom with a duster tied on to it to reach cobwebs and dust lurking in dark recesses.
* Alternatively use the vacuum cleaner dusting attachment.

Lampshades can be vacuumed lightly to remove dust.
* Plastic and glass shades can be taken down, washed and dried. Plastic shades sometimes attract dust: if this happens, it helps to rub the clean, dry surface with an antistatic cloth of the type sold for cleaning records. Do not wash fabric lampshades: the glues used are often water soluble. Instead dust and remove any marks by rubbing over them with a piece of bread or soft, clean artists' rubber.
* Real parchment can be wiped with a cloth dipped in a weak water and vinegar solution (see page 33) and allowed to dry. Take care though, as it is very weak when wet and should not be handled.
* Vegetable parchment should not be washed, only dusted.

Light fittings may need dusting or wiping (see page 14).

Paintwork can be washed with washing-up liquid in warm water.
* Wipe dry as you work and don't forget to wash the sides of stairs next to the stair carpet.

Pictures are best taken down before starting the hall. Dust, then rehang them once the room is clean.

Stairs will need vacuuming or brushing if carpeted.
* Take care when using a vacuum cleaner. Try to clean as much as possible with the cleaner at the bottom of the stairs. The last few steps may well require the cleaner to be placed at the top, but make sure it cannot topple down.
* Uncarpeted edges of stairs need washing as for paintwork.
* Real spring-cleaning buffs may want to clean any metal stair carpet holders with an appropriate metal polish. Cut a piece of thick blotting paper to fit round these, so that they can be easily polished without the polish spilling on to the carpet.

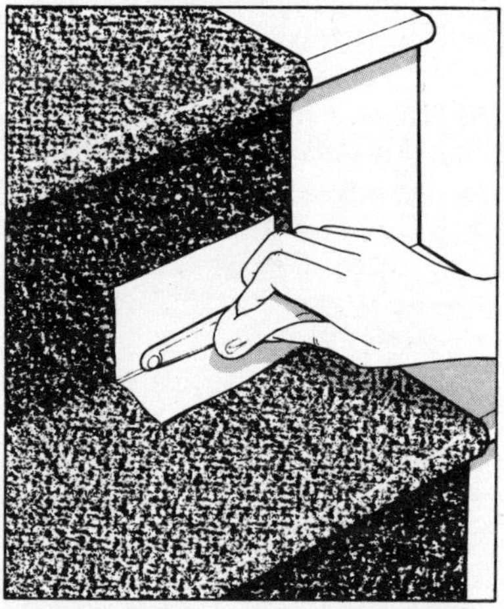

Telephones can be dusted and greasy marks can be removed with a little methylated spirit on a piece of cotton wool.
* Take this opportunity to tidy up the telephone message board. Revise the list of phone numbers and put up a few stern messages to the rest of the family to remind them about the cost of calls. An up-to-date call charges leaflet and an egg timer left next to the phone may jog someone's conscience!

Windows can be cleaned using a window cleaner or a solution of two tablespoons of vinegar in a bucket of warm water. Wash paintwork surrounds and dry carefully.

KITCHEN

As the place where most of the household work is done, this room is in constant use. Daily cleaning is needed for all surfaces that come into contact with food. Occasional major cleaning will help keep the room fresh and make daily cleaning easier.

Breadbins need wiping round every week or so. Use a little warm water and vinegar, and dry well before replacing the bread. If left-over bread has become mouldy, wipe and dry the bin before use. Stand the bin outside in the sunshine to dry it and get rid of any lingering mould.

Cupboards are now usually fitted with plastic shelves that simply need wiping with a cream cleanser.

* However, larder cupboards and old-fashioned wooden shelving need to be washed with warm soapy water and a small brush. Dry well and line the shelves with several layers of wallpaper. This means that once one layer is dirty, you can simply remove it leaving the clean layer underneath, ready for use. Don't use ready pasted vinyls though, as they tend to stick together and the pasted backing should not be used anywhere near food.

* While sorting cupboards, wipe the base of tins and jars to prevent them marking the shelves and write the date bought on the tops with felt pen. This way containers can be used in rotation.
* Greasy dust on top of wall cupboards is best cleaned off with a spray liquid cleaner.

Equipment: all the major appliances like cookers, fridges, washing machines need really to be pulled out away from the wall so that the floor behind them may be cleaned.

* This is often the time to find lost spoons and knives that have fallen down as well. Rollers are fitted on many appliances and can be bought separately for others, and, of course, these make life much easier.
* Beware of dragging heavy equipment across vinyl floors as this will damage them. The outside of appliances can be cleaned with a cream cleanser.
* Small scratches can be rubbed down, then covered with white appliance paint available from hardware shops.
* For cleaning the inside of various appliances, see the section on equipment.

Extractor fans

These often become quite greasy during use.

* Switch off the fan and unplug before cleaning. If there is no

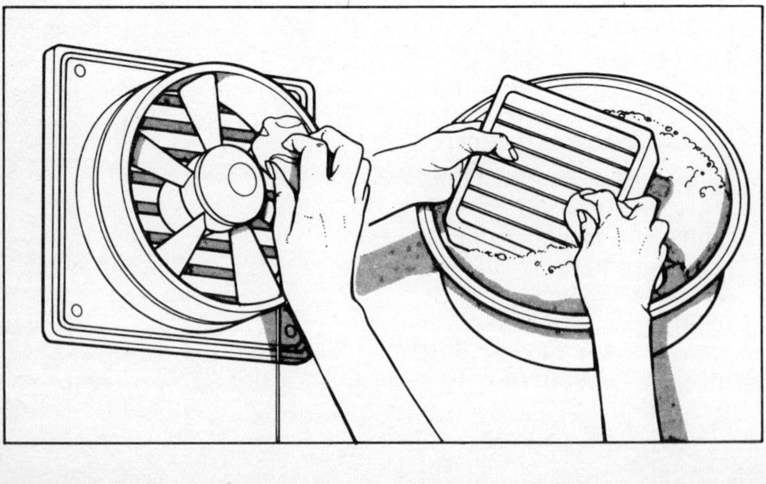

separate plug, remove the fuse from the spur socket or turn off at the mains. Then remove the outer cover, which can be washed in warm soapy water. The fan blades should be wiped with a just damp cloth. Do not wet this area. Replace the cover after drying.

* The outside grid, which is also usually removable, can be washed in warm soapy water and dried before replacing.
* Clean regularly to prevent a build-up of grease. The frequency depends on the type of cooking you generally do but once a year should suffice in most households.

Flooring in kitchens takes quite a pounding, but thankfully most floor surfaces need just a quick mop over to look good.

* Sealed wooden floors, sealed cork tiles, lino, thermo-plastic tiles and vinyl flooring can all be damp mopped daily. Use water sparingly on all of these surfaces.
* Glazed ceramic tiles can be washed with hot soapy water, then rinsed. Stubborn marks can be cleaned with a liquid household cleaner, or a damp cloth.
* The seal on wooden floors often wears unevenly, so needs removing and resealing. To do this, use fine grade steel wool dipped in white spirit and rub over the floor surface. Work in small areas, mopping up as you go. Make sure there are no naked lights (check gas fires and boilers) and work with a window or door open. Once all the remaining seal has been removed, very lightly mop the floor and allow to dry well before applying a new polyurethane seal.
* Fixed floor tiles that have been constantly polished with a self-shining polish often become rather cloudy around the edges of the room. This is because of a build-up of polish. To remove this use 2 tablespoons of powder floor cleaner to half a bucket of cold water. Add about a cup of household ammonia. Wash the floor with this mixture. Mop up and dry well before polishing sparingly with a self-shining polish.
* Carpet tiles can be vacuumed and individual tiles can be lifted and replaced or shampooed with carpet shampoo to remove stains and soiling.

Sinks can be cleaned with a cream cleanser, or filled with hot water and a little bleach.

* Stainless steel sinks benefit from the occasional spring clean

with stainless steel cleaner, but on a day-to-day basis, cream cleanser will do the trick.

* Occasionally put a handful of household soda in the sink and run the hot tap for a minute or two to clean the waste and pipes of grease.
* Overflows can be cleaned with a small toothbrush or bottle brush, but make sure your clothes are covered, as both tend to splash greasy particles at you.

Storage jars need sorting out, and often relabelling.

* Empty and wash the jars in hot soapy water. Stand them in a warm place, such as on a windowledge, to dry.
* Many foods are better stored in dark places, so try to place storage jars in cupboards, or use tinted glass jars.

Taps can be cleaned with warm soapy water or with a mild cream cleanser.

* Hard water deposits around the tap base can be tackled with a little cream cleanser on an old toothbrush, or mix in a little lemon juice and salt and apply on a toothbrush. Rub in well, leave for a couple of minutes, then rinse off thoroughly. (Do not leave for longer, as the acid may damage the chrome.)
* Hard water deposits around the spout of a tap may be treated with half a lemon. Cover the bath or sink with an old towel as the lemon juice might bleach it, then push the cut surface of the lemon on to the tap spout and work round. If this system does not work, try a water softener. This is usually sold in powder form at chemists, which is then mixed with water, using 2 teaspoons to ½ litre (1 pint).
* If there is a build-up of hard water deposits, hang a plastic container full of water softener and water around the tap, so that the outlet is immersed in the mixture. Leave for about two hours, then repeat if necessary.

Worktops are mostly laminates and are best cleaned with cream cleansers, or with a little dry bicarbonate of soda on a damp cloth.

* Wipe up spills as they occur and protect the surface from hot pans and dishes.
* Avoid cutting on laminate worktops as this will damage the surface and may make them difficult to clean.

HOUSEHOLD CLEANERS

The following alphabetical list gives details of cleaning liquids and powders (see also 'Stain Removal Chart' page 116). Some are proprietary solutions, in which case details of their use and suitability are given and some are household storecupboard items which have a secondary function as cleaners. In this case, there are details on how to make up your own solutions.

AEROSOL CLEANERS

These are generally multipurpose cleaners and polishers that can be used on glass, mirrors, wood, plastic and many other hard surfaces. They are convenient to use and quick to apply. Make sure you shake the can well and hold it upright when spraying, for the best results.

BICARBONATE OF SODA

Mix 1 teaspoon of bicarbonate with 250 ml (½ pint) of warm water for a good mild cleaner, that will not leave any lingering smells. It's ideal for the inside of fridges and freezers and for plastic food storage boxes.

Use neat on a damp cloth for stubborn marks and stains on worktops, plastics and household equipment.

BLEACH

Dilute this as directed on the container as strengths vary. Use for cleaning WC pans, drains and sinks. It is also useful on paths and any area that has had mould or mildew growing on it. Use diluted (as directed) on large areas or half and half with water on small areas of hard surfaces, such as the grouting between glazed ceramic tiles.

Never mix bleach with other household cleaners as toxic fumes may be given off.

BORAX

Use 1 tablespoon to 600 ml (1 pint) of warm water. This has a mild bleaching effect and is useful for removing acid-based stains. Soak fabrics for ten minutes or so, then remove to prevent the fabric becoming bleached. Always do a test piece before use.

CREAM CLEANSERS

These are good general purpose cleaners. The creamy texture prevents scratching on baths, basins and other hard surfaces and they are easy to use neat on small areas of paintwork and work-tops as well. Look for the VEDC (Vitreous Enamel Development Council) sign on cream cleansers, which shows they are suitable for vitreous enamel.

DISINFECTANT

This will kill germs but will not generally clean surfaces, so it is best used along with a detergent of some kind. Often cleaners combine the two to make a good multipurpose cleaner in one bottle. Dilute according to instructions on the container.

GREASE SOLVENTS

These are available in aerosol and liquid form. Follow the instructions on the container. They are useful to have on hand as many stains are grease-based. They can also be used for removing any residual colour left after the main stain has been removed. Avoid inhaling the fumes. Store safely.

HOUSEHOLD SODA

This is sold in powder form and can be mixed with water to clean any greasy areas. Follow the instructions on the packet. It is very effective for sinks and drains. As it is quite strong, do not tackle delicate items or areas and do not use to clean aluminium pans, as it can cause pitting. It may also be used as a water softener when mixed with detergent in hard water areas (see page 81).

LIQUID CLEANERS

Generally these are quite concentrated detergents that can be used neat or diluted. They are effective for removing greasy dirt, and some spray types are available which make cleaning inaccessible areas easier. Follow the directions on the container.

METHYLATED SPIRIT

Use neat on a white cloth, or for small areas apply on a cotton bud. This is a good general purpose solvent for cleaning and stain removal but always check that the fibre will not be affected, by doing a test first. It is highly flammable, so extinguish any naked flames and work in a well ventilated area. Store safely in a locked cupboard.

POLISHES

Liquid polishes are usually enriched, therefore are good for natural woods and other porous surfaces. Apply sparingly and rub in well. Paste polishes require a fair bit of elbow grease to produce a shine. The polish provides a protective layer, so pastes are good on older, more valuable furniture at risk from drying out.

VINEGAR

To make a *weak solution* use 1 teaspoon to 250 ml (½ pint) of water. For a *strong solution*, use twice this much vinegar to water. It is good for removing a light film of grease and for washing hard surfaces. On bathroom tiles in hard water areas, it can be used to remove the hard water stains that sometimes appear. Use half vinegar and half water for this purpose. Prevent stains from building up by rinsing tiles regularly with a weak vinegar solution.

WASHING-UP LIQUID

Use this when hot soapy water is required. Apart from general washing up it is also useful for cleaning paintwork and other hard surfaces. It can also be used for removing stains from upholstery and carpets by mixing 1-2 teaspoons with a cup of warm water and apply the foam only.

Note

Never mix different types of strong household cleaners, and do not use them in quantity with the windows closed. The fumes given off can be dangerous even when used on their own.

A-Z OF GENERAL CLEANING

ALABASTER
Wipe with a cloth wrung out in hot soapy water. Stains may respond to wiping with a very little turpentine on a cloth.

BAMBOO
Dust or vacuum regularly. Wash occasionally using warm soapy water plus a little borax or salt. Dip a soft brush in this and scrub the bamboo lightly. Rinse well with salty water and allow to dry naturally. Occasional polishing with a linseed oil will keep the bamboo supple and help prevent splitting.

BATHS
See Spring Cleaning – Bathrooms, page 12.

BLANKETS
See Spring Cleaning – Bedrooms, page 18.

CANE AND WICKER
Clean regularly with a spray cleaner. Varnished cane can simply be wiped over occasionally with a damp cloth. Unvarnished cane can be washed with warm water and washing soda mixture. Bleach stains with weak household bleach solution.

A sagging cane seat can sometimes be shrunk back by wetting well with hot water and a little bicarbonate of soda. Apply this mixture on a cloth to the top and the base of the seat, then turn the chair upside down to dry.

Spray small items of wicker with water from a plant spray occasionally (about once a month) to prevent them drying out.

Beware of buying old cane furniture that has woodworm. If you find small regular bore holes of the woodworm beetle on parts of your furniture, spray it with a woodworming agent, available now in small quantities from DIY shops. If in doubt, spray anyway for the sake of the rest of your furniture.

If cane is beyond cleaning, consider painting. Use a spray paint of the type sold for cars. This makes it easy to apply and gives a wide range of colours, including gold, or glossy black which looks lovely on cane.

CARPETS

Vacuum regularly to prevent dust and grit working its way deep into the pile. When a carpet is laid, save a spare piece to use for testing stain removers on. It's essential to know what can be safely used on each carpet in the house, so you can act quickly if necessary. Before using *any* cleaning agent or stain removal treatment on carpets you should do a test piece first on a spare piece or on a hidden area. (For general shampooing see Spring Cleaning section.)

Some carpets are now sold with a special stain-resistant finish. Most stains can simply be mopped up and blotted, but follow the instructions that come with the carpet. On other carpets, stains are best dealt with immediately. Mop up spills with plenty of tissues or kitchen roll or even tea towels. Cover

the spill, then stand on the tissues or kitchen roll to soak up all the spill. Use fresh tissues or move them around if necessary. Continue to do this until no more liquid is being absorbed. You may look a little strange standing on piles of tissues but it is the most effective way of blotting up spills. Often if you act fast enough it can prevent a lasting stain occurring. For other carpet stains, see the chart below.

STAIN	TREATMENT
Candlewax	Scrape up as much as possible. Cover the stain with blotting paper and iron this with a warm iron to melt and absorb the wax. Then clean the area with a little white spirit on a piece of white cotton to pick up any remaining colour. *DO NOT SOAK.* Allow to dry and brush or vacuum off.
Crayon	(As for candlewax)
Coffee, Tea	Blot well. Shampoo with a warm solution of carpet shampoo. Allow to dry and vacuum. Use solvent on a clean cloth. *DO NOT SOAK.*
Fruit juice	Blot to remove excess juice. Dilute with clean water, washing and mopping as you go to make sure the carpet does not become too wet. Finally shampoo with a warm solution of carpet shampoo. Allow to dry and vacuum.
Grass	Grass marks in the summer often appear on carpets and clothes. A little colourless methylated spirit applied sparingly will usually remove it. *DO NOT SOAK.*

Ink; ballpoint and felt pen	Use clear methylated spirit on a clean cloth. Keep refolding the cloth so that it does not redeposit inky marks on the carpet. *DO NOT SOAK*. When dry, treat with carpet shampoo.
Ink; fountain pen	Blot up excess, then treat with a detergent solution or carpet shampoo. Work gradually by applying a little of the solution, then blot with tissues or cloths and apply a little more. Continue until as much as possible has been removed, remembering to blot well as you go to avoid overwetting the carpet. Dried ink stains of any kind may need professional treatment. Some stains will be permanent.
Plasticine	Scrape off as much as possible, then use a spray stain remover.
Shoe polish	Lift excess off with a knife, then treat the stain with a little white spirit on a clean cloth, followed by carpet shampoo.
Tar	Scrape up excess with a knife. White spirit or a spray cleaner will remove this from most carpets. When dry, treat with carpet shampoo.
Urine	Treat quickly, use plenty of clear water, washing and mopping up as you go to make sure the carpet does not become too wet. Finally shampoo.
Wine	Blot as much up as possible, then rinse and blot the area. Clean with a carpet shampoo.

(See also Chapter 8, pages 333 to 336 for possible stains caused by little children.)

CERAMIC HOBS

These can be cleaned with a specialist cleaner and this should be done regularly to keep the finish in good condition. Stains sometimes respond to a paste of the cleaner. Mix the cleaner with a little water, then spread over the area and leave it to dry. Rinse and dry well afterwards. Always clean the hob when cold. To keep the ceramic top in good condition, avoid dragging pans across the hob and never use it for chopping on, as this could scratch the surface.

CHANDELIERS

Traditionally these were taken down once a year and each individual piece was washed in warm water and a little vinegar, then buffed up with a soft cloth. This method can still be used, although special spray cleaners are now available that allow the chandelier to be cleaned in situ.

CHROME

A little paraffin applied on a clean cloth will restore the shine to chrome. Alternatively, use a general purpose spray cleaner or special chrome cleaner sold in car accessory shops.

CORK TILES

Floor tiles are usually sealed with a polyurethane seal or waxed. Sealed tiles need only light mopping and can then be polished with a water-based polish. Waxed cork should not be washed but cleaned with a solvent-based polish. Cork wall tiles are not usually sealed, but can be rather dusty. Brush lightly and treat stains with a damp cloth.

DECANTERS

If put away while still damp these may become musty and cloudy. Avoid this by rinsing well and leaving the stopper off for storage. If possible leave them to drain upside down for a while but most decanters will need careful propping for this. Standing them upside down in a large plastic jug is ideal. To get rid of a musty smell, mix 2 tablespoons of white vinegar with about ½ litre (1 pint) of warm water and pour this into the decanter. Swill around well and leave to stand overnight. Finely crushed egg shell in warm water is an old remedy that often works. Use the same method.

DRAWERS
A musty smell in unused drawers can often be removed by filling the drawer with screwed-up newspaper and leaving it slightly ajar for a day or two, or, if possible, leave the drawer outside in the sunshine for a while. Another way of dealing with the mustiness is to put some lemon peel in the drawer. Mothballs can leave a lingering smell but usually a few pieces of cotton wool with a little vanilla essence on each will alleviate the smell, or try a fridge deodorizer. To keep a drawer smelling sweet, use perfumed drawer liners.

DUVETS
See Spring Cleaning – Bedrooms, page 19.

ELECTRIC BLANKETS
Some electric blankets can be washed with care but be sure to check on the label first and follow the instructions, as some need specialized cleaning and must be returned to the manufacturers. Usually underblankets aren't washable but some overblankets are. For washable blankets, measure the blanket before starting, so that you can check on shrinkage afterwards. Wash using a solution of liquid detergent in a bath of warm water. Lay the blanket in and leave to soak for an hour or so. Rinse at least twice to remove all traces of detergent. Do not wring but squeeze. Drape to dry over two lines or over an airer out in the garden. When almost dry, lay out and remeasure and stretch gently back into shape. Dry completely before using. Check that the elements are not crossed. This can be done by holding the blanket in front of a strong light. Store electric blankets rolled, not folded.

FABRIC BLINDS
Due to the stiffening in the fabric, these can't be washed. Give them an occasional dust.

GLASS
Glass shelves and coffee tables can be cleaned by wiping with a mixture of vinegar and water, or use a window cleaner or general purpose spray cleaner. Fine scratches can be removed using a metal polish on wadding. Rub round in small circles and rinse off.

GOATSKIN

Rugs made of goat and other animal skins should simply be vacuumed lightly at home. Professional cleaning is called for. If the skin moults, this is usually due to the curing process and cannot be remedied. (See also 'Sheepskin'.)

IRONS

The soleplate of an iron needs to be kept clean and smooth for best results. If fabric has melted and stuck to the iron, unplug and allow to cool down. While just warm scrape off the excess with a round-bladed knife covered with a piece of white cotton cloth. Then use a stick iron cleaner, following the manufacturer's instructions carefully. Use in a well-ventilated room as the process gives off fumes. For less major stains, one old-fashioned remedy is to warm the iron, unplug it, then run a bar of soap over the soleplate. Iron the soap off on to an old cloth. A steam iron cleaner, available from chemists, will clean the vent holes on a steam iron. To avoid the steam iron 'furring' inside, always use de-mineralized water unless instructions are given to the contrary.

IVORY

This needs little regular care apart from dusting. Use a small artist's paintbrush to dust intricate ivory pieces. Occasionally wipe over with a little methylated spirit on a piece of cotton wool. Avoid extremes of heat and cold and do not immerse in water. Valuable pieces should be professionally cleaned.

JEWELLERY

Most hard stones can be dipped in warm water and a little washing-up liquid, then gently rubbed dry. Alternatively, use a jewellery care kit. Pearls should simply be rubbed with a chamois leather. Soft stones, such as opals, are best cleaned this way as well. If in doubt or if the piece is particularly valuable, take to a professional cleaner.

KETTLES

In hard water areas use a defurring solution regularly, as a thick build-up of hard water deposits will slow down an electric kettle and increase running costs. Vinegar is a good alternative to defurring agents. Cover the element with vinegar, bring just to the boil, then turn off and allow to cool. Empty and rinse several times. Boil the kettle at least once and empty the water away before use.

Defurring solutions are stronger and should be used according to the instructions on the container.

Clean the outside of the kettle according to the finish; painted or enamelled finishes generally only need wiping with a damp cloth, stainless steel, or chrome finishes can be cleaned with a cream cleanser, rinsed and buffed up with a dry cloth. A specialist stainless steel cleaner, which comes with a double-sided sponge for use on satin finish and shiny finishes is also available.

LACE

Old lace is difficult to wash without the risk of damaging it, so if the article is valuable, consult a specialist cleaner. However, delicate lace can be soaked in plain distilled water for several hours. Amazingly, this often lifts a great deal of grime from the lace. Put a cotton teatowel in the bowl first, so that the wet lace can be lifted out without stretching.

Less fine or valuable lace can be washed in pure soap suds but avoid stretching and squeezing the lace as this can ruin its shape. Rinse well, then lay the lace out and blot dry with a towel. Sit the damp lace on a thick towel (or cover a piece of cardboard with old towelling) and pin it out in the correct shape. Put the pins through the gaps in the lace rather than in the threads to avoid damaging it. Allow to dry naturally away from direct heat.

Lace curtains can be folded and put into a cotton pillow case for washing to prevent stretching. Wash in pure soap suds. Leave them to soak for a while, then gently squeeze the whole pillow case and soak again. Rinse well, by soaking in cool water, then lay the curtains out flat to dry on a couple of bath towels or sheets.

Lace can be dyed using cold water dyes or using tea or coffee (which gives it a delicate shade of light brown). This is very often a useful way of dealing with discoloured lace that does not respond to washing.

LACQUERWARE

Lacquered metal just needs occasional dusting. It is possible to relacquer metal yourself using proprietary products first to remove and then to replace the original coat. Wooden lacquerware should be dusted and occasionally wiped over with a just damp cloth.

LAMPSHADES

See Spring Cleaning – Halls, page 25.

LEATHER

Leather furniture generally needs little daily care, although occasional treating with the recommended polish, used sparingly, will help keep it supple. Be careful with special finishes on leather, follow the manufacturer's instructions for these. Some specialist companies sell special renovation kits for improving the appearance of old leather. If leather furniture in daily use becomes covered in fingermarks, wipe with a cloth wrung out in water with a little vinegar added. Don't wet the leather, wring the cloth out well, and just wipe over the surface to pick up the grease. Leather desk tops can be treated with a squirt of washing-up liquid to 600 ml (1 pint) of water. Dip the cloth in the solution, wring out and wipe over the desk top. Ink stains are a common problem on desks; act quickly when these occur. Blot the ink up and wash the area with water for fountain pen ink, or milk for ballpoint. For small spots of ink wet a cotton bud and use this to remove the ink. If the leather desk top has become very sticky, wipe over with a damp cloth before using a light application of furniture polish. If using an aerosol furniture polish, hold it 8-12 inches away from the leather when spraying. Specialist leather shops and saddlers will sell suitable cleaners.

Dirty marks on leather luggage can be removed with a damp cloth. On old luggage that has become rather battered, use the water and vinegar mixture and add just a dash of ammonia to it, then wipe over the leather with a damp cloth. Finish with an enriched furniture cream.

LINOLEUM

The pattern on lino is often printed on the surface and strong detergents will eventually take this printing off. Therefore,

occasional mopping with warm water and washing-up liquid should be the regular cleaning method. Occasional polishing with a solvent-based polish will keep the flooring in good condition. Remove stubborn marks with a little turpentine, taking care to apply it on a cloth or piece of cotton wool. Do not pour neat turpentine on to the lino.

MARBLE

On a day-to-day basis marble simply needs wiping with a damp soapy cloth. As it is porous, it does stain easily. Using half a lemon on stains will fade them but great care must be taken to prevent the acid affecting the marble. It is best to leave the lemon for just a couple of minutes, then rinse the area well and repeat the procedure several times, so that the marble can be checked for signs of any damage. Specialist marble cleaners and conditioners are available, which will deal with light scratches, and very damaged marble should be treated by professional stone cleaners.

MATTRESSES

Using a cotton mattress cover or an old blanket under the sheets will help protect a mattress. For children's beds this is particularly important, and the best protector is a rubber or plastic sheet placed between the bottom sheet and the mattress. Old cot

sheets or even quilted cot covers can also be used. If accidents do happen, turn the mattress on its side to stop the spill soaking in, then blot up as much as possible. Urine will damage the fabric of the mattress, so needs rinsing out well. To do this without overwetting the mattress itself, use a garden spray filled with warm water into which a little bicarbonate of soda has been dissolved. This will help get rid of lingering smells. Spray the damp area, then lay the mattress on an old towel to absorb the moisture. Repeat this process as necessary, before leaving to dry naturally. If possible stand the mattress in the sunshine to dry, as this will help prevent a stain occurring.
See also Spring Cleaning – Bedrooms, page 19.

MIRRORS
Often old mirrors bought second-hand have lovely frames but the mirror itself has small flecks where the backing has come off. Improve the overall appearance by fixing a sheet of kitchen foil behind the mirror. Badly damaged mirror backs will need to be remirrored professionally.

ONYX
This needs regular dusting and can be given an occasional clean with just a little methylated spirit on a piece of cotton wool.

PAINTWORK
Small areas around door handles and light switches can be wiped with a cream cleanser. See also pages 14 and 15.

PEWTER
Pewter should be regularly washed in warm soapy water. Stains and spots can be removed with a little methylated spirit used sparingly. Copper polish, or silver polish that comes in an impregnated wadding can also be used, but take care to work with the shape of the article and follow the natural lines of the pewter. Old books also recommend warm beer and raw cabbage leaves, either of which are worth a try.

PIANO KEYS
If valuable or very discoloured, seek professional help. Otherwise, try equal parts of methylated spirit and warm water on a cloth. If the piano is battered, try a little toothpaste on a cloth.

PICTURES

Obviously, valuable oil paintings should be professionally cleaned but for less precious items a picture cleaner can be bought at artists' shops which will remove dust and brighten up an oil painting that has become dulled. Glass covered paintings can simply be cleaned with a general purpose spray cleaner.

Frames can be cleaned according to type. Wooden frames benefit from treating with a furniture cream. Gilt frames need regular dusting and can occasionally be treated with a little turpentine on a piece of cotton wool. Rub over the frame gently to brighten it. Specialist solutions can be bought from art shops to improve the appearance of gilt frames. With stainless steel frames, use a general purpose spray cleaner, provided the picture has a glass cover. Otherwise, hold a piece of card next to the frame, protecting the picture, and clean the frame with liquid furniture polish.

PILLOWS

See Spring Cleaning – Bedrooms, page 19.

QUARRY TILES

These are hardwearing tiles and generally only need regular mopping with a general floor cleaner. Unglazed tiles may need to be scrubbed with the same cleaner. For stubborn marks, cover with a paste of floor powder and a little water. Leave for five minutes, then scrub off. Old tiles that are looking rather patchy can be cleaned using white spirit on a fine grade steel wool. Make sure all naked flames are extinguished and open a window. Work in small areas mopping up as you go. Once clean, polish with a pigmented tile polish. Apply sparingly as excessive amounts will be slippery and may come off on to shoes. Apply the polish lightly, then buff up with a duster tied to a broom head. Newly-laid floors sometimes have white patches from the subfloor on them. These will fade in time. Rinsing with a little weak vinegar and water solution (see page 33) will help make them disappear.

SAUCEPANS

Wash aluminium pans in hot soapy water. Burnt-on foods can be soaked off, or use a saucepan brush and an abrasive powder. Black stains in hard water areas are harmless but they can be removed by boiling up lemon skins or apple peelings for about 15 minutes. To prevent a black stain appearing, add a slice of lemon to the water when steaming or pressure cooking. If washing in a dishwasher according to manufacturers' instructions, do not leave them inside the machine once the cycle is finished, as they will become pitted if left damp for any length of time.

Burnt food in enamel pans can also be cleaned by soaking or using a saucepan brush and cream cleanser. Colour from foods such as carrots is often deposited on enamel and this can be removed by soaking with a mild bleach solution (according to directions on the bottle). Rinse thoroughly before re-using.

Cast iron pans are often finished with an enamel interior, so can be cleaned as enamel. Frying pans and skillets sometimes are made completely from cast iron and washing should be avoided if at all possible. Instead clean with a little oil and kitchen paper to leave a protective film on the iron.

Stainless steel is not really stainless. Pans can develop a rainbow mark from heat which is permanent and pitting can occur from soaking and from salt or highly acidic solutions. For best results when cooking, avoid the use of high heat and use a radiant or gas ring of a slightly smaller diameter than your pan. Wash in hot soapy water. Do not use metal scourers or scouring powders as these will scratch the surface. To remove stubborn deposits, soak in warm water. To restore the appearance of your pan, use either a proprietary stainless steel cleaner, or a mild culinary acid, such as lemon juice or vinegar. Apply with a cloth or sponge and wipe over both the inside and the outside of the pan.

Nonstick finishes generally only need washing in hot soapy water. For old pans, boil a little warm water and washing-up liquid in the pan, then brush well with a saucepan brush or nonstick cleaning pad. The black nonstick finishes in pans can be cleaned using a cup of bleach and 2 teaspoons of bicarbonate of soda. Three quarters fill the pan with hot water and boil this mixture for 10 to 15 minutes. It makes an awful smell, so open the window and leave the room. Then rinse and dry the pan before conditioning it. To do this, rub around the whole of the inside surface with a little oil on a piece of kitchen towel. This method works very well for old nonstick pans and brings them up like new but must only be used on black nonstick finishes. It is not recommended for white or silvery finishes.

SHEEPSKIN

Coats need regular professional cleaning but spots and stains can be cleaned with a specialist suede cleaner. Alternatively, use Fuller's earth. Use it sparingly; a small sachet should treat several stains. Rub it in well, then brush off after about an hour. The woolly side will be improved by using dry hair shampoo occasionally. This is especially useful for the collar which becomes dirty more quickly than the rest of the coat.

Rugs can be improved by applying the lather only from soap flake solution on a small brush. Work in sections, wiping off the excess lather as you go. Allow to dry and brush or vacuum.

SILVER

There are a wide range of silver cleaners on the market, including a dip that is very useful for small, intricate pieces of silverware. Protect your hands by wearing rubber gloves.

Silver can also be cleaned by immersing it in a bowl containing a handful of washing soda and a handful of milk bottle tops. Add sufficient hot water to cover the silver. The tarnish is removed and collects on the milk bottle tops, but it may also collect on any silver protruding from the water, so ensure it is all submerged. Fumes may be given off by this process, so work with the window open. Once the mixture stops fizzing or as soon as the silver is clean, remove it and buff up with a soft cloth. An impregnated silver cloth is useful either to shine up silver quickly, or to wrap around silver that is to be stored. These can be bought or you can make your own. Use 10 parts cold water, 2 parts ammonia and 1 part long-term silver polish. Soak some squares of cotton in this, then leave them to drip dry.

SLATE

General cleaning simply involves washing or scrubbing with hot soapy water. Dull slate can be brightened up by mixing equal quantities of linseed oil and white spirit. Apply this on a soft cloth and buff up well. Specialist cleaners are also available.

STONE
This can be cleaned by scrubbing with plain water, or specialist cleaners are available. If you have trouble tracking these down, try your local builders' merchant or a specialist fireplace show-room.

STRAW MATTING
Sweep or vacuum any straw matting regularly. It is better not to wash it, as it takes ages to dry.

TAPS
See Spring Cleaning – Kitchens, page 30.

TORTOISESHELL
Tortoiseshell sometimes becomes cloudy when exposed to light and this generally needs expert attention. It can be cleaned with a little jeweller's rouge mixed with a spot of cooking oil. Mix to a paste, then apply on a soft cloth, wrapped round the tip of one finger. Work in small circles. Wipe the mixture off with a clean cloth. This is good for old and neglected tortoiseshell. Any in good condition simply needs occasional polishing with a rich furniture cream.

UPHOLSTERY
See Spring Cleaning Section – General Rooms, page 24.

VACUUM FLASKS
These often become quite musty in storage. After use, rinse well and drain. Store with the lid off. Use a tea or coffee stain remover, available from chemists, or half fill with warm water and add a little bicarbonate of soda (about 2 teaspoons). Put the lid on and shake well. Soak overnight if necessary.

VENETIAN BLINDS
These need regular dusting either with a special blind cleaning tool or with an old cotton glove. Put the glove on and run your hand along the slats. Very dirty blinds can be washed in the bath. Protect the bath with an old towel and wash the blinds in a little warm soapy water, taking care to keep the mechanism out of the water. If the blinds are too big for the bath, there are specialist steam cleaning companies around who will do the job for you.

VINYL FLOORING

This generally needs only light mopping. Do not overwet and work in circles. Scratch marks can be improved slightly by using a little metal polish on a cloth.

WALLPAPER

An international set of symbols is now being used in wallpaper pattern books and on product labels. It includes symbols on wallpaper care, and these should be followed when treating marks. Use a spray dry cleaner for greasy marks, but remember to do a test area first to ensure that the colour is not affected. Other marks may respond to a soft, clean artist's rubber, or a piece of bread rubbed over the spot.

Washable wallpapers are really only spongeable; use a sponge dipped in warm water with a little washing-up liquid. Squeeze the sponge well, so that it is damp rather than wet, then wipe over the wallpaper.

Vinyls are tougher; even crayon marks can be removed with a damp cloth. This makes them an ideal choice for children's rooms.

Hessian and similar wallcoverings cannot be washed. Instead, vacuum them with the vacuum cleaner dusting attachment.

WOOD

Floorboards can be scrubbed with hot soapy water as long as they are mopped up well. Do not make the wood too wet as too much moisture will cause the wood to swell and the floorboards to buckle. Sealed wooden floors simply need light mopping and can be buffed up with a duster tied to a broom or with a special cotton mop.

Most furniture can be cleaned with a spray polish. French polished wood generally needs only dusting and occasional polishing with a good wax polish. Remove sticky marks and a build-up of wax by wiping over with a cloth dipped in warm water and just a little vinegar. A chamois leather gives the best results. Buff up when dry.

Most modern furniture is veneered and this simply needs regular dusting and occasional polishing with a spray polish. Some modern woods have special finishes (such as a plasticized finish), so always check with the maker's instructions before cleaning or removing stains. Always do a test piece, when tackling stains and marks on any furniture.

Heat marks on polished wooden furniture may respond to rubbing with a cloth dipped in just a little turpentine. Rub with the natural pattern of the wood and use sparingly. Water marks usually show up as white rings or splashes and these, too, may respond to a little turpentine. If not, try using a little cream metal polish. Rub in carefully, then wipe off. Repolish when dry.

Teak is often oiled and should only need regular dusting. About twice a year oil lightly with teak oil, applying it sparingly to prevent the article becoming sticky.

Valuable or antique furniture is best treated by a professional to maintain both appearance and value.

One old country remedy for cleaning oak and mahogany is to use a cloth dipped in warm beer. It works if you can stand the smell!

WORKTOPS

See Spring Cleaning – Kitchens, page 30.

WHEN ALL ELSE FAILS

Panic usually sets in when the cooking is not going as rapidly as planned, the children are restless and you are expecting guests in ten minutes, one hour or that evening and the house is a total mess. The golden rule here has to be not to try to clean and tidy everywhere; parents-in-law or great aunts are sure to arrive while you are up to your knees in brooms, cleaners and general debris and looking like Cinderella at home. Far better to do the absolute minimum, then concentrate on distracting and entertaining your guests. With a little luck this will work so well that they will not have time to notice the dust, or sticky fingermarks on the doors.

Carpets are best vacuumed if time allows. If not, move a rug around since it is likely to be clean underneath, and add a couple of floor cushions.

Cheer up a spare bedroom with flowers, or a pot plant from another room, a carafe of water and a few books and magazines. These touches will demonstrate that you care about your guests' comfort and they will be far less likely to notice the dust, or dirty windows.

Collect all the odds and ends that make a room look untidy. Load them on to a tray and hide this in the bedroom.

Collections usually impress people and make a topic of conversation. Make lots of odds and ends look like a collection by linking them together; fill odd containers such as glasses, boxes, jars, little trays, sea shells, shallow dishes, and so on with miniature soaps, tiny sweets or fabric flowers. Group together on a shelf or table to make a focal point.

Keep a couple of wicker baskets, or painted boxes in each room so that small objects like coins, papers, and anything else left lying around can be quickly hidden away.

Keep guests busy; offer drinks, be it tea or gin-and-tonics as soon as possible, and supply biscuits or other nibbles as well. Stay with them if at all possible; left alone they will have time to inspect the room!

Newspapers are best collected and removed. Other papers, like letters, circulars and bills can be straightened up and held in place between a couple of jars, ornaments or books. Make sure final demands are hidden in the middle!

Open fires are so welcoming that it is worth the effort to light one, even if it is not really cold enough to need it. If you can borrow a cat to curl up in front of it, so much the better!

Plants and flowers cover up an amazing amount of untidiness. Borrow them from the bathroom and bedroom if necessary. Position them in groups for best effect and use them to cover up the odd tear in the wallpaper or stain on the carpet, if necessary.

Smells are very evocative; cover unwelcome ones with pot pourri, incense, perfumed candles or, if desperate, air freshener. Create pleasant smells by making fresh coffee, warming a loaf of bread in the oven or burning a few herbs, such as rosemary, under the grill.

Sofas often become quite tatty, and oddly enough you never notice until other people are coming. Make your sofa instantly prettier by collecting all the small cushions in the house and arranging them on it. Alternatively, throw an ethnic style bed-spread over it.

Spend 3 minutes in the bathroom. Put out fresh towels and pretty soaps. Wash round the hand basin and spray a little air freshener around.

Toys are best collected together. Throw them into a wicker tub, toy box or an old laundry basket and sit the nicest ones on top.

Turn the lights low, and light a few candles if at all appropriate. Dim candlelight seems to make everything look a little better, but it might alarm parents or great aunts if you do this for Sunday tea!

Wallpaper past its best can be covered with a wall-hanging. Use a piece of patterned fabric, or a rug, or even pretty wrapping paper. Hang lightweight things on reusable adhesive, and heavier weights on picture hooks from curtain rails.

Windows without curtains look bleak. If you are entertaining in a new house, make instant curtains from sheets, or yards of fabric. Wrap these around the curtain pole or track, and swag back with brightly-coloured ribbon or even shoe laces. Alternatively, line the windowledge with an attractive display of empty glass bottles, so the light shines through them. Avoid gin bottles though if you want to create a good impression with Great Aunt Ethel!

MAKING THE MOST OF EQUIPMENT

Household equipment has replaced the laundry maids, housekeepers and cooks of yesteryear. Even so, many of us underestimate what the various appliances in our house can do, so here is a guide to how to get the best from major appliances. It is also worth remembering that this equipment needs some care and attention to keep it in good working order.

COOKERS

We demand a great deal from our cookers. They are the mainstay of the kitchen equipment, and we expect the same cooker to produce anything from a single boiled egg to Christmas lunch for twelve. On the whole, cookers serve us well and generally last many years, so it is worth choosing a new one with care.

Choosing a Cooker

Between gas and electricity, the choice is largely made according to personal taste.

Nowadays, however, it is important to consider the origin of the cooker as there are a number of both gas and electric cookers being imported into the UK. We tend to do more baking than cooks in other countries and many Continental cookers are not designed to cook some of the more basic British foods such as scones, small cakes and Victoria Sandwiches. Many Continental (and some British) cookers have the grill fitted into the roof of the oven which can be inconvenient should the user wish to use the grill and oven at the same time. It is therefore worthwhile checking the basic construction of the cooker and the recipe book to establish the cooking functions.

On either gas or electric cookers, think seriously about which extras are worth having.

* An autotimer may be worthwhile if the whole family is out during the day or if you wish to cook overnight, but it must be easy to set and reliable in use.
* Check how easy the cooker is likely to be to clean. Look for spillage bowls or trays under the hob that can easily be fitted into the sink. Large spillage plates are a nuisance if they cannot easily be soaked clean.
* See if the oven is well lit, for checking on the progress of food.
* Many gas and electric cookers now have self-clean oven linings. These oxidize the splashes and spills as they happen, so the oven remains quite clean. Occasional wiping with a damp cloth and alternating roasting with medium to high temperature dry cooking (i.e. baking) is all that is needed to keep most of the oven in good condition.
* Many cookers now offer second ovens, which are useful for any family that does little weekday cooking but does need to cook a great deal at weekends. So a single casserole or cake can be cooked in the small oven and a full scale Sunday roast made in the main oven.
* Fan ovens, in which the hot air is circulated around the oven cavity, are widely available on electric cookers and a similar feature is now available on a few gas cookers. The major advantage of this system is that the oven can be filled with food, which will bake or brown reasonably evenly, without you having to move the trays around. Cooking times and temperatures can also be reduced slightly, thereby cutting running costs and splashing of meat.

Using a Cooker
Keep running costs down by filling the oven whenever possible.

* Vegetables can be cooked in the oven alongside a casserole or roast meat, and puddings and cakes can often be fitted in as well.
* Electric ovens retain heat very well, so it is worth making a

habit of switching them off ten minutes before the food is cooked (except for short operations, for example when cooking scones).

* Adjust gas flames, so that they just match the size of saucepan. Flames licking around the edges are wasteful.
* Use steamers where possible to cook two or more foods at once and pressure cookers often cut cooking times dramatically. Clean a cooker regularly to keep it in good condition.
* Self-cleaning linings need little attention, but vitreous oven interiors are best cleaned with an oven cleaning pad. Follow the manufacturer's instructions carefully, wear rubber gloves and protect the floor.
* A microwave cooker can be cleaned by standing a dish of hot water in it. Add a slice of lemon and boil the water in the oven until plenty of steam is produced, then wipe over the interior with a damp cloth.
* Gas grill pans can be lined with foil to catch drips and so cut down on the need for cleaning.
* Wash the whole pan and grid in hot soapy water.
* If the pan is very greasy, soak in hot water to which a little household soda has been added.
* A cream cleanser will usually keep the hob and outside of the cooker clean, particularly if care is taken to wipe up spills as they occur.
* Any removable parts of the hob can be soaked in hot soapy water, while the hob is cleaned. Dry each piece and replace, making sure that pilot lights on gas cookers are relit before using the cooker.

DISHWASHERS

To the British these still seem the ultimate luxury. Indeed we have the lowest ownership rates in Europe. However, since the average family spends 10 hours a week washing up, it may be worth investing in a dishwasher, as they may be more economical than using quantities of hot water from the tank.

Choosing a Dishwasher

For family use, choose a 12 or 14 place setting machine, since the most economical way to use one is to load it throughout the day and only run it once in the evening.

* Check that the shelves and baskets can be adjusted to fit your glasses and plates. It may even be worth taking a plate or two along to the shop to try them out for size before buying.
* Most machines need dishwasher powder, salt for the water softener, and a rinse aid to prevent streaks on glasses and china. Check where all these go and how easy they are to load.
* Finally check that the filter is easy to empty and clean.
* A cold water fill machine is slightly more efficient than a hot and cold water fill and more convenient if your hot water supply is limited.

Using a Dishwasher

Most families find it worthwhile to buy any necessary extra cups and plates, so that they have enough crockery for all the meals throughout the day. The machine can then be loaded after each meal and switched on only after the evening meal at night.

* Most machines have a rinse and hold setting, for rinsing the crockery should the machine not be used for a day or two.
* Remember that dishwasher detergent is much stronger than washing up liquid and, like all household cleaners, should be stored safely away from children.
* Ordinary washing up liquid should not be used in a dishwasher.

* The rinsing cycle is useful for washing little-used crockery and glasses before use, and the heated drying cycle on some machines is a quick way of warming plates for a dinner party.
* Very dirty saucepans and casserole dishes should be soaked before putting in the dishwasher, just as they would be before washing up by hand.
* Check the manufacturer's instructions booklet carefully as many recommend that lead crystal, bone-handled cutlery and fine handprinted china should not be washed in a dishwasher.
* Avoid washing silver and stainless steel cutlery in the same section of a dishwasher, as this can cause pitting on the surface of the metal.
* The most common problem with dishwashers is caused by using too little powder, so always measure the powder before putting it in the machine.

FOOD PROCESSORS

These have become popular in recent years. They are powerful machines that can chop, mince, slice, shred and purée foods as well as making small quantities of cakes and pastries.

Choosing a Food Processor

* Check the maximum capacities for foods, such as cakes, biscuits and bread mixes: many processors can only deal with very small amounts such as 225 g (8 oz) or 450 g (1 lb) of bread mix.
* Most food processors will not whisk egg whites or cream to the same bulk as is possible by hand whisking or using an electric mixer. The design of the processor means that less air is incorporated into the mixture, so meringues and the like are not usually successful. Some machines have special whisking attachments, but even so the results are not as good as with hand whisking.
* Look for a model with a pulse button, which allows it to be run for just a couple of seconds. Processors are so powerful that it is easy to overprocess foods. The pulse button makes controlling the degree of processing much easier.
* Check whether the bowl, lid and all the various attachments are dishwasher proof.

* Look for good storage arrangements for the accessories. Most are very sharp and need to be safely kept in a rack, not left in a kitchen drawer.
* Check the range of accessories available. Many machines offer extra discs, such as a coleslaw disc or a chip making disc. Some have whisks and juice extractors as well. A good range of optional extras is useful if you later decide to add to your collection.

Using a Food Processor

* Always underprocess foods. Stop and check the consistency, then turn the machine on again for a few seconds if necessary. This saves spoiling food by overprocessing.
* Avoid overloading the machine. Process large quantities in batches. Overloading will cause uneven processing and may strain the motor.
* Always use the plastic pusher provided when slicing and shredding. Never push food down with your fingers.
* Take care when removing the metal blade after making cakes and biscuits. Tip most of the mixture out, then reach in and grasp the blade by the central plastic spindle, not by the metal parts as these are very sharp.
* Take care when washing up. Leave the sharp blades and discs on the worktop until you are ready to wash them. If you leave them in the washing up bowl you may forget they are there and then cut yourself. Clean under running water, using a small brush.
* Most processors are not designed for crushing ice or grinding coffee beans. Check in the instruction leaflet before attempting to use your processor for these functions.
* Use the processor to the full. A good recipe book will guide you, but they are very versatile and can make most dishes from home made pasta to quick choux pastry, and even beat half frozen ice cream for a light and creamy texture.

FREEZERS

Freezers are a great boon for most large families, keen gardeners and those of us who have sudden urges to cook grand dishes in the middle of the night. They also enable town dwellers to take advantage of seasonal gluts in the market.

Choosing a Freezer

Most families find a 150 or 180 litre (5 or 6 cu. ft.) freezer a useful size as it will fit under the worktop, although for bulk buying and keen cooks and gardeners, a larger model is usually worthwhile.

* Check that the controls are easy to see and adjust but not within easy reach of small children.
* Uprights are easy to use and keep organized but check that at least one shelf can be removed to accommodate large joints and the Christmas turkey.
* Plastic fronts to shelves keep the cool air in when the door is opened.
* Chest freezers are cheaper to run than uprights and can take a great deal of food. However, they do take up more space than an upright, are quite difficult to keep organized and short people generally find it difficult to reach the base.

Ideally the freezer needs to be placed somewhere cool but close to the kitchen.

* A garage is fine, but it is a nuisance to keep going out for a few peas or ice cream, so many families find having a fridge freezer in the kitchen as well is a good combination.

Using a Freezer

Some degree of organization is necessary with a freezer.

* Labelling food is very important, since once frozen and covered with ice, you won't be able to tell whether it's plum purée or tomato soup.
* Label the food with name, quantity and date frozen so that you can use similar foods in rotation.
* Foods should be well wrapped, in heavy duty polythene bags, foil-lined bags, waxed cartons or plastic boxes. Yogurt pots and margarine tubs can be used as well.
* It makes sense to freeze in small quantities, since you can then remove as many packages as necessary, rather than having to saw lumps off a gallon of frozen soup.
* A colour coding system is useful; by using coloured bags and tags, you can at least find the right sort of foods easily. So red tags might indicate chicken, blue fish, yellow meats and green

sweet dishes. This way you can easily find a meat pie for tea, even if the label has come adrift.

* Another possible system is to keep specific shelves and baskets for different types of food.
* Highly organized people keep freezer log books, with an up-to-date record of what is in the freezer at any one time. This saves a finger-numbing search for foods that have worked their way to the bottom. However, you do have to train all the family to use the book, otherwise whilst you are feeling smug about how full the freezer is, your teenager's late night snacks have reduced the stock to half a pound of peas and a few packets of ice cream.
* When freezing down large amounts of food, use the fast freeze setting for best results. Check the instruction booklet for the maximum quantities that should be frozen in 24 hours. When freezing just one dish or the odd loaf of bread, this is not so important but with large quantities of fresh food the results will be much improved by using the fast freeze setting. It also helps prevent the food already in the freezer from increasing in temperature.
* Many foods can be open frozen, then packed into bags or containers. This is useful for fruits, vegetables, biscuits and small cakes as the individual pieces remain free-flowing, so that you can use them in any quantity required.
* Nonstick baking trays are ideal for open freezing.
* Delicate foods, such as iced cakes and gâteaux can also be open frozen until hard, then overwrapped or boxed for storage.

The freezer can be a useful method of storing leftover food.

* Dregs of wine can be frozen in ice cube trays, ready to be added to casseroles and stews straight from the freezer.
* Left-over cheese can be grated into a plastic box and again used straight from the freezer for topping and sauces.
* Bread that has gone hard can be made into breadcrumbs for stuffing and you can keep a constant supply of pastry mix by rubbing the fat into the flour to breadcrumb consistency, then freezing. This mixture will remain free-flowing and can be removed by the tablespoon and used to make pastry; or add sugar and nuts for an unusual crumble topping.

* Freeze concentrated home-made stock in ice cube trays, so they are quickly usable.
* Keep a supply of pie fillings ready to be topped with pastry for a quick and easy meal.

Defrosting and Cleaning

To avoid anyone accidentally unplugging the freezer, cover the plug and socket with a large piece of tape, or use a coloured plug top to remind you which is the freezer.

* A freezer alarm is useful, especially if the freezer is in the garage, as this gives an audible warning when the contents begin to thaw.
* In the event of a power failure a full freezer should remain completely cold for about 8 hours. Do not open the lid during this time and keep the surroundings as cool as possible.
* When going away on holiday, it is worthwhile freezing a small quantity of water in a plastic container. Wedge the container on a slope while the water freezes, then stand it upright in the freezer. If there is a power failure while you are away, the water will thaw and refreeze on the level, so you will know what has happened. Ask a neighbour how long the power was off for and this will give you some idea of how the food may have been affected. If it was less than eight hours, and the freezer was full of food, it is unlikely to have thawed.

Defrosting is usually a major job, but it only needs to be done a few times each year; usually two to three times for an upright and once or twice for a chest model.

* If possible run down the contents of the freezer, then load the food into freezer boxes and the fridge.
* If this is not possible, place an old blanket in the freezer for a few hours to become really chilled. Place the food in cardboard boxes and cover with the blanket.
* Speed up defrosting with bowls of hot water placed in the freezer.
* A chest freezer without a drainage channel will need old towels placed in the base to soak up the water.
* Once defrosted, wash out the interior with warm water and bicarbonate of soda, about 1 teaspoon of soda to ½ litre (1 pint) of water. Finally wipe round and replace the food. Turn on to the fast freeze setting for several hours in accordance with the manufacturer's instructions, then return the control to normal.
* If the food has thawed and been left for days, defrost and wash out as above, then wash again using sterilizing solution of the type sold for babies' bottles. Wipe round the surfaces, avoiding the metal pipework. Fill with screwed-up newspaper and leave for a day or so with the door ajar.

MICROWAVE COOKERS

These were originally used mostly for thawing and reheating foods, but basic modern cookers are far more versatile and can be used for cooking fresh foods, with very good results. They are excellent for fish, vegetables, poultry, larger joints of meat and sauces. They can be used to cook foods such as steaks and chops, but if browning is required then you can buy a separate browning dish, or use your conventional cooker grill to achieve the desired effect. Cakes and similar foods also suffer from the lack of browning, and bread and pastry do not cook very well in a microwave cooker.

They are useful in busy family households, or in homes where everyone needs meals at different times. The fact that they save time and energy makes them popular with families and single people living alone.

Choosing a Microwave Cooker

First, decide if your family really needs a simple model for thawing, reheating and occasional cooking. The alternative is a more sophisticated model, perhaps with a heat probe, variable power and browning facilities built in, but this will mean taking a little time to get used to the cooking methods involved.

* Look for a defrost setting to make thawing foods easy. The defrost setting helps to ensure that the food thaws evenly and does not begin to cook. Even with a defrost setting some foods need to be allowed to stand before cooking to ensure even thawing.
* A low power setting is useful for cooking tough cuts of meat and other dishes such as egg custards.
* A turntable is convenient but it can restrict the size and shape of dishes that can be used in the cooker.
* Make sure the timer is clear and easy to set. Check that small amounts of time, such as 30 seconds, can be set easily.
* Look for a good instruction and/or recipe booklet. Ask to see one in the shop; check it has clear guidelines about what can and cannot be used in the cooker, a run-down on how a microwave cooker works, and a good selection of the sorts of recipes your family likes.

Using a Microwave Cooker

Take a little time to get used to the cooker and new cooking methods. Experiment a little, and be aware that cooking times are likely to vary quite a bit. Cook by eye at first and make notes as you go along.

* Do not use metal dishes or foil containers in the microwave. Small quantities of foil are sometimes allowed to shield small areas of food, such as chicken drumsticks or the tail end of fish, but check in the instruction booklet.
* Undercook foods, then allow them to stand, as many dishes continue cooking once they come out of the cooker. It is easy to return them to the oven for an extra minute or so if necessary.
* Place the cooker near the main worktop, so that you can keep an eye on what is happening to the food. This will also make stirring, and adding ingredients easier.

* Avoid turning on the cooker when it is empty. Some manufacturers recommend that you leave a glass of water in the cooker in case it is accidentally switched on.
* Clean by wiping with a damp cloth. If very dirty, stand a cup of water with a slice of lemon in the cooking cavity. Heat until steaming, then wipe round.

REFRIGERATORS

Keeping food cool was always a problem before efficient cheap refrigerators became widely available. Rich households relied on the Ice Cart calling regularly; many country estates had their own Ice Houses, usually a cave on the north side of a hill. Here winter ice could be stored for most of the year. Refrigerators are thankfully cheaper and easier to install.

Choosing a Refrigerator

When choosing a new fridge, look for plenty of door storage space and check to see whether tall bottles of wine or squash will fit into the bottle rack.

* Movable and sometimes reversible shelves make fitting in the weekend shopping easier and some fridges have flap-up sections on shelves to allow tall bottles and containers to be fitted in.
* Two separate salad drawers allow fruit and vegetables to be stored separately. They are also easier to remove and wash.
* Star markings on the evaporator of a refrigerator show how long ready-frozen foods can be stored. One star indicates frozen food may be stored for one week, two stars means one month and three stars shows food may be stored for three months. Unless the evaporator shows the freezer symbol, fresh food must never be frozen in a refrigerator.

* For anyone who already has a freezer, a larder fridge is a good buy. This has a flat evaporator plate at the back of the fridge and no evaporator, so all the shelf space can be used for storing fresh foods.
* Three temperature fridges have a section for frozen foods, a refrigerator section and a cellar area, whick keeps foods such as cheese, wine, fruits and cold meats at just the right temperature. Usually these foods benefit from being removed from the fridge an hour or so before use to allow the flavour to develop.

A fridge needs careful siting; it should ideally be near your main worktop, to make transfer of heavy shopping easier, but not next to the cooker or tumble drier, as proximity to heat makes the fridge work harder to keep cool and so increases the running costs.

* Remember that the back of a fridge does get warm, so always allow a little space, about 1.5 cm (3 inches), for the air to circulate easily.
* Cats are often quick to realize that there is constant warm air floating up from the back of the fridge and they sometimes have to be evicted from the fridge top. This is a good reason for not storing any foods on top of the fridge.

Defrosting and Cleaning
Manual defrost fridges need defrosting when the ice on the evaporator builds up to about 1 cm (½ inch). Avoid leaving it until the evaporator door is impossible to open, and you are desperate for the last beefburger locked inside! Defrosting is rather a nuisance, but less so if it is done regularly.

* Turn the fridge off, remove the food and speed up defrosting by placing a bowl of very hot water on one of the shelves.
* Use only plastic or wooden scrapers to clear the ice, not knives or any other sharp object as these can easily puncture the metal parts.
* Most families find it is worth the extra initial cost to buy an automatically defrosting fridge. These work by one of two methods, the first by turning themselves off every now and then, and letting the water from the evaporator run through to the back of the fridge where all the warm air will evaporate it away. Very clever, as long as you do not allow the water channel to become blocked. Avoid this by remembering to clean the fridge occasionally. It is surprisingly easy to forget if the fridge does not need defrosting. The second method is by pressing the special defrost button. The refrigeration system then stops and the ice melts. When the defrosting is over the refrigeration cycle starts up again. Usually, the evaporator tray which collects the water has to be emptied.
* There is sometimes a rapid defrosting device whereby heat is introduced into the evaporator. Follow manufacturers' instructions with regard to removal of food.
* Remove the food and wipe the inside of the fridge with a cloth wrung out in warm water and a little bicarbonate of soda.
* Stubborn spots or marks can be cleaned with dry bicarbonate of soda on a damp cloth. A purchased refrigerator deodorizer will help keep the inside smelling sweet.
* Do not use washing-up liquid as the smell is absorbed by the plastic and will linger.

Using a Refrigerator
It is worth making the effort to cool foods completely before placing them in the fridge, as hot foods will increase the running costs and will also create a faster build-up of ice around the evaporator.

* Foods should be covered as well, since smells tend to be transferred, so unless you like milk lightly flavoured with kipper or butter with delicate hints of Stilton, wrap foods or place in plastic containers.
* Bacon, in fact, keeps far better wrapped in cling film or foil than in a bacon box.
* Avoid over-packing a fridge. Air circulation is essential to keep the foods cool and once over-packed some foods inevitably get pushed to the back and left there until they become so mouldy that the smell leads you to them. If this happens, wash out the fridge with bicarbonate of soda in warm water. If the smell lingers, use a little sterilizing solution, as described for freezers on page 63.
* If the fridge is very full, as it often is at holiday weekends or when entertaining, milk and wine can be kept cool in a bucket of water with a few ice cubes in it.

The refrigerator can be very useful when cooking.

* Stocks and home-made soups are easier to skim if they are allowed to cool, then placed in the fridge for an hour or so. The fat will solidify and can be skimmed off with a spoon.
* Tinned meats such as corned beef and hams are easier to slice if chilled in the fridge for an hour before opening.

It is not only food that keeps well in the fridge.

* Films are best stored at low temperatures, nail polish remains smooth and cling film does not tend to cling to itself if it has been stored in the fridge.
* In the summer, keep toilet water and cologne in the fridge to make them more refreshing.
* Even candles can be placed in the fridge for a while before burning as this makes them burn for longer. Leave them for 2 to 3 hours before you use them.
* It is easy to forget to adjust the refrigerator as the weather changes, but this will keep the running costs to a minimum and keep food in the best condition.
* A noisy fridge can sometimes be cured by levelling it. Some models have adjustable feet at the front to level them, or you may need to slide a thin piece of wood under one corner.

* Before going on holiday, turn off the fridge, empty it and wash it out, then prop the door ajar to prevent it smelling musty.

TUMBLE DRIERS

Tumble driers are a great boon during rainy weather. They mean you don't have to festoon the house with damp clothes and they ensure that towels, nappies and jumpers are soft.

Choosing a Tumble Drier

Most take about 4.5 kg (9 lb) of clothes, although a few worktop models hold only 3.5 kg (6 lb).

* Choose a model that has two drying settings (one for natural fabrics and one for synthetics) and look for one that has a cool-down period at the end of drying. This will ensure that clothes stay as free from creases as possible.
* Some sophisticated machines sense when the clothes are dry and turn themselves off – useful if the drier is going to be used in a separate utility room or garage, and for saving energy.
* Check how easy the filter is to clean, as this should be done regularly.
* A venting kit is a useful method of getting rid of the hot steamy air, but the drier needs to be placed near an open window or on an external wall, so that the vent can be fixed through the wall.
* Some driers have a system of condensing the hot moist air and pumping it out as water. This is useful in small kitchens that would otherwise steam up rapidly, but does tend to increase the running costs.
* If space is at a premium, remember that some small models can be wall mounted, others can stack with a matching washing machine.

Using a Tumble Drier

Never overload the drier as this tends to make clothes very creased and can extend the drying time.

* Try to avoid mixing small and large articles; a sheet and a collection of underwear will inevitably become tangled and not dry evenly.

* If synthetic fibres tend to cling to each other, use a fabric conditioner in the final washing rinse, or a fabric conditioning cloth that is added to the tumble drier.
* Cotton polyester clothes can often be taken straight out of the drier and hung on a coat hanger without needing to be ironed.
* Many garments can be worn without ironing, provided you hang or fold them carefully.
* Towels and nappies dried outside can be softened by tumbling for fifteen minutes.

VACUUM CLEANERS

Almost every home has a vacuum cleaner, although many are vintage hand-me-down models that are still merrily sucking up dirt and dust every day.

Choosing a Vacuum Cleaner

There are various types of vacuum cleaner, suited for different cleaning operations.

* Upright vacuum cleaners are the most convenient way to deal with large areas of fitted carpets. They have a beating action along with the suction, so the dust is loosened and then sucked up. Attachments which can be used for other cleaning jobs are sometimes supplied with upright vacuum cleaners and are sometimes offered as an optional extra.
* For cleaning upholstery, heavy curtains and large areas of carpet, a cylinder cleaner may be more useful. The tools are very efficient and often easier to fit and use than those on an upright cleaner.
* Wet and dry cleaners are designed to pick up large scale debris, such as in a workshop or on a patio, and to cope with minor floods. These cleaners are often noisier than conventional models and sometimes not as easy to move around.
* Small battery-operated or rechargeable cleaners are useful for clearing up crumbs and for cleaning cars.

Using a Vacuum Cleaner

Whichever type of cleaner you use, it can be a useful aid to daily cleaning. As well as being the most effective way to cope with carpets, it can also be used for regular cleaning of upholstery and curtains, for dusting shelves, window ledges and above doors and around curtain rails. The area under beds, hard floors and the backs of cupboards can all be cleaned with a vacuum cleaner.

* Remember to empty the bag regularly, as a full bag will prevent the machine from working properly. Some have full bag indicators to remind you when it is time to change the bag.
* Try not to pick up paper clips, pins and other metal objects as these could damage the cleaner.
* If the hose becomes blocked, remove it from the cleaner and clear with a metal coat hanger, unwound to make a long straight wire.
* Some machines can blow as well as suck, which makes clearing a blocked hose easy, although do remember to do this outside.

* Replacement parts such as beater bars, brushes and belts are usually available in electrical shops, but only use those which are made by the manufacturer of the vacuum cleaner.

WASHING MACHINES

Washday Mondays used to be grim days for the whole family, with the house full of steam, damp clothes and an all-pervasive smell of starch and bleach. Washing machines are great labour savers and need little care and attention, so are a worthwhile investment.

Choosing a Washing Machine
The choice to be made is between twin tubs and automatics.

* Twin tubs are still popular: they are economical to run, use little water and powder and are ideal for anyone who likes to remain firmly in charge of what is happening.
* Automatic washing machines are timesaving, since they can simply be loaded and left, and they are kind to the fabrics. They are either loaded from the top or front. Automatics tend to use larger quantities of water than twin tubs, which may be important if the water is metered. They generally spin more slowly than twin tub machines, so look for a good spin speed when buying, otherwise drying clothes made of natural fibres will take longer. An automatic washing powder must be used as ordinary powders will not give the best results and may damage the machine since they produce too much foam. A hot and cold water fill is useful if you have lots of hot water, especially if you are on an economy tariff which heats your hot water during off-peak hours, but most machines can be used on cold water only if a 'T' piece is fitted to the inlet hoses.

Using a Washing Machine
For either type of machine, the clothes to be washed need to be sorted into separate loads, to minimize running costs and possible damage to the clothes, see also pages 81 and 82.

* In an automatic, mix small loads of different types together for fewer, larger washes, and wash on the programme suitable for the more delicate fabrics.
* In twin tubs wash the cleanest clothes first, then, using the same water, work through the loads until the very dirty clothes can be washed last.
* On an automatic machine, clean and dry the dispenser drawer occasionally and check the filter, if there is one. This often collects quite a bit of fluff, as well as the odd button, pin or coin.
* The door seal should be wiped out after use to dry it, as

leaving it constantly wet could damage it over a period of time.

* Nappies soaked in sterilizing solution should be rinsed before washing as this too can affect the door seals and other parts of an automatic washing machine.
* After use turn off the hot and cold water supply if possible, as this protects the valve within the machine.
* Twin tub machines need little regular care apart from wiping round after use.
* Lay the outlet hose down into a bowl placed on the floor to drain out any remaining water.
* Use an automatic washing machine at night if there is a cheap night-time electricity tariff. This is not so easy to do with twin tub machines, but often you can heat domestic hot water overnight and use this in the washing machine the next day.
* In hard water areas, the amount of washing powder used can be cut down by using a water softening agent along with the powder. This is available from chemists and hardware shops in a powder form. Add it to the water at the same time as the washing powder.

HOUSEHOLD PESTS

Many pests of one sort or another can gain entry into the house. Avoid this as far as possible by careful hygiene, by storing food properly, and keeping dustbins clean and well away from the house. Use proprietary products with great care. Always read the label carefully and follow the instructions given; wear protective gloves and clothes where necessary. Store them out of reach of children and away from pets, and try to keep both out of the way when you are using the products. Most local councils will advise on household pests; some may charge.

PESTS	WHERE FOUND	WHAT TO DO
Ants	Almost anywhere. Nests are usually outside, but they often trail into the house.	Trace the nest and pour boiling water in – or use a proprietary ant killer.
Bed bugs	In cracks in walls or under skirting boards. Occasionally in secondhand furniture or beds.	Spray with a proprietary insecticide. Spray the bed, mattress and frame, also check wall cracks and skirting boards and spray these. In severe cases, contact your local authority.
Carpet beetles	On carpets, wool and feathers.	Use a proprietary insecticide.
Cat and dog fleas	On cats and dogs, but also lay eggs on carpets and furniture.	Use proprietary defleaing agent, then use a defleaing collar.

		Vacuum furniture and carpets as well, as the eggs can live for up to two months. Your vet can supply a very effective spray for the animal and one for the house, if ordinary sprays don't work.
Cock-roaches	In kitchens, under floorboards and in cupboards.	Very difficult to get rid of. Try a spray killer but otherwise call local council to fumigate.
Flour mites	Small creatures that appear in flour stored for long periods.	Throw away flour and clean cupboard well with disinfectant.
Flies	Almost everywhere in summer.	Keep foods covered, wipe worktops, keep dustbins clean. Use slow release sprays. Flies don't like the smell of basil, mint or tansy.
Mice and Rats	Under floorboards and behind skirtings.	First, borrow a neighbour's cat, then use traps or poison with great care, especially if children or pets in house – or contact local council.
Moths	Larvae laid on blankets, clothes, etc. especially if stored.	Lavender and rue are supposed to discourage them. Use mothballs to prevent larvae surviving. Wrap clothes well before storage and check under collars and in pockets. Use aerosol spray for carpets.

Silver fish	Damp areas, cupboards, larders, bathrooms.	A little borax will discourage them but do not use this if children or pets are around. Use insecticide sprayed on to affected areas.
Wasps and Bees	Nests usually in gardens but may be in pipework under eaves and similar places around the house.	Contact local council, as interfering with nests could be dangerous.

1. ~~About the House~~
2. Clothes Care

CARE LABELS

This symbol gives the recommended washing instructions.

This symbol means do not machine wash.

The figure above the line indicates the machine code that the fabric should be washed at. This may correspond with your washing machine. These are also shown on the side of the detergent pack. The temperature shown below the line is a guide for water temperature.

This indicates that the article must not be washed.

This indicates that the article can be bleached with chlorine bleach in solution.

Do not use bleach on garments bearing this sign.

The circle indicates that the garment should be dry-cleaned only.

The letter inside the circle indicates the kind of dry cleaning fluid that should be used on the garment. This will not concern you unless you are attempting to clean it in a laundrette dry cleaning machine, in which case you should check that the symbols correspond with fluid in the machine you are using (see opposite).

This symbol provides you with a guide to ironing the garment.

One dot means use a cool iron on such fabrics as acrylic, nylon, acetate, polyester and viscose.

Two dots mean use a warm iron. This should be used on such fabric as polyester mixes and wool fibres.

 Three dots indicate a very hot setting which should only be used on cotton and linen.

 This indicates that the article should not be ironed because it would harm it to do so.

 This symbol indicates the drying instructions.

 Tumble dry.

 Line dry.

 Drip dry.

 Dry flat.

If the dry cleaning symbol has an A in its circle then any type of dry cleaning fluid can be used. This is useful if you want to use the laundrette dry cleaning machine.

in the circle means that many dry cleaning solvents can be used, i.e. you can use a laundrette machine. Both these symbols mean that any dry cleaner can cope with the garment.

in the circle and a line underneath means do not use a laundrette machine and that cleaners should be made aware of the symbol as certain precautions have to be taken.

indicates that only a certain number of cleaners will be able to deal with this. It usually appears on a delicate fabric. When you take a garment bearing this sign into a cleaners, point it out to the cleaner and ask if he has the chemical. It indicates that solvent 113 should be used on the garment.

Aftercare: After either dry cleaning the clothes yourself, or having them cleaned, make sure that they are well aired before they are put away as the fumes are quite poisonous. Articles you should never dry clean yourself include padded materials, duvets, or anything that is likely to house the fumes for a long time.

Wash code	1 95°	2 60°	3 60°	4 50°	5 40°	6 40°	7 40°	8 30°	9 95°
Machine Washing	Very hot to boil Maximum wash	Hot Maximum wash	Hot Medium wash	Hand-hot Medium wash	Warm Medium wash	Warm Minimum wash	Warm Minimum wash	Cool Minimum wash	Very hot (95°C) to boil
Hand Washing	Hand-hot (50°C) or boil	Hand-hot (50°C)	Hand-hot (50°C)	Hand-hot	Warm	Warm	Warm Do not rub	Cool	Hand-hot (50°C) or boil
Agitation	Maximum	Maximum	Medium	Medium	Maximum	Minimum	Minimum Do not rub	Minimum	Medium
Rinsing, spinning, wringing	Spin or wring	Spin or wring	Cold rinse Short spin or drip-dry	Cold rinse Short spin or drip-dry	Spin or wring	Cold rinse Short spin Do not wring	Spin Do not hand wring	Cold rinse Short spin Do not wring	Cold rinse Drip-dry
Suitable fabrics	White cotton and linen fabrics without special finishes	Cotton, linen or viscose fabrics without special finishes and colour-fast at 60°C	White nylon; white polyester/ cotton fabrics	Coloured nylon, polyester, special finish cotton and viscose; acrylic cotton; coloured polyester/ cotton	Machine washable wool, cotton linen or viscose fabrics with colours fast at 40°C, but not at 60°C	Acrylics: acetate and triacetate, including mixtures with wool; polyester/ wool blends	Wool, including blankets and wool mixtures with cotton or viscose; silk	Silk and printed acetate fabrics with colours not fast at 40°C	Cotton articles with special finishes capable of being boiled, but requiring drip-drying

WASHING WISDOM

GOOD PRACTICE

Bicarbonate of soda is one of those magic substances that can work all kinds of wonders, from improving your baking to cleaning the oven quickly, so it's hardly surprising that it can help with the weekly wash, too.

* If you substitute a tablespoon of soda bicarbonate for a quarter of a cup of your normal washing powder it will not only save you the cost of that powder, but it will also help to free the grime from the fibres as well as acting as a water softener. Make sure it is rinsed out thoroughly afterwards.

Bulky articles can be wetted before putting them in the washing machine, to make fitting them in easier but be careful not to overload your machine (follow the instruction booklet to find out about maximum loading). Bear in mind that a full load is harder to rinse.

Check and empty the pockets of any garment before you put it into the washing machine. Soggy pound notes which go through the whole washing cycle won't buy the groceries; paper clips, coins or pen tops can wreak their own particular kind of havoc with the wash!

Garment labels are always the best guide to how something should be washed.

* Don't take a guess at the programme for any fabric. Instead, take a few minutes to go through the clothes to be washed, looking at each label and sorting them into little heaps according to the instructions.

* If, of course, you find you only have a few things to be washed on one programme and you don't want to waste time, money and electricity, then you can mix garments requiring a quite different wash treatment, but in this case you must wash *all* of them on the programme given for the most *delicate fabrics* and do not mix dark and light colours.
* Remember (if your machine has one) that you can always use the economy half load programme on your washing machine for a small wash.
* Some garment labels giving the fabric content are as long as a laundry list as there are so many different fibres in the one material. For practical purposes and to be safe, pick out the most delicate of the fibres in the mix and wash according to the instructions on its care label.

Load your machine properly following the machine manufacturer's instructions, if you want to get clothes washed well.

* Some wash programmes should only have small loads, so check the instructions for your machine carefully.
* Always remember that it's better to do two washes than stuff a few extra things in; big loads rarely give the best wash.

Low lather powders designed for automatic machines can be used for any other kind of machine too.

* A good reason for using them is that you end up with much less scum in the water than with the powders intended for non-automatics.
* Always use powder as recommended by the manufacturer (see page 86).

Ordinary washing powder should not be used in a front-loading automatic or a top loader with a revolving drum, at least not if you want to keep your clothes in good shape. The drum action causes too much froth with an ordinary powder, which in turn causes fabrics to get squeezed hard against the side of the drum and prevents them from getting a proper wash. An excess of powder will also mean the rinsing will not be so effective. Then, powder left in garments can often irritate sensitive skin.

* When you're washing garments by hand it's absolutely essential to make sure that the powder is properly dissolved before you put the garments into the water. If you don't, you'll get nasty little white bits sticking to the clothes when they're dry. If you're using warm water for the wash, put the required amount of powder into a container, pour boiling water on to it, stir until thoroughly dissolved, then add the solution to the warm water in the bowl or sink.

Soaking heavily soiled clothes before you put them through the regular washing programme will usually result in cleaner clothes. However, *always* check the garment label first.

* Don't be too impatient, a long soak gives the powder time to get to work and flush out the worst grime and stains. So organize yourself and your clothes the night before washday and soak white things overnight and coloured articles for at least two hours.
* Start the soak with hand hot, never boiling, water.
* Never soak garments made of silk, wool, leather or any fabrics which are not colourfast (see page 84 for how to test) – and be wary of any fabric with a special finish (such as waterproof or flame-resistant clothing).

* Any garments with metal trimmings, buckles, heavy zips, metal buttons and so on don't take to soaking too well either, so if you can't remove the trimmings, don't soak.

Soap is splendid stuff and is essential to keep many of our clothes clean, but too much of it can definitely have a dulling effect on clothes. Black garments end up with a 'bloom' on them and white things can either go grey or yellowish.

* One way to make sure you get all the soap out of them is to add 1 tablespoon of vinegar to the rinsing water.
* And if you see that during the last rinse on the washing machine cycle there still seem to be suds left in the water, or the clothes feel ever so slightly 'slimy' when you take them out, try the vinegar treatment here, too. Pop the things back in again for one more rinse and put a teacupful of vinegar into the drum.

Test for colour fastness by dipping a small section of the garment into a solution of washing powder mixed in warm water, then place the material between two sheets of blotting paper on your ironing board and press with a warm iron. If the colour goes on to the paper or the shade of the garment changes appreciably through the application of heat (if it goes dark, for instance, then goes back to the same shade as the rest of the fabric), then wash the item separately.

* If you've forgotten to test garments for colour fastness, or your husband has slipped a pair of bright new socks into the washing machine when your back was turned, and you get colour transferring on to other garments, the best chance of getting rid of it or lessening the impact is to take prompt action. Should you be lucky enough to spot what's happened as the clothes dance past the glass door of the machine then switch off straight away. Turn the dial to allow the water to drain away, switch on and, when drained, switch off again. Take out all the clothes. Separate those affected by the colour and put these back into the machine again, add powder and select a wash programme as hot as the fabrics will take and let everything go right through the wash cycle again. With a bit of luck and some help from the washing powder and the water,

the colours will fade considerably, perhaps disappear altogether.

* If you don't spot the disaster until your wash is done, it is still worth trying the re-wash treatment.

Water softener is useful in hard water areas to reduce the amount of scum in your washing water.

TRICKY BITS

Collars of shirts or blouses which are particularly grubby benefit from a pre-wash.

* Dampen, then rub a bar of soap along the soiled area and leave for five minutes. Scrub with a soft brush (a nail brush or even an old, clean toothbrush will do). Then wash in the usual way.
* This treatment can be given to cuffs and hems too.

Elastic is useful stuff since it holds things up and holds us in as well. But when it begins to sag, so do the garments made from it. It's not too difficult to replace a length of elastic in the top of a pair of jogging pants, but where the elastic has been woven into, say, the ribbing, replacement is much more complicated, if not impossible. Therefore it pays to wash elastic very carefully indeed as incorrect washing can consistently weaken it.

* Never, never boil any garment with elastic in it, don't wring it out or pull it.
* Always wash it in lukewarm water and give it a very short spin or pat dry with a towel.
* Check the care label on the garment before attempting to tumble dry.

Flame-resistant finishes on clothes, such as nightdresses, can easily be damaged by the use of washing powders, if you wash them in the normal way. Check the care label on the garment first.

* Always look on the washing powder packet for specific instructions and follow them to the letter.

* Usually the only programme you can use for such fabrics is the one designed for delicate fabrics.

Grey tinges to washing aren't simply something dreamed up by the advertising moguls, they can happen. However, the chances are this is not due to the particular brand of powder you use, but more a result of the quantity of powder used.

* It's a fact that when whites are constantly washed some of the whitener in the fabric washes down the drain with the dirt, hence the grey tinge. Washing powders usually help to put some of the whitening agent back, but to do that successfully you must use enough. Manufacturers sometimes give over-generous quantities on their packets, but many women suspect this and so they 'underdose'. However, too little powder fails to restore the whiteness. If you find the recommended quantity doesn't produce the best results, try using a little more (using the same quantity over several washes because it may take two or three to restore whiteness) and compare the results. Alternatively, try soaking the garment before washing.
* If white underwear begins to dull as a result of frequent washing, use one of the special whiteners you can buy in either powder or tablet form. These whiteners are available for various fabrics and can be added to the washing or rinsing water. Follow the packet instructions.

Perspiration odour sometimes clings to clothes even after they've been washed.

* Add a little vinegar to the rinsing water next time you wash the garment and finish by rinsing again thoroughly in clear, clean water.
* An alternative treatment is a soak in a solution of 1 teaspoon of laundry borax to ½ litre (1 pint) of warm water. Leave for an hour, then wash in soapy water with a few drops of ammonia added before rinsing in clear water.
* Try soaking the garment in biological detergent before washing it.
* Fabric conditioner can also help to get rid of perspiration odour.

Shiny bottom on skirts and trousers? Try a touch of vinegar in the rinsing water, 1 tablespoon, which may make the surface more matt, but don't expect miracles, and the cure will only be temporary.

Static electricity may be an indication of your electrifying personality but you might not consider it to be much of an asset with clothes crackling and popping as you take them on and off. Static is a problem associated with certain synthetics, mainly nylon, polyester and acrylics.

* To help reduce the build-up of static electricity, just add fabric conditioner to your next wash and avoid tumble drying the clothes.

Tangles in the wash can be lessened if before you put shirts and blouses in the washing machine you button the cuffs to the front of the shirt.

Zips on items like jeans are big and tough but, with the constant battering they are subjected to as they rotate in the drum of a washing machine, they can get damaged. To avoid this, close them so that the overlap of cloth protects the metal.

TYPES OF CLOTHING

Blue jeans all fade in the wash to a greater or lesser degree.

* However, if they begin to fade in streaks and lines it's not the fabric that's at fault but the way you're washing them. To avoid the streaks, turn the jeans inside out before washing.

Bras take a lot of punishment from perspiration which can rot elastic.

* Wash them every day if at all possible or at least every other day. They should dry overnight. If hand washing, do not rub, twist or wring. Rinse two or three times in clear warm water. Gently ease into shape and hang to dry away from heat.
* Padded bras need special treatment if they, and you, are to keep in shape. If they have an interlining of foam rubber, a washing machine can damage it. Wash in hand hot water, rinse thoroughly and dry well away from heat.

Cotton shirts, blouses and similar garments may have some 'dressing' in the fabric which will form a scum when the detergent gets to it.

* You can remove a lot of the dressing by soaking the garment in cold water for thirty minutes before popping it into the washing machine.

Dungarees, overalls and other such protective garments worn in the garden or the workshop can be difficult to launder.

* Dip the garments in a fairly thin starch after you have washed them, then allow them to drip dry in the garden: washing will be much easier the next time round.

Girdles, too, have a longer life if they are washed every day.

* Latex and nylon should need only a quick dip, a quick spin and then be left to dry overnight.

Hand-embroidered blouses and scarves often come from third world countries, and such garments sometimes do not have labels giving wash instructions, while those which do are not always as clear as they might be, so it's always wise to take a few precautions.

* Before you wash any embroidered item put it into a solution of salt and water (1 tablespoon of salt to 1 litre (2 pints) of water). This will sometimes help set the colour and prevent any tendency to run. Leave in the solution for a couple of hours, then rinse out the salt with lots of cold water before washing very carefully in cool to warm water. It is best to wash by hand, unless the care label recommends otherwise.
* A touch of vinegar in the final rinsing water (a tablespoon to a bowl of water) will help revive the colours and bring them back to freshness.

Jogging and leisure wear (and even some of those chunky sweaters) made from synthetics have 'Hand wash only' tags on them. If you don't discover this until you take your purchase out of the carrier bag at home, then don't despair, hand washing needn't be all that much of a chore!

* The quickest and most efficient way to get the dirt out of even the grubbiest garment is to use the same powder as you do for your automatic – this makes the grime literally flow out before your very eyes.
* For one sweater add something less than 1 tablespoon of powder to a basin full of water. Give the garment a gentle squeeze, pop it into your washing machine and programme it to a cool rinse and a short spin. When the label on the garment says 'Don't machine wash' the 'Don't' doesn't include rinsing and spinning, it's quite safe to do it.

Leg warmers and chunky socks usually come in bright and cheerful colours, but be wary about washing them along with other items of clothing unless you're quite certain they're colourfast. While many garments, cord jeans for instance, do make it clear on the label that they need to be washed separately, socks rarely seem to provide such information. So it's better to be safe than sorry – a simple pair of maroon socks have been known to give the rest of the wash a lovely rosy glow!

* Test for colour fastness, see page 84.

Silk blouses are extremely luxurious to wear but can be laborious to wash.

* Wash by hand using warm soapy water, then lots of cool to rinse.
* Make sure you haven't got any ragged nails or rough skin which can snag the silk as you wash it.

Swimsuits suffer from salt in sea water and chemicals in pool water.

* If you're putting a swimsuit away for the winter give it a good soaking in cold water to take out the salt, then wash and dry.
* If, on the other hand, you haven't got further than the local swimming pool, the suit could be affected by chemicals in the water, so soak it in 2¼ litres (half a gallon) of water, to which you've added 2 teaspoons of borax, before washing in the usual way.
* Always rinse swimsuits in fresh water after every wear.

Synthetics are unfortunately not always as easy to care for as one might imagine. Washing them the wrong way, for instance, can lead to nylon blouses acquiring a permanently crushed look, body-hugging ribbed polo neck sweaters can very easily turn into loose baggy garments if you wash them at too high a temperature.

* To retain that spring and cling, wash at a lowish temperature, and keep handling down to a minimum.

Tights tend to get snagged in the washing process if you do not take precautions. It can happen all too easily if they go into the washing machine along with a jumble of other items with zips and hooks and sometimes the drum itself can develop a slight roughness which is equally hazardous.

* Pop the tights into something like a pillowcase for protection before putting them into the washing machine.
* An alternative 'tights protector' is a square scarf. Knot it securely round the tights to form a pouch similar to Dick Whittington's.

Wool garments need specific care.

* If you find the words 'Machine washable' on the label, then you can put them in the machine, but be sure to follow the other instructions on the label.
* Check that the powder and the machine programme you plan to use is suitable for wool and is approved by the International Wool Secretariat. Look for the Woolmark.

Certification Trade Mark
Pure new wool

* Ordinary wool clothes should never be machine washed; they need a gentle handwash. Rub as little as possible.
* Turn the garment inside out as this will mean less damage to the surface of the wool.
* To keep the shape, fasten all the buttons.
* Any very special sweaters which you don't want to run the risk of spoiling can be washed with a special cold water solution. You can buy it in powder form in small packets.
* A small amount of glycerine (1½ teaspoons) in the rinsing water gives wool a nice soft texture and keeps it bouncy.

Wool socks need frequent washing. If they become dirty and full of perspiration they can become hard, flat and matted.

DRYING

Berets, the flat styles, that is, should be stretched over a plate after washing. The plate should be about 2 cm (1 inch) shorter in diameter than the berets. They'll keep their shape that way. Make sure you don't overstretch them, though. If you go in more for the peaked type of headgear, then prop it over a pudding bowl and plump out any loose areas with crumpled up paper.

Coats and jackets made of nylon pile fabric should be shaken several times as they're drying on the line. This will help restore the fluffy look to the pile.

Corsets need cosseting after they've been washed.

* Boned corsets should be pulled gently along the bones, then pegged out to dry. If the corset has a zip all the way down hang it lengthways along the line, then zip it up over the line.
* It's very important not to use suspenders, shoulder straps or hems for hanging, since the constant flapping about on the line will weaken the corset at these points.

Detachable lace collars should be rolled in a towel after washing, then dried flat.

Dresses which are washable can be dried on hangers in much the same way as they are hung in a wardrobe, but those with pleated skirts should be hung by the waistband with the pleats falling straight. Don't skimp on the pegs – use them along the waist seam.

Drip drying something large like a coat can be rather messy – no one wants puddles all over the floor. So if the weather won't allow the garment to be hung outside, try the towel treatment.

* Absorb any excess moisture, or as much as possible, by rolling

the coat in a towel before hanging up. Any tiny creases which result in the process can be given a quick run-over with the iron later.

Radiators come into their own when time's short, the weather's wet and the tumble drier's developed a fault.

* Things like socks and leg warmers will dry much more quickly if you hang them on a clothes' drier near a radiator.
* Shirts and blouses can be put on a hanger and then hung on the clothes' drier. This minimizes the need for ironing as most of the creases will drop out.

Running colours can be a problem with some fabrics even at the drying stage.

* Hang striped garments, which have a tendency to run, with the stripes running down vertically.
* The quicker such garments are dried, the less chance there is of dye running. You can spin dry after washing in coolish water, then shake the garment out immediately.

Starched clothes should not be left out on the washing line after they've dried if there's a sharp wind about. The wind can have the effect of blowing out all the newly acquired crispness from collars and cuffs and leaving them quite limp.

* Keep an eye on starched items and take them in as soon as they are dry.

Trousers often seem perfectly dry until you feel the pockets, which are still soggy.

* Avoid this by turning the trousers inside out before pegging them out on the line. The pockets will flap about in the breeze and will keep pace with the rate at which the rest of the fabric is drying.
* Open zips too (which you will have taken care to close during the washing process, of course, to avoid damage) then the air will be able to circulate all round the double thickness of material at these points.

Tumble driers, given the great British climate, can sometimes be the only answer if we want to wear our clothes fairly soon after washing them!

* Don't overload the machine and don't put your socks and underwear in with large items like sheets if you want to get good results.
* Dripping wet clothes should never be put straight into a tumble drier; spin them first following the instructions on the care label.
* Taking out the garments just as soon as the cooling period finishes also helps to prevent any creases setting into the fabric.
* Try not to mix several types of fabrics in the one load as each may require different heat settings and drying times to get the best results.
* Dry for the shortest possible time, as overdrying can harm fabric.

White wool garments must be dried well away from the noonday sun. Sunlight has a tendency to turn such garments yellowish. Other forms of direct heating inside can have a similar effect. Sunlight can also fade coloured fabrics so always take care when drying in very sunny weather.

Wool clothes don't need to be dried flat. They are surprisingly robust garments and are likely to come to more harm in the washing than in the drying.

* They can be hung on the line. Take a pair of old tights and put them in one sleeve, right through the garment and out the end of the other sleeve and peg the tights, not the wool, to the line.
* Incidentally, do fasten buttons and zips before you hang wool garments up.
* However, particularly heavy items may not be suitable for hanging up in case the weight of the garment stretches them. To be absolutely sure that a sweater is the same size and shape *after* drying, you can draw its outline on a piece of wrapping paper before you wash it, then when it's ready to dry, put it down over the pencilled outline and gently pull it into the required shape as necessary.
* Any seams which have become slightly rucked, or buttonhole bands on cardigans which have wrinkled in the wash, can also be pulled back to their proper length just before the drying stage.

Ironing

Checklist of points for making ironing easier:

* Look at the care label on the garment for instructions.
* Set iron at the correct temperature.
* Check that the item is at the right degree of dampness for ironing.
* Fill a steam iron and select the steam indicator before switching on the iron. If not using steam, then dampen very dry items and roll up.
* Make sure the iron and the board are clean before you start.
* Always start ironing on a part of the garment hidden in wear, just to be on the safe side.
* If you can sit down and be comfortable, then do.
* Put your basket of clothes on one side of the board and have a clothes drying rack on the other – small items can be draped over the rack, things like blouses can be hung on with hangers. To take longer things like dresses you can screw a piece of wood on to the back of the kitchen or cupboard door near where you do your ironing – put a few cup hooks into the wood, then simply hang the ironed dresses on hangers on to the hooks.
* A top cover of silver milium fabric over your board can make ironing easier. It reflects the heat, retains the damp.
* Always iron in the direction of the selvedge.
* Iron a garment methodically – going from one section to the next in sequence – don't dash about all over the place with the iron.
* Iron double parts first on thick materials and last on thin materials.
* Iron with smooth, slow strokes – back and forwards at the same pace. Varying the stroke makes extra work, takes more effort.
* Iron on the right side for a shiny finish and on the wrong side for a matt finish.

* Fabric softeners used in the wash can make fabrics easier to iron.
* Begin by ironing garments needing a cool iron and progress towards those needing a hotter iron (see page 103).
* Give the iron time to stabilize at the correct temperature, when moving to a hotter temperature.
* Iron until dry.

A reminder of the ironing symbols/see also page 78):

 Cool iron
 Very hot iron

 Warm iron
 Do not iron

Baubles, beads, metallic threads and sequins certainly add a sparkle to clothes but that sparkle might quickly be dulled if you use an iron on them carelessly.

* Steam may tarnish metal, so always use it sparingly, or, better still, not at all.
* If it's possible to test a bit of the fabric on the inside first, do so; steam, allow to dry and check for tarnish.

Buttons, zips and other metallic fasteners don't get creased, so don't press them! If you do, you run the risk of their shape showing through on material beneath.

Clean the floor underneath the ironing board. Sheets and long dresses drag on the floor as you iron them and can pick up dust in the process.

* If you put an old sheet or blanket down on the floor and stand the ironing board on top of this, hems of garments shouldn't get marks on them.

Crisp creases in the legs of your trousers are smart, a good crisp crease down the centre of your sleeves is not. The only way to get sleeves ironed properly and without that nasty centre crease is to buy a sleeve board. There are other gadgets, too, which are essential if clothes are to be ironed to professional standards; all can be bought cheaply or in some cases you can make your own.

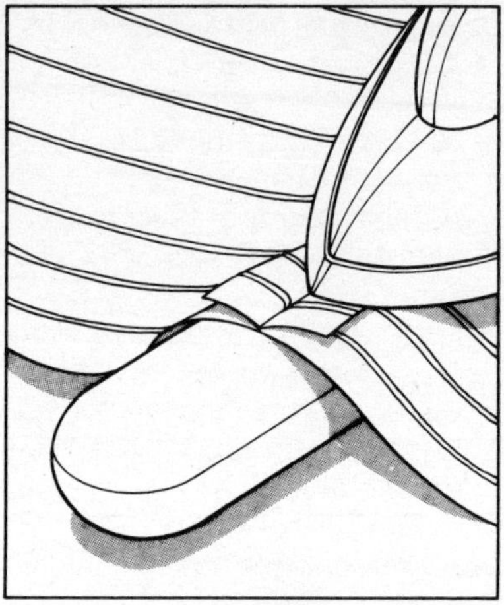

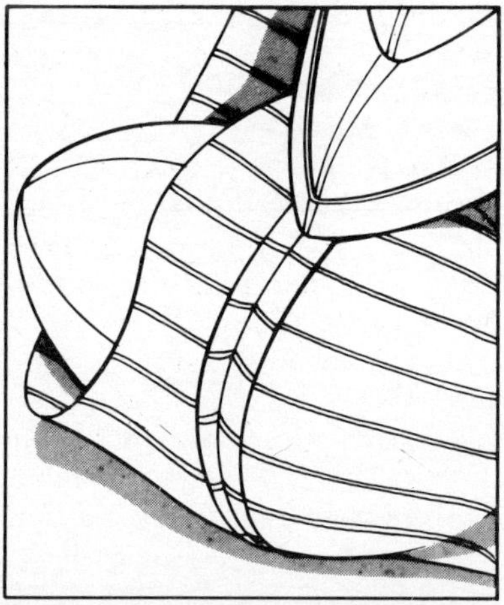

* For darts, shaped seams and rounded parts of garments (the top of a sleeve, for instance) you can get an egg-shaped item which looks rather like a pin cushion and is called a tailor's ham.
* If you wear a little padded mitt on your hand you may be able to reach awkward places that even a ham can't get to. In an emergency you can use a good, thickly padded, clean oven glove as a substitute.
* An item called a seam roll will solve the problem of ridge marks caused by the extra material in the seam. The roll, which is rather like a long narrow stuffed sausage of cloth, is placed between the material and the seam overlap.
* If you do not have one of these, roll up a small hand-towel or even a tightly rolled magazine.
* If you do your own dress-making, you'll need a gadget made of wood and shaped rather like an anvil with a point at one end. It's the only way to get really sharp points in your collars and to cope with other awkward shapes.
* For a crease you could cut butter with, turn trouser legs inside out and rub some hard yellow soap down the inside of the crease, then turn right side out and press with a damp cloth. Don't soak the pressing cloth or you'll run the risk of the soap forming suds.
* Alternatively use starch on the reverse side of the creases, as described above.

Damp cloth is your greatest ally when it comes to ironing materials like corduroy and crêpe.

* Turn the garments inside out and iron with a damp cloth using gentle pressure.
* If you are dealing with a double thickness of material, trouser legs perhaps, then try this: fold a towel to approximately the same width as the leg and slip it inside before ironing; this will save the pile being damaged as it rubs against the other side of the leg.
* To obtain the crease in the trouser leg, turn the right way round again, put a folded towel underneath and a damp cloth on top and press very lightly.

Double-sided sections of garments need double pressing, but, as with all ironing jobs, there's a proper way to do it to achieve a well-groomed look.

* Collars, cuffs, pocket flaps, belts and so on should always be pressed on the wrong side first, then on the right side. That way if you do get a slight crease developing (it can happen if the material on both sides isn't exactly the same measurement or the padding between the two has slipped), it develops where it can't be seen.

Embroidery looks lovely when it's just been washed and has lots of body and texture, but if you thud an iron down on top of all those threads you'll flatten them.

* Get a thick towel, spread it out on your ironing board and put the embroidery face down on the towel. Iron it from the wrong side and not with too much enthusiasm – gentle pressure will do the trick.

Fine fabrics can sometimes be marked just by the action of running the iron over them, regardless of how little pressure you apply.

* You can avoid this by putting a piece of tissue paper on top of the garment and by ironing on to the paper instead of directly on to the fabric.

Follow a routine when ironing blouses and shirts.

* Tackle those areas where there's a double thickness of material first at collar and cuffs, pressing first on the wrong side, then on the right.
* Iron sleeves next, then work your way round from the right side via the centre and finish with the left front. If, of course, you happen to be left-handed, then you'll want to start with the left front and work round that way.

Fragrance can begin on the ironing board. When it's the turn of your favourite undies, sprinkle one or two drops of cologne or toilet water on the ironing board cover (not on to the underwear). The heat of the iron will persuade the sweet smell through to your underwear.

* If you do not wish anything else to be perfumed, leave this ironing until last and the fragrance will have worn off the ironing board before you next use it.

Freshly ironed garments should ideally not be worn straightaway. Anything which is still warm and sometimes ever so slightly damp as well, will crease twice as easily as when it's completely cool.

* For precisely the same reason, do put blouses, jackets, trousers and dresses on to a hanger the moment they are off the ironing board . . . if you drape them over a chair they'll develop creases at an amazing rate and without any help from you!
* What you can't put on a hanger, lay out flat – on the bed perhaps – and wait a little before packing it away into a drawer.
* Freshly steam-ironed garments should be well-aired before they are put away otherwise they will develop mildew.

Gathered yokes and sleeves lose their pretty effect if they are flattened into pleats by heavy-handed ironing.

* The trick is to use the tip of the iron only and push it into the gathers rather than over the top of them. This takes time, but it's worth it.

Modern fabrics are very often a mixture of more than one fibre.

* One rule which will steer you clear of accidents is to set the thermostat on your iron for the fibre which requires the lowest temperature.

Never go against the grain, even when ironing. Always move in the direction of the grain of the fabric and use long smooth strokes, with the following exceptions: very fine wool should be ironed with a light circular motion; viscose should be ironed diagonally.

* Never iron round the hem of a bias cut skirt, but always on the straight of the material.

Perfect finishes come from clothes that are neither too wet nor too dry.

* Garments which are too wet will have a poor finish, those which are too dry won't come up smooth and crisp.
* But as with every rule, there's always an exception! Shantung, tussore, chiffon, georgette and crêpe should be quite dry before they're ironed.

Pressing pleats can be a nightmare because if you're not terribly careful, the part that folds underneath can show right through the material leaving a very obvious line.

* Take a tip from the professionals. You need a thin piece of cardboard. Pop it inside the pleat on top of the piece which folds under and you won't get a line showing through.

Puff sleeves on children's dresses can be awkward to deal with but the chore is made considerably simpler if you 'stuff' the sleeve with a towel or something similar before ironing.

Seams on delicate garments can become unsightly and obvious if ironed the wrong way so that the extra material used in the seam shows through the surface as a hard ridge. There's no denying that it takes time and care to avoid the seam showing on the right side, but if you want your clothes to look as though they are treated with care, it's well worth making the effort.

* Make up some long narrow strips of brown paper (save the paper from parcels or even from grocery bags) and keep them in a drawer near where you usually do your ironing. Push a strip under the seam allowance before you iron and no impression will show through.
* Sometimes after you've washed a garment you get a seam puckering badly. If this happens don't despair, you can take out the kinks with a strong right arm and the iron! This should last for the first few hours of wear.
* Lay the seam on the board, give a firm tug to the hem, or the bottom of the leg if it's trousers, and while you are pulling the seam straight with one hand, iron with the other using a fair amount of pressure and a good head of steam.

Silks, satins and viscose should never be spotted with water. This can make them patchy and marked.

* If fabrics are too dry when they get to the ironing board, dampen a towel and roll the garments up in it, leaving for a few minutes so that they absorb a little of the moisture.
* Even the best steam irons have a habit of spluttering every so often, so try to avoid using steam when ironing these fabrics.

Skirts and trousers often have soft tucks around the waistband area instead of pleats. How do you preserve their natural-looking fullness when you iron them?

* From the right side first, press under the fold, then from the wrong side, inserting strips of brown paper tucked under the fold, press again. Finally finish by ironing on the right side without the paper.

Soiled clothes should never be 'freshened up' by ironing. They may look a little better but the long term results can be disastrous as you could simply have set stubborn stains hard into the fabric with the heat.

* It's also sensible to brush clothes lightly before ironing, so that any loose particles of dust and dirt are removed instead of being pressed into the fibres where they can cause damage.

Sort all the garments to be ironed into different fabrics, then iron those which need a cool iron first.

* Progress through the temperature range ending up with the hottest. Doing it this way you are also less likely to have such accidents as when, for example, the iron thermostat hasn't quite caught up with your changing of the dial and a cool iron item gets the full force of searing hot metal.

Starched collars and cuffs should be kept until last in the ironing heap, because the starch can cling to the base of the iron and can all too easily be transferred on to the next garment as an unsightly brown mark.

* Clean the base of the iron immediately you have finished ironing a starched item. A quick rub over with the rough side of a damp foam washing-up pad (the sort designed for non-stick pans) should do the trick.

Steam satisfyingly hissing and rising up from the fabric tells you that the iron's doing its work effectively (dry fabrics rarely iron up crisp and crease-free). There are various ways of keeping clothes damp; pick the one which suits you best.

* Get one of those little plant sprayers, keep it by the ironing board and use it to put a fine mist of water over clothes.
* A cleaned flour or sugar shaker filled with water can also be used to spot the fabric with droplets of water.
* Alternatively, roll up the clothes before they are really dry and store them in a large plastic bag (a bin liner will do the trick). Clothes will then stay damp until you're ready to iron them. But a word of warning here: don't leave them encased in plastic for more than twenty-four hours, otherwise you'll have mildew to get out of the clothes as well as the creases!

Ties can be tricky, because if you press them the chances are that the seam will show through and you'll get a line down the middle. Cut out a piece of cardboard to correspond to the shape of the tie and put it in between the two sides of the tie before pressing.

* If you have narrow ties, medium ties and wide ties, then it's not a bad idea to cut out a cardboard shape to suit each of them to have on hand when you come to do the ironing.
* Use a damp cloth when pressing ties.

Trousers can be pressed under the mattress overnight using an old bachelor's trick, but be careful not to strain your back lifting the mattress.

* Moisten the creases with a damp cloth first.

Velvet, even velvet ribbon, should not be ironed or it will end up a mess of matted pile.

* Steam it instead. Small items can be put over the spout of a boiling kettle or suspended over a bowl of boiling water.
* To get the best of the steam and to achieve results in the shortest possible time, try putting the item on a plastic coat hanger with a bar at the bottom, then drape a piece of polythene over the top of the hanger and down over the sides of the basin to form a 'tent'. That way the steam will be contained within the tent and will work quickly.
* Larger items like velvet trousers or skirts can be suspended over a hot bath. Don't fill the bath especially; wait until

someone's having a bath, so as not to waste water and fuel.

* When travelling, try the above trick with the steam from a shower.

Wool clothes, such as a suit, benefit from a padded ironing surface.

* Put a piece of fine wool material (an old remnant from the workbasket will do) between the fabric to be ironed and the ironing cloth.

Wool garments will lose their bounce if you iron them and it shouldn't be necessary anyway, but you can re-fashion a woolly which has become somewhat shapeless by using a steam iron. This is an 'at-a-distance' ironing technique where the metal never actually touches the material.

* You may need a surface slightly larger than your ironing board for this. The kitchen table, well covered by a thick blanket, may be suitable. Stretch the garment to the desired shape and fasten it down with pins. Hold your iron half an inch above the wool and let the steam penetrate. Move slowly over the whole surface.
* Sometimes the cause can also prove to be the cure! For instance, shine on the seats of skirts and trousers is often caused by ironing. The 'at-a-distance' ironing technique can often remove the shine. Hold the iron about an inch above the material, let the steam penetrate for a few minutes and brush lightly with a very soft brush.

STORAGE

Always make the effort to put your clothes neatly away on their hangers, or in the case of sweaters, folded away, no matter how late you get to bed, how tired you feel or how cold it is. Throwing them over the nearest chair may suit you, but it won't suit your clothes. Trousers are particularly prone to developing double creases if they are persistently left to their own devices.

Belts are best hung up by their buckles.

* Fix some hooks to the inside of a cupboard or wardrobe door. Hook the buckles of your belts over these and let the rest hang down.

Blouses and shirts should be kept on hangers.

* Fasten the top and middle buttons as well. If you don't do this the fronts will sag and you may get small folds of material

forming, particularly around the neck and yoke area, which then show as a crease when you put the garment on.

* If, however, you don't have the space to put shirts and blouses on hangers, then fold them in the following way to keep them as crease-free as possible. Fasten the buttons at the front, then lay the garment face downwards. Turn in both sides towards the middle, so that the sleeves lie flat down the back of the shirt level with the collarband. Turn up the tail and fold an equal amount of material twice more.

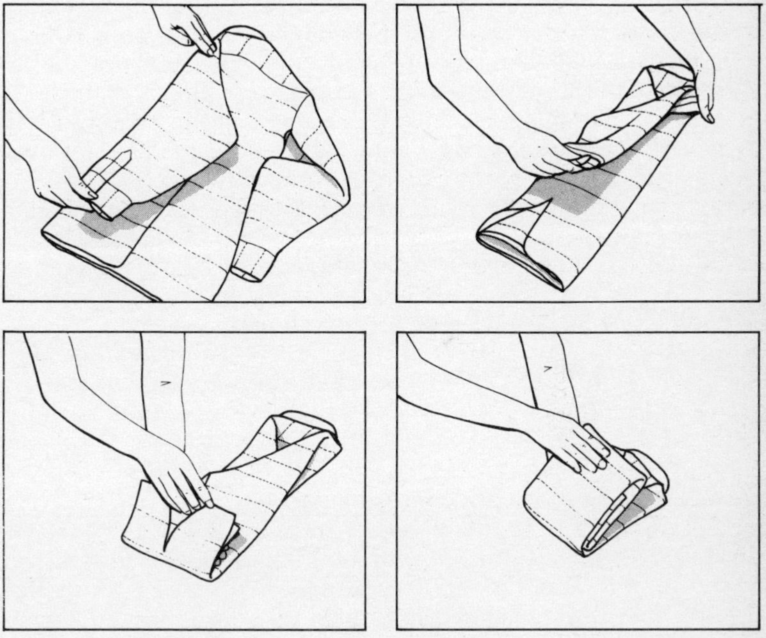

Clothes, like people, need lots of space and room to breathe if they're to be at their best. So, if you can avoid it, don't cram all your garments tightly together in the wardrobe like sardines in a can, or you will find they are permanently creased.

* Use the spare room to take up the overflow; alternatively, buy an extra wardrobe or add a built-in unit in the bedroom.

Coathangers are such commonplace things that most of us are content just to put our clothes on them and hang them up. However, a hanger should fit the garment it's being used for, otherwise all kinds of damage can result. If you, for instance, use a wooden or a metal hanger which is actually wider than the shoulders of the jacket or dress hung on it, then you will end up with a nasty 'bump' on the upper sleeve where the hanger has left its mark. Hangers that are not wide enough should not be used either as shoulders droop and lose their shape. Similarly, hard hangers can leave ridges on delicate materials.

* Use padded hangers where possible.
* For really special clothes it's worth making a hanger to fit the width of the shoulders exactly; you can carefully cut the ends off a wooden hanger, then pad it using wadding you can buy by the yard from any fabric shop and any old scraps of leftover material you happen to have in your workbasket.
* Of course human error, or carelessness, can cause problems even if your hanger is a perfect fit for the garment! Always check that a jacket, dress or whatever, is properly aligned on the hanger with the centre of the collar at the hook, otherwise you'll get one end digging into the fabric.
* To keep things properly on their hangers and to stop them slipping sideways, stick some strips of foam rubber at each end of the hanger. Alternatively, wind rubber bands round the ends of the hangers.

Dust gets everywhere in a house and the wardrobe is certainly no exception. In fact those which have louvred doors seem to draw dust straight in and a fair portion of it always seems to settle on the collar and shoulder areas of clothes. You may only realize this when you haven't worn a dress for some time and then, when you want it for a special occasion, discover it's grubby round the top.

* There's only one way to avoid this, either buy hanger covers in heavy plastic or make a cover yourself from a plastic bag.
* For a sleeveless article you could make the cover quite long, but if it's a bulky item with sleeves, something which just covers the shoulder area is best, so that the sleeves are not pulled in.

Folding clothes is far from simple – it's a skill in itself. The more skilled you are, the smarter your clothes will look.

* The first basic rule is to fold crossways not lengthways, then you've got the force of gravity on your side which means that the weight of the clothes as you hang them will tend to make the creases drop out easily.
* Take a tip from the professional packers and always fold away sweaters in exactly the same way as they are folded when you buy them. Lay the sweater flat, face downwards, then fold in one side and arm towards the back, then the other side and fold the sleeves back on themselves. Next fold it in two with the sleeves inside the fold and put away carefully in a drawer.

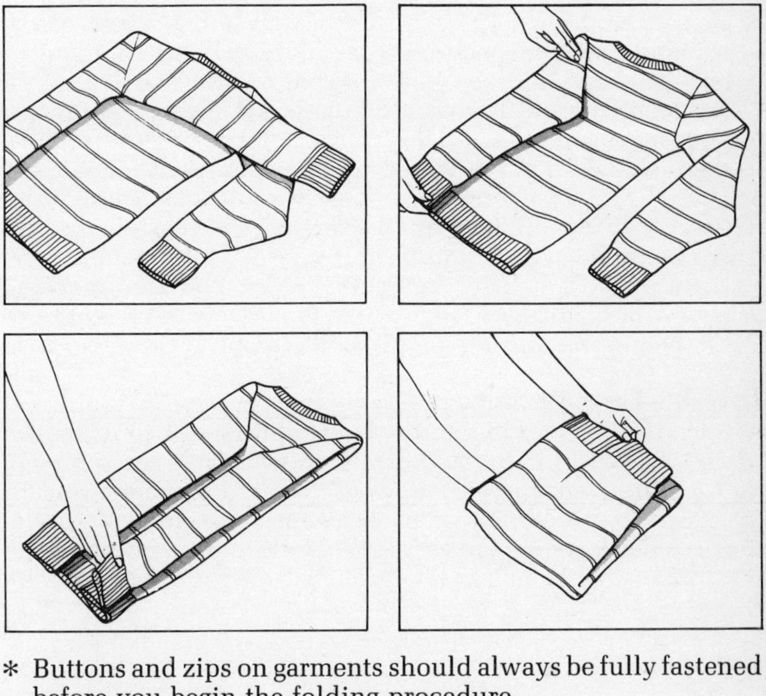

* Buttons and zips on garments should always be fully fastened before you begin the folding procedure.
* As you fold a garment always run your hand along inside the fold just to make sure that the material is lying smooth. Rucks will cause unsightly 'double' creases.

Grade your clothes, not according to size as they do with eggs, but according to kind, and you'll always be able to find things in your wardrobe.

* Put all the coats next to each other at one end, then suits, next dresses, evening wear, skirts, trousers and so on. And always make a point of putting them back into the same section. It makes life a lot easier because you can see at a glance what you have to choose from if you're looking for a particular kind of outfit to wear.

Hats need proper storage. Some hats are meant to be floppy, but most are not.

* There's nothing quite like the old style hat boxes classy milliners used to pack hats in. These are still supplied in exclusive hat shops. However, if your new hats come in just a carrier bag use cardboard boxes of a suitable size begged from your local supermarket or off licence to store them in. Stuff the inside with crumpled up tissue paper and don't jam too many hats into the one box.
* Berets and woolly hats can be popped into plastic bags and kept on the top shelf of the wardrobe or in a drawer.
* One thing to watch out for are pom poms. Don't put anything heavy on top, otherwise next time you wear the woolly cap the pom pom will loll about all over your head.

Lavender bags may be rather reminiscent of sweet old ladies and days gone by, but grandmother knew a thing or two when she placed these bags in her underwear drawer. They cost a lot less than perfume and they produce a delicate fragrance ideal for daytime when you don't want a heavy perfume wafting around. So buy some lavender bags at the next village fête or local jumble sale, or even better, make your own if you have the plant growing in the garden.

* To make your own lavender bags, cut the plant in July when it's at its best. Dry on newspaper in an airing cupboard for a week, then crush into small pieces. Make the bags 5-8 cm (2-3 inches) square from remnants of muslin, cheesecloth or some other loosely woven material.

Leather gloves can be blown into shape.

* Fine skin can wrinkle very easily but gloves can be kept in good shape if you blow into the gloves, rather as though you were blowing up a balloon, the moment you take them off and while the warmth of your hands is still in the leather.

Long dresses should be stored with particular care as they are worn much less frequently than ordinary day clothes. They tend to be relegated to the corner of a wardrobe with the hems trailing on the floor. This can cause two problems: first, delicate material can snag if the floor isn't too smooth; second, dust will be caught in it.

* Stitch two loops of tape inside the seams at waist level, turn the bodice over the skirt and hang up by the loops on a hanger. This way the fabric is kept well away from the floor.

Plastic bags are excellent for storing sweaters – use heavy ones designed for the job, rather than lightweight ones which can very easily be damaged.

* Always make sure the bag is big enough for the garment; if it has to be crushed up at the edges to fit, a sweater isn't likely to emerge from the bag in prime condition.

Precious lace things, blouses or dresses for instance, which are almost in the antique category, should be stored in blue paper, not white. (White lets in the light which may damage precious lace.) Make sure that the lace is completely covered by the paper to keep the garment in the best possible condition.

Rubber boots are essential in the British climate and if you live in the country they can positively be your best friend, but when not on your feet they do tend to fall about on the floor and get in the way. There are two ways you can store them tidily.

* For practical black Wellingtons, punch a hole on the top edge of the rubber, thread a thin (but strong) piece of thread through them and 'hang' them up.
* For smart boots you need a clothes peg, preferably one of

those old-fashioned wooden pegs. Put the inside parts of both boot legs together and clip them together with the peg.

Shoes should never be left to loll about at the bottom of the wardrobe or even under the bed! The dark ones can mark the light ones, uppers can become squashed and so on.

* Buy one of those plastic-covered wire storage racks and make a point of putting your shoes away in it.
* For families with lots of footwear it's an even better idea to put a rail right across the bottom of the wardrobe somewhere near the back and about 150 mm (6 inches) off the floor and pop your shoes on to that. A piece of dowelling picked up from a DIY store is ideal for this and doesn't cost very much. It can be fixed in position at either end with holders similar to those used for carrying towel rails or hanging rails for wardrobes.

Ties tend to get left lying about, draped over the back of a chair or even over coathooks in the hall.

* If you do not have a multiple tie rack, one way to keep them tidy and together is to stretch a curtain rod across the back of the wardrobe door. Just screw in the small hooks provided with the wire, then stretch it tightly across. Ties can be popped over the wire and its stretchy properties will keep them from flapping about.

Trousers are best stored on hangers, but those with a narrow metal bar can leave a crease mark right across the legs.

* Avoid this by covering the bar with a roll of cardboard. The inside section of a roll of household foil for instance, can be cut lengthways and popped over the hanger bar, then taped closed at the cut edges.
* Equally effective is a piece of foam rubber rolled round the hanger and taped in position (you'll often find foam used as packing in the boxes you get with some household appliances and electrical equipment).
* The best hangers for trousers are the grip-type which hold the trousers by the bottom ends and let them hang straight down.

STAIN REMOVAL: 10 GENERAL PRINCIPLES

1. Tackle any stain immediately, because once a substance has had a chance to get right into the fabric it can stubbornly remain there. If you're at home, there's no excuse at all for not doing a thorough job – drop everything to see to the stain. If the waiter spills wine on your skirt, don't just mutter that it doesn't matter and dab at it ineffectually with your hanky, insist on the mark being removed there and then (a spoonful of salt from the kitchen, for instance, will stop wine spreading further over fabric).

2. It's useful to memorize the three broad categories of stains and the general treatment of each. Basically, there are greasy stains, water-soluble stains and protein stains. The first usually take to treatment with grease solvents of one sort or another and to hot soapy water; the second respond to the cold water sponge and a slick of soap if needed; the third can be dealt with by cold water and biological powders. But that's only a rough guide to help you cope in an emergency. Many fabrics can't be washed and so all sorts of other substances like borax or vinegar have to be brought into use. The stain removal chart goes into all this in detail, see pages 116 to 125.

3. Try to keep a few bits and pieces together to make up a stain removing kit which will be readily to hand when you need it. Small sponges, for instance, are ideal for applying remedial treatment to some stains, so buy one large one and cut it up into several pieces. Keep the sponges in a box along with a pad of some material to put behind stains (this saves you resorting to a towel and ending up with a stain on that, too), a few paper tissues for blotting up moisture, a couple of men's old hankies, a small clothes brush and a wad of cotton wool which is useful as a 'pad' if you don't have a proper one, to mop up excess moisture and it can also come in handy for applying soap and water or solvents. A medicine dropper or small syringe is useful to avoid overwetting with detergent or solvents. It can also be used to squirt liquid through a cloth to remove a stain on to a backing pad. Put these various items, and any extras you can think of yourself, in a polythene bag or an old plastic ice cream carton and keep it under the kitchen sink, in the bathroom or some other readily accessible place.

4. There's a right and a wrong way to use solvents and this is the right way: deal with the stain from the *wrong* side of the garment and use a pad on the other side to absorb the substance. That way you are pushing the substance from the surface of the fabric straight on to the pad and if there are any stubborn little traces left they will be on the wrong side and not visible. Dampen a pad of cloth with some of the solvent. Make a ring with the moistened pad a few centimetres outside the actual stain where the fabric is clean, then work inwards. Do it the other way round and you run the risk of a 'ring' being left round the outside of the stain which will mean the whole garment having to be washed or dry cleaned.

5. Even in the middle of winter work fairly near to an open window when you are treating stains with some of the solvents and chemicals needed for the job – that way you'll avoid getting the full blast of the fumes which will escape out of the window instead.

6. Acetates, viscose, delicate materials and coloureds can be totally unpredictable in their reaction to cleaning chemicals, so always test any chemical you plan to use on a hidden part of the garment which won't be seen if you do damage to the fabric or the colour. The overlap left at seams is a good test spot; avoid hems whenever possible, because you never know when you might want to let them down!

7. Don't ever soak garments made of wool, silk or with a flame-proof finish in an attempt to get a stain out; you may get the stain out but you'll ruin the garment.

8. Unless you are sure of what has been spilled and how best to remove it, be very wary of using hot water on a stain. Heat can easily set stains rather than remove them.

9. If you wouldn't normally wash any particular material and you're not sure whether you can or not, then always play safe and try something simple, like plain cold water.

10. Get rid of any stains on clothes before putting them into the laundry basket. Some stains, of course, come out in the wash, but others can become a permanent fixture in the washing process. It's best not to take any chances.

11. Don't try to remove the very last traces of a stubborn stain if you've tried more than twice to remove it. It's better to leave a faint trace of a stain than run the risk of damaging the fabric by too much rubbing or chemical action.

STAIN REMOVAL CHART	
ACIDS	Flush with running *cold* water. Neutralize with a solution of 1 teaspoon of borax to 600 ml (1 pint) of warm water. If you don't have borax, use bicarbonate of soda in the same proportion. Sponge on the solution, then rinse thoroughly with clear water.
ADHESIVES Adhesive tape	Remove with methylated spirit or white spirit.
Animal and fish glues	If the fabric is washable, soak in hot water with a tablespoon of vinegar added to it; for non-washables dab with a similar solution.
Contact & clear	Dab gently with acetone or a nail varnish remover. DON'T USE ON ACETATE FABRICS, such as Tricel.
Epoxy resin	Remove *before* it sets. On natural fabrics use cellulose thinner or methylated spirit; on synthetics, lighter fuel.
Latex	While wet, remove as much as possible with cold water – when dry simply peel off and any residue can be dabbed with a grease solvent.
Modelling cement	Remove with acetone or non-oily nail polish remover. Don't use on acetate material.
PVA glue	Remove with methylated spirit.
Superglue	Apply cold water – on a pad or hold the item under a running tap.
ALCOHOL Beer	**Washables:** Soak in biological washing powder, then wash. *Non-washables:* Blot up as much as possible with a piece of kitchen paper or a paper handkerchief, dab with white vinegar, then blot again.
Spirits	**Washables:** Wash in cold water. **Non-washables:** Blot with a paper handkerchief, then sponge with a little

	methylated spirit. Blot again, then dab with a little cold water and blot again.
Wine	**Washables:** Stretch the material over a basin straightaway and pour hot water through the material from above, until the stain fades. Any stubborn marks can be removed with a bleach solution (follow the manufacturer's instructions). **Non-washables:** Sponge with warm water and blot with blotting paper. Sprinkle with talcum powder to absorb the stain for an hour, sponge again and blot.
BIRD DROPPINGS	**Washables:** Scrape off the surface of the fabric and soak in a biological powder before washing as usual. If there are coloured stains (due to a bird's diet of berries) you may have to bleach white cottons to remove all traces. **Non-washables:** Scrape off the worst; make up a solution of 1 part ammonia to 6 parts water and sponge this into the stain, but do a test first on coloured fabrics. Blot off any excess moisture and finish by dabbing with vinegar. If there are still traces left take the garment to the dry cleaner's immediately.
BLOOD	**Washables:** Soak the item in a strong solution of salt and cold water. Leave for five minutes, rinse and then put into another salt solution. Repeat until you can rinse out all traces. Do not rub stained wool, let the salt water run through the fabric. **Non-washables:** Blot up any surface blood, then sponge the stain with cold water to which you have added a few drops of ammonia. If there are still traces, cover the area with a paste of starch and water and when dry, brush off.
Dried stains	**Washables (silk and wool excepted):** Soak

	overnight in a biological powder and water solution. **Non-washables:** Dampen with lemon juice, sprinkle with salt, then iron between two sheets of dampened blotting paper.
CANDLE-GREASE	**Washables and non-washables:** Put the stained item in the fridge or freezer to harden the wax. This makes it easier to scrape off. Scrape off what you can, place a piece of white blotting paper over what's left and press with a warm, not hot, iron. You may have to do this more than once, using a fresh piece of blotting paper each time. Any left-over wax can be removed with a solvent. If the wax is coloured use methylated spirit.
CARBON PAPER	**Washables:** Sponge with liquid detergent, then a little ammonia. **Non-washables:** Sponge several times with white or methylated spirit. If this doesn't remove the stain, take to the dry cleaner's.
CHEWING GUM	**Washables:** There are two options. Apply a little egg white or proprietary grease solvent (whichever is available) to soften the gum, scrape off what you can, then wash in the usual way. Or freeze the gum solid, either by putting the garment in a plastic bag and then into the freezer, or by putting a few ice cubes in a plastic bag and rubbing the gum with them. When hard, peel it off the fabric. Any residue can be removed by covering with brown paper and ironing. **Non-washables:** Give the gum the freeze treatment and take away any marks remaining with a dab of proprietary grease solvent.

CHOCOLATE AND COCOA	**Washables:** Scrape off any deposit, then wash in cool soapy water. If it's still marked, sponge with a warm borax solution – 25 g (1 oz) to 600 ml (1 pint) warm water. Another method is to sponge with warm water, sprinkle with dry borax, rub it in with your fingertips, leave for half an hour, rinse and launder. If the stain remains, use a proprietary grease solvent. **Non-washables:** Scrape off as much as possible and use a grease solvent.
COFFEE AND TEA With or without milk	**Washables:** Soak overnight in a biological detergent. If you want immediate results then sponge with a cloth dipped in a warm water and borax solution – 25 g (1 oz) to 600 ml (1 pint). **Non-washables:** Sponge with borax solution, blot with a tissue and any traces left can be dabbed lightly with a proprietary grease solvent.
CRAYONS	**Washables:** Sponge with methylated spirit, then wash as usual or rub in undiluted detergent, then rinse out thoroughly. Treat any residual colour with methylated spirit. **Non-washables:** Dab gently with a proprietary grease solvent; if unsuccessful, take the garment to the professionals for treatment.
CREAM	**Washables:** Soak in warm or cold water, then wash. Once dry, any remaining grease marks can be removed with a proprietary grease solvent or acetone if the fabric isn't rayon or Tricel. **Non-washables:** Sponge with a proprietary grease solvent and leave to dry, then use a clean cloth to dab with warm water. Rub dry with an old towel or similar.

CURRY	**Washables:** Soak in biological powder, then rinse as usual. **Non-washables:** Sponge with borax and warm water – about ¼ teaspoon to ½ litre (1 pint).
DEODORANT OR ANTI-PERSPIRANT	**Washables:** Try soaking in biological powder, following the packet instructions. **Non-washables:** Take to the dry cleaner's.
DYE	**Washables:** Small stains will usually respond to sponging with methylated spirit to which a few drops of ammonia have been added. But TEST FIRST with coloureds and rayons. Alternatively, try lots of cold water and a long soak in biological detergent. If all else fails, you can use a proprietary dye stripper on the entire garment. **Non-washables:** Get to the dry cleaner's fast.
EGG	**Washables:** Scrape off any excess, rinse with *cold* water then wash in biological detergent. **Non-washables:** Scrape off any excess, then dab with a proprietary grease solvent.
FRUIT JUICE	**Washables:** Rinse in cold water. If there's still colour left, then stretch the fabric over a bowl and pour hot water through the material. **Non-washables:** Sponge with cold water, then with glycerine. Leave for an hour, then sponge with white vinegar. Finish by sponging with a clean damp cloth and leave to dry.
FURNITURE POLISH	**Washables and non-washables:** Dab with a dry cleaning solvent. Washables can then be washed.
GRASS OR FOLIAGE STAINS	**Washables:** If warm soapy water doesn't shift the mark, try sponging with methylated or white spirit, then washing.

	Non-washables: Make a paste of equal quantities of cream of tartar and salt plus water, rub into the stain with the finger-tips, leave for 10 minutes, then brush out.
GRAVY	**Washables:** If the stain's only slight, wash straight away in cold soapy water and rinse. Any traces can be removed with a proprietary grease solvent. **Non-washables:** Dab gently with soapy water – but don't soak. Blot dry, then use a solvent.
GREASE	**Washables and non-washables:** Most fabrics respond to sponging on the WRONG side with a grease solvent.
INK Ball point	**Washables:** Rub with warm soapy water, then wash. If stain remains, dab with nail polish remover – but don't use on acetate fabrics. **Non-washables:** Dab with nail polish remover – but not on acetate fabrics. Some stains may be permanent.
Felt-tip	**Washables and non-washables:** Dab with methylated spirit.
Fountain pen ink	**Washables:** Liquid detergent if applied quickly enough will usually remove stains. If you get stubborn stains on white cotton or linen, rub with lemon dipped in salt, then pour boiling water through the fabric. On very stubborn stains, you can try a bleach solution (follow the manufacturer's instructions).
Indelible ink	**All fabrics:** Remove *immediately* with a proprietary solvent.
Printer's ink	**All fabrics:** Sponge with white or methylated spirit.
Typewriter ribbon	Use a dry cleaning solvent and/or sponge with methylated spirit. For stubborn stains try a bleach solution (follow the manufacturer's instructions).

MAKE-UP Eye pencil Foundation	**Washables and non-washables:** Treat with a grease solvent. **Washables:** Sponge with detergent and warm water. Any traces can be removed with a dry cleaning solvent. **Non-washables:** Dab the area with methylated spirit.
Lipstick	**Washables:** Sponge with methylated spirit, then dab with washing-up liquid (neat) and rinse through. For severe stains, rub in petroleum jelly to loosen, leave for a few minutes, dab with ammonia, then rinse. **Non-washables:** Use a grease solvent.
Mascara	**Washables:** Sponge with washing-up liquid, then with ammonia, then rinse. **Non-washables:** Use a proprietary dry cleaning fluid.
MAYONNAISE	**Washables:** Sponge with warm water immediately, soak in biological powder and wash as usual. **Non-washables:** Sponge with warm water and if the stain is severe, sprinkle with bicarbonate of soda, leave for five minutes, sponge with cold water and blot dry.
METAL POLISH	**Washables and non-washables:** Use white spirit and when the stain is dry, brush lightly to take off any dried particles of polish.
MILDEW	**Washables:** Ordinary laundering should be sufficient. If not, flush through from wrong side with a bleach solution (follow the manufacturer's instructions). **Non-washables:** Dry clean.
MILK	See 'Coffee and tea', page 119.
MUD	**Washables and non-washables:** Leave the mud to dry thoroughly, then brush off as much as possible and wash as usual. Any

	traces should be dabbed with a dry cleaning solvent.
NAIL POLISH	**Washables and non-washables:** Most fabrics respond well to dabbing with nail polish remover. If the fabric is viscose rayon, then test first on the inside of a seam, but DON'T use on acetates. If in doubt, sponge with amyl acetate.
PAINT Oil-based/ gloss/enamel	**Washables:** Wipe straight away with turpentine or white spirit. Sponge with soapy water, then wash. **Non-washables:** Same treatment but don't wash afterwards.
Emulsion/ water colours	**Washables and non-washables:** Sponge with cold water. If dealing with very delicate fabrics, have them professionally dry cleaned.
PERFUME	**Washables:** Rinse out in warm water, then wash. **Non-washables:** Dab in a solution of half glycerine, half warm water (well mixed), then sponge with clear, warm water.
PERSPIRATION	If not removed in normal wash: **Washables:** Sponge with a weak solution of ammonia, rinse and then wash. Another trick to try is two aspirins dissolved in the rinsing water. **Non-washables:** Sponge over the area with a solution of 1 teaspoon white vinegar to 250 ml (8 fl oz) warm water.
PLASTICINE AND PUTTY	With all fabrics, first chill in fridge or freezer and scrape off as much as possible with a knife. **Washables:** Sponge with a proprietary grease solvent, then wash. **Non-washables:** Just sponge with grease solvent. If the treatment doesn't work with either substance – go to a dry cleaner.

RUST	**Washables and non-washables:** Make up a solution of 1 teaspoon oxalic acid to ½ litre (1 pint) water and sponge the stain lightly with this. N.B. Oxalic acid is a poison, so use with care. On whites you can try lemon juice.
SCORCH MARKS	**Washables:** Light marks will disappear if you soak the fabric in cold milk. Any traces should be dabbed with a solution of soapy water with 1 teaspoon of borax added, then rinsed. **Non-washables:** Sponge repeatedly with a warm borax solution – dissolve 2 teaspoons borax in ½ litre (1 pint) hot water. Wring out a cloth in the solution and rub the scorched area. Do this several times, then sponge with a cloth wrung out in clean water.
SHOE POLISH	**Washables and non-washables:** Treat with white spirit or a dry cleaning solvent.
SOUP	**Washables:** Wash immediately. **Non-washables:** Put a thick towel underneath the marked area and sponge with warm water. Blot dry with a towel or tissue and dab with a proprietary grease solvent.
SUNTAN OIL	**Washables:** Sponge the fabric with a proprietary grease solvent using a thick pad underneath. If there is still a touch of colour, soak the garment in warm water with 1 teaspoon of borax added, then wash in detergent and rinse. **Non-washables:** Dab with a proprietary grease solvent.
TAR AND CRUDE OIL (off beaches)	**Washables:** Scrape off as much as possible, sponge with eucalyptus oil working from the back of the fabric. Lighter fuel can be used to take away any traces left, then wash.

	Non-washables: Scrape, soften with a little glycerine, rub gently with lighter fuel, then dab with a cloth wrung out in warm water.
URINE	**Washables:** Rinse by holding under the running tap. Soak in biological detergent and wash in the usual way. **Non-washables:** Sponge with cold water, blot up the excess; repeat this several times, then sponge with a solution of 2 teaspoons white vinegar to 1 litre (2 pints) of water. The vinegar will also help get rid of any smell from the garment. If possible, hang in the open air after cleaning.

LONGER LIFE CLOTHES

BE YOUR OWN VALET

Banish baggy knees on trousers with a special ironing technique.

* Lay the garment on the ironing board with the leg seams together, not the creases as would be normal, and cover with a damp cloth. Hold a hot steam iron just above the cloth and press down on the fabric very gently from time to time and you'll be surprised at how easily the excess material 'shrinks' back to its original shape. Have a look under the pressing cloth from time to time to check on progress and to see that you're not just ironing in folds and creases. When the knee's

back in shape again, put the legs in their creased position and carefully iron a crease into the area you've just shrunk.
* To banish bagginess on a more premanent basis, sew a piece of firm lining material across the front of the trouser leg to cover the knee area. The material should be stitched into the seam, so that the stitching doesn't show through. Use a fine fabric and always iron with care, so that no ridges show through from the lining.

Collars on coats, jackets or dresses often become more soiled than the rest of the garment. Rather than dry clean the whole thing, clean the collar by rubbing it with powdered magnesium, or dab it gently with a little proprietary grease solvent on a cloth or pad.

Develop a disciplined attitude to your handbags and you'll never find yourself the butt of all those 'clutter' jokes.

* Empty and sort it out once a week.
* Clean out all the dust and fluff and remove any spots in the lining.
* Leather bags should be stuffed with tissue when unused.
* Plastic bags should be sponged with soapy water, then wiped with a cloth wrung out in clean water.

Feathers can be refurbished if they are sprinkled with French chalk or even talcum powder and given a 'dry shampoo'. Work the powder in with your fingertips, leave there overnight, then brush with a soft brush the next day. It may be necessary to repeat the process to get feathers really clean.

Fluffy dinner suit? Remove hairs and fluff with a good clothes brush. Alternatively, pick off the fluff with a strip of sticky tape.

Gilt or silver footwear needs to be kept in top condition for glittering occasions.

* Any scuff marks can usually be removed by rubbing with cotton wool dipped in soapy water.
* Banish tarnish with a silver cleaning cloth rubbed lightly over the surface.

* Store metallic type shoes which are easily tarnished in black tissue paper which should prevent damage.

Improve your limp handshake by restoring your fabric gloves to their former crispness. Next time they're nice and clean after a wash dip them into a thin starch before ironing them dry. A medium to thin starch can be made with 2 tablespoons starch powder to 2 litres (4 pints) water.

Lace doesn't look good if it's limp, nor does a garment made of silk.

* To restiffen a lace veil and put a bit of body back into a silk blouse, use a gum arabic solution instead of starch because the latter can cause patchiness and even discolour a garment. To make the solution, first wash 100 g (4 oz) gum arabic crystals in cold water, then add to ½ litre (1 pint) of hot water in an old saucepan and allow to dissolve slowly. Strain through fine muslin and put into a bottle with a stopper of some sort. When you use the solution it will need to be diluted – 2 teaspoons to ½ litre (1 pint) of water is sufficient, and in the case of lace, cut down the amount to as little as ½ teaspoon per ½ litre (1 pint). Wash and rinse the garment in the usual way, adding the gum arabic only to the final rinse. Iron while the fabric is still damp, for the best results.

Little bands which are intended to secure the end of a belt are rarely secured themselves, so they can easily slide right off, never to be seen again. A flapping belt end isn't very smart, so you have three options to solve the problem.

* First, you can take a small piece of reusable adhesive and attach it to the end of the belt and it will press flat against the main part.
* Second, you can pop a rubber band over the buckle end and slip it round into position, tucking the flap into the band.
* Third, you can glue a self-stick fastening strip to the belt – one piece to the end and a matching piece on the main belt where it will meet. The trouble with this option is that should you have to tighten your belt or let it out on a future occasion, the sticky strip will be in the wrong place.

Nasty little balls which form on knitted and woven garments are officially called 'pilling'; they can be removed by using a safety razor, providing you use it with great care, of course. (Note, however, that pilling weakens the fabric and the more you remove the pills, the quicker the fabric is weakened.)

Next time you're vacuuming the carpet – give heavy clothes a quick run over at the same time.

* If you use the suction attachment of a cleaner (intended for upholstery and curtains) it will draw out any dust and grime which has settled on coats and suits. Hold the garment by the hanger and, using the nozzle half closed, work the cleaner gradually over the surface of the fabric. Incidentally, don't try this with lightweight fabrics or you may find them being sucked right up the hose.

Shiny seats on trousers are hard to avoid.

* Dry cleaning may possibly restore some of the mattness to the material but for more instant (and, unfortunately, temporary) results, sponge the fabric with a solution of 1 teaspoon of ammonia per ½ litre (1 pint) of warm water. Sponge again with clean water, then press until dry using a damp cloth – don't iron directly on to the fabric.

Shoulder straps slipping can be an untidy nuisance. There are two alternatives which can help solve the problem.

* Fix a piece of ribbon to the shoulder seam of a dress with snap fasteners at either end – the ribbon need only be about 25 mm (1 inch) long. You can then anchor the strap of your slip to the ribbon.
* Alternatively, if you can't be bothered stitching these on to a number of garments, you can change the slip itself. Unpick the straps at the back of the slip, cross them and sew back in place. They will no longer be able to slip.

A slight mark on a light-coloured felt hat can sometimes be simply rubbed away by using a piece of very fine grade glass-paper very gently.

* More stubborn marks will respond well to a paste of white spirit and French chalk rubbed into the fabric, left until dry, then brushed off.

Slipping straps on sling back shoes are not always immediately apparent when you're in the shop buying them, but if the problem does develop later, it can reduce you to a hobble!

* Line the inside of the straps with a length of the narrow foambacked draught excluder for doors and windows, to keep the straps on your heels. It can be replaced when necessary.

Smarten up your pale-coloured straw hat with a touch of lemon leftovers.

* Dip an old toothbrush in a solution of lemon juice and hot water – 1 tablespoon juice to ½ litre (1 pint) water – and rub the straw with it. Rinse thoroughly, otherwise the straw will get sticky, and leave to dry – outside if at all possible.
* If your hat happens to be of black straw, sponge it with the beaten white of an egg to give it a gloss and stiffen it.

White and light-coloured socks and tights get stained on the feet as a result of perspiration and dye coming out of shoe linings. If you add 1 teaspoon of bicarbonate of soda to the water in which you are washing them, it will help restore them to their former brightness.

White stitching on shoes goes grubby with amazing speed. One way to slow it down is to paint a coat of clear nail polish carefully over the stitching when it's new.

PATCHES AND REPAIRS

Beeswax can bridge the gap in a raincoat by filling in a tiny leaky spot and forming a rather unusual, but effective, patch.

* Rub some beeswax over the leaky spot and over the edges of the affected area. Cover the beeswax with a piece of brown paper and press with a hot iron. You'll find you are fully waterproofed once again.

Buttons sewn on to garments made from delicate fabrics benefit from reinforcing action! The chances are that the button came off in the first place because it tore away a little of the fabric it was stitched to, so put a small piece of material of matching colour on the inside, behind the button, and stitch through the two thicknesses of material. This will strengthen the material and make it more resistant to constant buttoning and unbuttoning.

Cigarette burns can leave a nasty hole in a garment and the charring round the edges makes matters even worse. If this happens in heavy garments, then leave the patching to the professionals. But if the damaged fabric is lightweight, you can do what amounts to an invisible patch yourself, just as long as you have a matching bit of material to hand (and if you have no remnants, then consider taking a piece from a hidden area of the garment, such as a hem or seam allowance. Do this very carefully to ensure a neat job.)

* Here's the patch technique:
  First trim off the charred fabric with sharp scissors. Next cut out a piece of matching fabric larger than the hole and cut a

piece of polythene of the same size. You need to use a light polythene – not heavy duty stuff – so a bit cut from one of the bags you use in the kitchen would be fine. Now set down a sheet of brown paper on your ironing board or table and put the garment with the burn right side down on the paper. Next put the polythene between the garment and the patch of material and press with a hot iron; the polythene will weld the patch to the garment with the heat of the iron. And, as if by magic, when you pick up the garment from the table you'll find that the polythene previously exposed in the hole has completely gone from the face of the fabric – the heat will have melted it and transferred it to the brown paper.

Frayed edges on jeans and trousers are a nuisance.

* If you sew a strip of leather, about 10 mm (½ inch) wide, around the inside of the hems, this will take the worst of the wear from rubbing shoes. Alternatively, use strong bias binding or similar material around the hems.
* If you find it's only the back portion of the trouser leg which wears as a result of shoe rubbing, sew a small button inside the bottom of each leg where the heel of the shoe catches it. This will act as a barrier.

Invisible repairs to trousers, skirts or outer garments are miraculously made with iron-on mending tape. Even better, the job takes only minutes!

* Get a colour which matches the garment as nearly as possible, then iron a piece on to the wrong side of the material, making sure you get the edges of the tear exactly together. Use a damp cloth with your steam iron.

Knitted patches can prove an interesting alternative to leather and suede on finer garments. The patch can be knitted in either purl, plain or even moss stitch, depending on which appeals to you and seems to suit the sweater.

* If you've knitted the garment yourself then there's no problem – simply knit a rectangle (one for each elbow) in the same wool, then stitch it over the hole.

* Contrast wool looks equally good and will probably be a necessary choice for bought sweaters.

Ladders strike at any time and the worst thing about them is that other people have no way of knowing your tights have only just laddered – as far as they're concerned you could simply be a sloppy dresser by nature! So the moment a ladder develops, either change your tights or do an emergency repair.

* A little soap will stop the run progressing further; since you may not always be near a ladies' loo carry a few scraps in your bag in a small container of some sort.
* Alternatives are clear varnish or hairspray.

Leather and suede patches nowadays form part of the style of many expensive sweaters and tweedy jackets. These patches not only look good but will allow you to keep wearing the garment for many more months – even years, if you're lucky.

* You can buy them ready-made from most haberdashery departments, and if you intend putting them on to something you wash frequently, make sure you get the washable sort.
* You can make your own patches out of old scraps of suede or leather – the legs of discarded long boots for instance are ideal for this purpose.
* Ready-made patches usually have little stitching holes punched round the edges but if you make your own, machine round the edge about 6 mm (¼ inch) from the outside edge, and leave the thread out of the needle. What you want is the hole only, no stitching!
* If you're applying patches, copy the look of ready-made luxury sweaters and add matching pieces of skin across the top of the shoulders.

Let down hems live up to their name. Even if there is no obvious difference in colour between the old and the new, the crease marking the old hemline doesn't seem to come out even with heavy pressure from a steam iron.

* Try a touch of white vinegar, applied with a brush along the crease line before you press with a steam iron and cloth.

* If you let the legs of a pair of jeans down, you're left with a white line. Do a cover-up job by brushing a little diluted ink along it.

Material patches should be washed before they are attached. That way if there's any tendency to shrink, it will be taken care of before fitting to the garment.

* When you put the patch into position, always check that the straight grain of both old and new follow the same line.

Printed fabrics call for two measures if you want a patch to look professional.

* Either pick out one of the colours in the print and use a plain fabric in that colour, or take a portion of fabric very carefully from the hem, or wherever there's any excess, so that it fits in precisely.

A safety pin, so they say, is a girl's best friend – and it can certainly come in handy if your elastic breaks, both for a temporary solution and for a longer-term remedy.

* Use it to pin one end of the new piece of elastic to one end of the old. Pull the other end of the old elastic and as you pull out the old you pull in the new.
* If the old elastic has come out altogether you can still use the pin. Just pin through the end of the new elastic, then put the closed pin into the seam and push it along from the outside of the material. As it works its way along it will take the elastic with it.

Satin shoes which have suffered as much as your feet from a clumsy dancing partner should be treated as soon as possible, preferably the moment you take the shoes off.

* For white satin, remove any surface dust with a soft brush, then dab a piece of cotton wool in surgical spirit and lightly rub the marks.
* Treat coloured satin shoes in the same way, but use either benzine or petrol.

Scuffed heels can be improved if you carefully stick the torn leather back into position with a dab of clear glue.

* If the tiny scuffed piece of leather has wrinkled, then stretch and pull it back to fit before you press it down firmly with the glue.
* Keep an eye on the heels of your shoes and always get them repaired (or do the repair yourself with heels and soles bought from a chain store) before it's absolutely necessary. If you wear a heel down too much, it can very rarely be made to look as good as new again.

Sock darns will last that bit longer if you combine a strand of matching cotton thread with the wool in your needle. If you haven't a 'mushroom' to put into the heel, then use an old light bulb.

Zips are a wonderful invention, but when they break at the bottom, they usually do it when you can't run for cover.

* Use a needle and thread (begged, borrowed or carried in your handbag if you're cautious) to do a quick repair. What you are faced with is the slider part of the zip left attached to one side only.

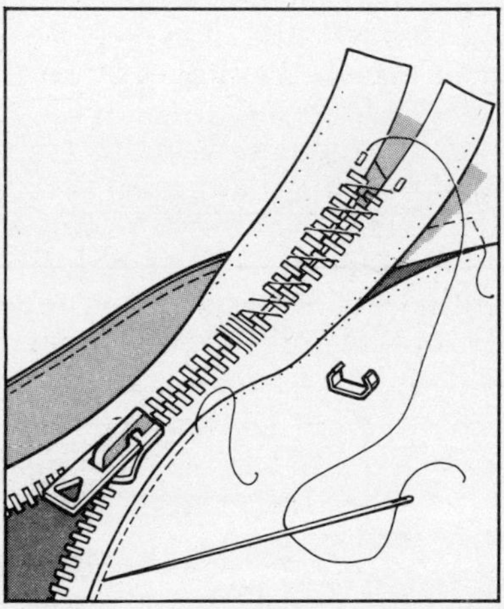

* Unpick the stitching at the bottom of the zip, then remove the little metal 'stop' at the bottom (it's not always easy to dislodge but it will give in to pressure in the end). Next move the slider back into its proper position and gently pull the zip up a little. Stitch several times back and forth over the teeth of the zip just above where the damage was. Don't forget to restitch any gaping hole you've left after unstitching the zip. Later, when you have a bit more time, you can improvise a new 'stop' by stitching one of those bars for skirt and trouser fastenings across the teeth above the spot where you've stitched a temporary stop.
* If the stops at the top of the zip come away (and this can often happen if the material at the top of the zip gets frayed so that the stop simply eases off) then you can, again, improvise a new stop. This time take one of the eyes you get with hooks and eyes and bend it in two so that the small circles are back to back, then slip the material in between the two sides of the bent eye and stitch it in place, going through one circle, right through the material and through the circle on the other side.
* If a zip isn't actually damaged but sticks (not much fun when you have a bus to catch or someone's ringing the doorbell) rub a lead pencil over the teeth if they're made of metal and a piece of soap if they're made of nylon.
* Not all zips have those convenient little slivers of metal underneath the slider pull, which then slots into position to make sure the zip can't slip down. If your zip isn't self-supporting, so to speak, try this treatment. Attach a little circle of very strong thread (not the kind you use for your sewing machine, but preferably the sort you'd sew leather with) to the top of the zip pull, threading it through the little hole. Then pull the zip shut and stitch a very small button into position so that it's hidden by the overlap of the waistband fastening. Now the loop of thread from the zip pull can be popped over the button and so keep the zip firmly fastened.

LOOKING AFTER FUR

During the summer months (if you can afford it) put your coat into storage with a furrier. There it goes into a proper air conditioned, refrigerated plant. If you want to keep it in the house, then avoid a stuffy, airless wardrobe or cupboard. A fur requires good ventilation and should be stored well away from central heating. It will then need a quick brush up after it's been stored in the wardrobe during the summer.

Friction from the strap of a shoulder bag (or even a clutch bag, which is always held in the same position against the side of a fur coat or jacket) can wear the fur. Try to vary the position in which you carry your bag.

Fur should always be cleaned by a professional furrier, who uses bran and a special mixture of spirits in a drum and then puts the garment in a 'cage' to shake out the cleaning mix.

Jewellery should never be pinned on to a fur: if you put a brooch into fur you will tear the skin and weaken it.

Perfume should ideally not be sprayed directly on to fur. The alcohol content will dry the skin and stiffen the hair as a result.

Some furs are harder wearing than others. Ermine and squirrel, for example, are light in wear, while musquash and mink can stand up better to tough treatment. But the amount of care and attention given to any type of fur can often be the deciding factor when it comes to how long it will last.

Wet fur should not be dried anywhere near direct heat. If your coat has been rained on, shake it to get rid of as much excess water as possible, then hang it up in a well ventilated place.

LOOKING AFTER LEATHER AND SUEDE

BOOTS AND SHOES

Keeping shoes smart is an art, as any shoe shine boy will tell you. And to do it properly you need the right equipment.

* If you use tinned polish, you'll need three different brushes. A stiff one to take off the mud and grime, a soft one to apply the polish and a medium one for polishing. To get the kind of shine Fred Astaire used to have on his dancing shoes you'll need a 'buffer'. This is a rectangular cushion covered in an old piece of velvet from the scrapbag. Make one about 15 cm (6 inches) by 10 cm (4 inches) and stuff it with cotton wool or old tights. Use it to give your shoes a good buff after polishing with the brush. Wash it regularly to avoid the surface of the velvet becoming clogged up with polish.
* Shoe trees keep shoes in good shape. It may not be quite so important for casual styles, but the ones you wear on special occasions really ought to be 'treed up' every time you take them off, so that they'll look good for as long as possible. Trees for bots are also worthwhile, mainly to keep the legs straight and prevent the leather or suede being creased by bending. If you don't have boot trees, try the old magazine trick instead. Any old magazines can be rolled up lengthways and put into the leg of each boot to keep them upright.
* If your shoes are wet through, newspaper's what you want: crumpled not rolled. Stuff this right into the shoes and let them dry away from any direct heat source (including a strong summer sun).
* Patent leather is expensive so it pays dividends to look after it

and keep it soft. Clean shoes by removing any soil with a damp cloth, then use a neutral shoe cleaning cream or a proprietary aerosol spray to brighten them up.

* Shoes of leather or suede shouldn't be stored near heat, nor even near boilers or gas cookers where there's any risk of the fumes reaching them. A dark, dry cupboard well away from the sunlight is best.
* If you've ever tried getting a shine on damp shoes, you'll know that nine times out of ten you'll be disappointed. In an emergency, moisten the brush or cloth with paraffin, then apply the polish. Alternatively, rub the leather with the inside of an old lemon, leave to dry for a little, then polish.
* If you happen to have aniline-dyed shoes, they will need special treatment. Every time you wear them, pamper them! Take a piece of cotton wool, dip it in soapy water and wipe over the leather. Rinse with a cloth which has been wrung out in clear warm water, then dry and polish with the product made for this kind of shoe.
* 'These boots were made for walking', but, unfortunately, after you've worn them a few times and the leather begins to wrinkle around the ankles, you begin to wonder if they're really fit for their purpose. You can't avoid this 'concertina' look whatever you do, but if you clean the wrinkled area and rub in lots of polish regularly there's a reasonable chance that the wrinkles won't become cracks.
* Badly-stained brown shoes can benefit from a rub with turpentine. Leave the turps to work into the leather overnight, then polish as usual.
* New shoes not only squeak, then can slip as well. So give them a bit of grip by going over the soles with a rough sandpaper before you wear them for the first time.
* Waterproof footwear wouldn't get wet even if it was dipped in a bath of water, but it's expensive to buy and the styles available in the waterproof footwear ranges can be rather limited. Since there's nothing worse than wet feet, and puddles can be hard to avoid, try waterproofing your existing shoes. To do this you have several alternatives and the choice may depend on price. You can buy polishes and sprays which do the job for you. You can rub linseed oil into leather or you can try this old-fashioned recipe which the ploughmen found worked very well in the days of horses and tackety boots!

Recipe: Mix together 2 parts of beeswax and 1 part of mutton fat and apply this to the leather at night. Next morning wipe with a soft cloth. The shoes will be dull to start with, but once you've used polish two or three times, the shine you get will be even more brilliant than before the waterproofing treatment.

* If you have 'seasonal' footwear you may well find that after being stuck in the back of a wardrobe for some months the leather has become hard. Castor oil is just what the doctor ordered! Rub it into the leather and it will soon be smooth and supple again.
* Blue suede shoes, or ones of any other colour for that matter, can shine unpleasantly after a few months' wear. Try the steam iron treatment. Hold the iron about an inch above the suede, letting the steam get into the pile, and brush with a very soft brush. Alternatively, hold the shoes over the spout of a boiling kettle (take care not to soak the shoes, though, or scald yourself in the process) and brush. An emery board, or a piece of very fine grade sandpaper from the toolbox, can be used to raise the nap on worn spots on the suede. Rub the area lightly.
* If your shoes happen to get splashed with salty water from the road in winter snow conditions, the result can be a nasty white tide mark on the leather. Make up a solution of half vinegar, half water and rub it into the leather. Dry the shoes, then polish as usual.
* When you're cleaning the sides of the soles on suede shoes you need a steady hand because the slightest bit of polish on the adjacent suede of the upper will cause instant shine. Use a very narrow brush or an old toothbrush for the job.

GLOVES

Use a soft India rubber to erase some of the grubby marks from kid gloves. But clean the rubber before you use it, you don't want black pencil rubbings transferred to your gloves. Rub gently, so as not to damage the leather. Alternatively, raid the bread bin. Take a piece of white bread and, with the gloves on your hands, crumble the bread between your palms and roll it around, concentrating on the soiled areas in particular. Finish by brushing all the crumbs off with a soft brush.

* Put suede gloves on when they need cleaning. Rub some Fuller's earth into them well with a small brush, but not so firmly that it will damage the skin. Then brush it out with a clean brush and finish by giving the gloves a good shake.
* For white suede use dry pipeclay instead.
* If you have a pair of chamois leather gloves, soak them for about fifteen minutes in some warm soap suds to which you have added 1 teaspoon of ammonia for every 1 litre (2 pints) of water. With your fingers, press the gloves gently to get the dirt out, but on no account squeeze or wring them. Then rinse them with fresh warm water. This isn't as simple as it sounds and needs a great deal of patience! Just move them up and down and try to get any soap out; use several lots of water if necessary. Finally, hold them under a warm shower spray and gently press the water out with your hand, working from the wrist to the fingers. Put the gloves in a clean towel and press as much moisture out as you can. Spread them flat on a dry towel and leave them outside in the garden until they dry, but don't put them in strong sunshine. As chamois (and every type of leather) has a tendency to stiffen as it dries, check the gloves every so often and rub them a little just to keep them supple.

HANDBAGS AND BRIEFCASES

* Beeswax furniture polish, the colourless kind you'd use on your best Chippendale chairs, cares equally well for leather handbags and briefcases, however modern they may be. Just rub in, shine up and your bags may continue to look good for as long as your antiques have.
* If a leather handbag is looking rather sorry for itself and polishing doesn't do a lot to improve its appearance, it's time to give it a good clean. Use saddle soap and apply it with a small sponge, working it into the leather in a circular movement. Once clean, rinse off using a soft cloth dipped in warm water, leave the bag to dry, then polish in the usual way.
* And if you want to give it a real tonic, try this 'reviver'. Mix 200 ml (⅓ pint) of vinegar with 400 ml (⅔ pint) of boiled linseed oil and shake in a bottle until it looks like the texture of cream. Rub some of this into the bag, then polish with a soft cloth.

LEATHER COATS AND JACKETS

* Mud and surface dirt should be wiped off leather coats and jackets with a soft cloth.
* Any stains should not be treated at home because solvents can often take the colour out of leather and leave a lighter patch. Take the garment to a dry cleaner who specialises in cleaning leather and explain what has caused the stain so that they know how to deal with it.
* Always make sure buttons are securely fixed because if they match the coat as is often the case, a replacement can be impossible to get.
* Any tiny tears in the leather can be repaired by carefully sticking the material which has lifted off back down with a touch of clear glue. A match is ideal for pushing the surface piece firmly back down on to the skin.
* Always have garments cleaned regularly and before they become too soiled.

LEATHER EXTRAS

* Leather buckles and trimmings on clothes should always be mentioned to the dry cleaner, or the results can be disastrous. It may well be that the cleaner will want such things removed

or protected in some way (e.g. with kitchen foil) in case they are damaged by the cleaning fluids.

* Similarly, if you are washing garments with leather trims yourself, unless you know they are made of washable leather (most elbow patches for sweaters, for instance, are washable these days), then remove them.

SUEDE JACKETS AND COATS

* You can never hope to clean suede jackets and coats successfully at home, so don't try. However, you can cope with the odd mark. Fuller's earth well rubbed into the surface, then left in for ten minutes before brushing out with a soft brush (NEVER a wire suede brush) may do the trick. If the skin is not so much dirty as just tired looking, then hold the area over a bowl of boiling water or a kettle spout, let the steam penetrate and brush up the nap with a soft bristle or rubber brush.
* However tempting it may be to try to save on cleaning bills, don't ever attempt to use any proprietary spot cleaners or any sort of chemical fluid on a suede garment. The worst that can happen is that the colour will go completely haywire and at the very least 'ring' marks will be left around the stain which will make it even more obvious than it was before.

TYPES OF LEATHER

The different kinds of leathers used in bags and shoes need quite individual care and attention.

White buckskin needs a good brush to get rid of any surplus dust, then should be cleaned with any of the proprietary brands sold for the purpose. But if badly marked you may find that the marks still show through the cleaner: the first step, in this case, is to wash it using a cloth and water. When dry, check for any bad marks still left and, with a piece of very fine grade sandpaper, gently rub the affected areas with a circular movement. Use a cleaner in the normal way.

Calf – if you've been careless and dried this leather near heat it may have become dry and stiff. Soften by rubbing a mixture of half milk and half water into the surface.

Crocodile Buff shoes with a soft cloth after wearing. If you do this, you should only need to use shoe cream occasionally, which will save you time and money.

Lizard is designed for the lazy, since it doesn't need polishing at all. Just remove any dust or dirt with a soft brush and give a quick wipe with a soft dry duster.

Pigskin needs fairly rough treatment. Use a wire brush after wearing and a suede cleaner on it from time to time.

1. ~~About the House~~
2. ~~Clothes Care~~
3. Make Amends

How to Cope in an Emergency

Household emergencies of one sort or another crop up all too often. A little prior thought can turn a major emergency into just a small hiccup in the smooth running of the household.

First of all, there are 8 points to observe in any household.

1. Check where the water stopcock is. This is usually under the kitchen sink. If the stopcock is not under the sink, you may be able to trace the pipework back from the tank, provided the pipes are exposed. If not, check where the water supply enters the house or check with neighbours to find where their stopcock is. Do not wait until an emergency, as the last thing you want to be

doing when water is pouring out of a burst pipe is playing 'hunt the stopcock'.

2. Once or twice a year, check that the stopcock is still movable and has not become jammed. If jammed, give yourself extra leverage by grasping the stopcock with a ring spanner.

3. Check that you know where the gas lever is and that you know which way to turn it off.

4. Have emergency 'phone numbers, such as 24-hour plumber or gas-leak service, written down somewhere handy. Find a reputable plumber by recommendation or by checking whether he is a member of a professional plumbing body.

5. Keep a fire blanket and powder extinguisher wall-mounted and easily accessible in the kitchen.

6. Check your lofts for a build-up of snow in really bad winter-storm weather. Shovel it out with a plastic shovel, then lay sacking around the edge of the roof space to prevent snow blowing in again.

7. Give your neighbour a spare door key and a work number where you can be contacted, if appropriate.

8. Sort out some emergency heating and lighting in case of a power failure. Store them somewhere easily accessible. Trying to climb into the loft or searching the garage by torchlight is not easy. Check them to see that they are in good working condition at the beginning of each winter. (See also page 153.)

BLOCKED SINK

This is generally caused by putting fat or grease down the sink, along with tea leaves and food debris.

* Usually it can be cleared if you sprinkle a handful of washing soda around the plughole, then pour plenty of boiling water down it.
* It may be necessary to bale out any cold water already in the sink first, which is not a pleasant task. Use a ladle, or tie an old cup to a wooden spoon to avoid having to dip hands into the water.
* If this does not work, a sink plunger usually clears blockages quickly. It works best if the outlet pipe is covered, so that a slight vacuum is made. Wedge a piece of wood over the end of the pipe at the drain; with a double sink put the other plug in

place. It may take several attempts with the plunger to loosen the blockage, but once cleared, remove the covering on the outlet and clean the sink and pipework with washing soda and boiling water.

* If this too fails you will need to get at the U-shaped pipe underneath. Lead pipework will have a metal nut to be unscrewed, plastic pipe fitting will have a pull-off section. If it has been installed within the last ten years, you are likely to have a two-piece U bend or a bottle trap, either of which can be unscrewed by hand quite easily. Place a bucket under the sink first, then use a thin stick or a piece of wire carefully to hook out the blockage.

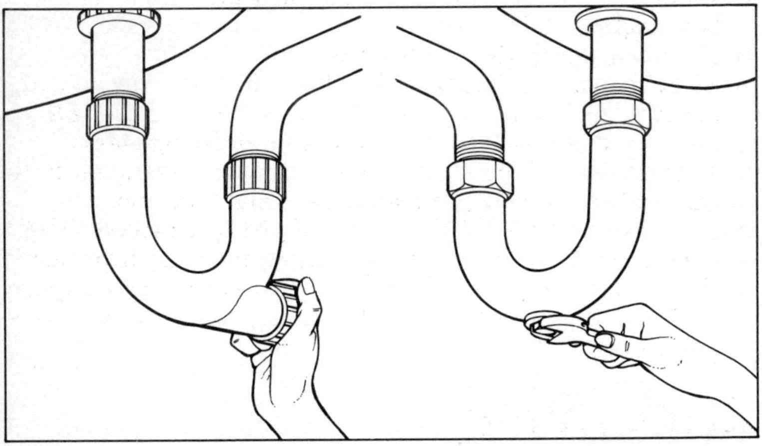

* After all this, resolve never again to throw tea leaves or grease down the sink. Alternatively, fit a waste disposal unit.

BROKEN WINDOW

Broken glass is always dangerous, but especially so if there are children around.

* Cracked panes of glass can be held together with two strips of waterproof sticky tape across the crack, one each side of the window pane, until it can be properly repaired. The pane should be clean and dry, so that the tape will adhere properly.

* Once a window is broken the rest of the glass should be removed and disposed of safely straight away. To do this, stand to one side and hold a sheet of thick card or an old blanket at the window. This will prevent splinters breaking off indoors, while you knock out the remaining pieces of glass.
* Knock from inside to out against the card or blanket using a hammer.
* Lay sheets of newspaper on the ground outside to make collecting up the glass easier. Wear old gardening gloves to protect your hands, and goggles or an old pair of sunglasses for your eyes.
* Wrap and double wrap the glass, then put into a cardboard box, seal and label well.
* Never put loose glass in the dustbin.
* Clean out the fragments of glass from the frame rebate with a pair of pincers and replace the glass. Use a chisel on any remaining pieces of glass, but beware of flying glass.
* Take a piece of the broken glass, carefully wrapped, to the glaziers so that you can match the weight and type.
* Carry the new sheet of glass with care. Make a pad with sheets of newspaper to hold it top and bottom and carry it vertically.
* If the window is often broken, or in a particularly exposed position, consider having reinforced glass or acrylic sheet fitted instead.

BURST PIPE

Pipes are liable to burst during the winter, when they have not been well enough insulated. The water within the pipe freezes and expands, thus cracking the pipe. It is generally not noticed until it thaws, although sometimes you notice that the pipe is blocked, then every plumber in the book is inundated with calls from frantic householders.

* To avoid joining the queue to pay a happy plumber his emergency call-out rate, check that all the pipes in your house are well insulated.
* It is usually the pipes in the loft that are affected, especially if over-enthusiastic loft insulation has left exposed pipework in the icy loft space. Remember, when insulating, to leave the

area directly under the cold water tank uncovered, so some rising heat will keep the chill off the tank and pipes. So insulate the cold water tank on top and round the sides but not underneath.

* Insulate pipes well, either with old rags wrapped around them, or with proprietary foam pipe insulation.
* If you have a dripping tap and conditions are icy, keep the plug in the sink during the night (unless the problem is so bad that the sink would overflow).
* If a pipe has burst, put a bucket underneath and turn off the water supply at the stopcock. It usually turns off clockwise, and is usually very stiff (see page 147). The next step is to turn off the central heating system; this cannot run if the water supply is not working. Turn on all the taps to empty the system, but keep a bath full of water for emergency use. Then call a plumber.
* Waste pipes from sinks can sometimes freeze up too; sprinkle salt down them in cold weather to prevent this happening. If it does occur, thaw by wrapping cloths wrung out in warm water around the U bend.

CEILING FALLS IN

Once the ceiling has actually fallen in, there is not a lot to do except clear up the mess and call in someone to do the repairs. However, there are generally warning signs before the actual disaster. If it is due to flooding from above, for quite a while before the collapse the whole ceiling usually bulges with the weight of water above it. A burst pipe may have caused the water to seep through but under certain circumstances snow can blow in under the eaves and cause a flood as it thaws. If you notice that the ceiling is unnaturally bowed, you can act quickly to prevent it collapsing.

* First, place as many bowls and buckets as you can muster under the middle of the ceiling. Next turn off the lighting at the mains, then carefully make a small hole in the ceiling using a screwdriver, to let the water run through. Repairing this hole is a minor affair compared to coping with a collapsed ceiling. Be sure to move or cover furniture before making the hole, if there is time.

CHIP PAN FIRE

This is among the most common and thankfully the most easily dealt with of domestic fires.

* Do not use water on a blazing chip pan or attempt to move it. Instead, turn off the heat, cover the pan with a lid, baking tray, or better still a fire-blanket.
* If the fire has taken a hold and the cooker, kitchen units and other areas are affected, do not attempt to deal with it. Make sure everyone is out of the house. Close the door and call the fire service. Do not under any circumstances return to collect things or tackle the blaze.

FLOOD

Most households with small children will have experienced a flood in the bathroom, however minor. Usually this can simply be mopped up, but if the water seeps under the floorboards it can affect electrical wiring. A great deal of water can, of course, cause the ceiling underneath to bow or collapse (see Ceiling Falls In, opposite).

* Switch off the electricity at the mains, and mop up as much water as possible.
* Lift carpets and floor coverings and dry thoroughly, preferably outside.
* If there seems to be a great deal of water under the floorboards, lift one or two and allow the air to circulate. Open a window to aid drying. Only then turn the power back on and try turning on a light. If the lights fuse, call an electrician.
* Street flooding is a more major problem as the water is often very dirty. Try to move as much furniture as possible upstairs, so that it is not affected.
* Large scale floods usually mean that local councils are on hand with advice and sandbags.
* Once the water has receded, large scale cleaning is needed on the ground floor. Carpets are best lifted and may be sent to a specialist company who will clean flood-damaged carpets.
* Sometimes water under the floorboards needs pumping out. Use a wet and dry vacuum cleaner for small scale problems and call your local council for help on a larger scale.

GAS LEAK

If you smell gas, put out cigarettes and extinguish naked flames.

* Open doors and windows to get rid of the gas and keep them open until the leak has been stopped.
* Do not use electric switches – including doorbells – as these may cause a spark.
* Check to see if a gas tap has been left on accidentally or if a pilot has gone out. If not, there is probably a gas leak.

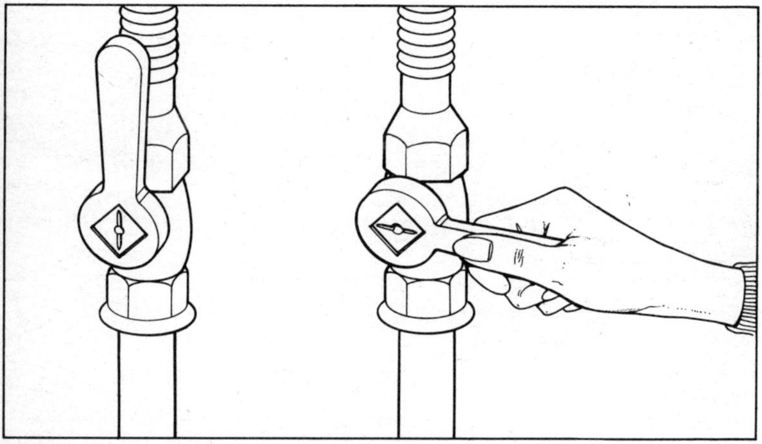

* Turn off the whole supply at the meter and call gas service – the number is in the telephone directory under 'GAS'. They run a 24 hour a day, 365 days a year emergency service and are quick to respond to any suspicion of a gas leak.
* Checking a suspected escape and simple gas escape repairs will usually be free because the first 30 minutes of work will not be charged for, including parts and materials up to the value of £1.
* Although most escapes can be made safe within 30 minutes, if the work takes longer, or if a second visit is necessary or more expensive parts needed, you will usually be charged for the extra time and materials.

LOCKED OUT

If you have forgotten or lost your door key, check first if anyone else has one; a husband or wife, a teenage son or daughter, etc.

* If you cannot locate another key, the next step is to see if there are any open windows that you or someone else can climb through. Remember though, that if you can easily break into your own house, then so could a burglar. For free advice on making your house secure, contact your local Crime Prevention Officer (see page 357).

* If it is impossible to get into the house, call a locksmith. If the lock is simply jammed, powdered graphite may loosen it enough to turn the key.
* If there is a child trapped in the house, call the Police.
* If you are at a complete loss, phone the Police, who will be able to advise you.

POWER FAILURE

This always seems to happen in the depth of winter, when the lack of heat and light are far more noticeable.

* Heat only one room, and keep the warmth in by hanging old curtains or blankets against internal doors.

* Candles must be used carefully; make sure each one is well fixed in a holder or in a tin and out of reach of children.
* Freezers will usually keep cold for eight hours as long as they are full and unopened (see page 62).
* If you have warning of the power failure, cook a casserole and place it in a freezer box lined with screwed up newspaper to keep it warm. This will hold its heat for a couple of hours.
* Make up flasks of hot water for drinks and/or soup and make hot water bottles for beds.
* Wrap up warmly and keep as active as possible.
* Clearing snow from the drive is an ideal way to pass the time, as long as you are fit!
* Finally, leave a light on, so that you know when the power comes back on again.

RUNNING REPAIRS

Blunt scissors can be sharpened around the neck of a milk bottle. Alternatively, cut up a sheet of sandpaper for a slightly sharper edge.

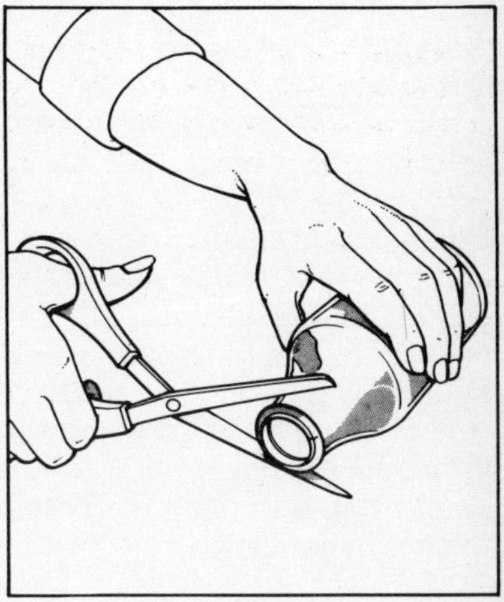

Carpets that are badly burnt or stained can only be improved by cutting out the affected area and fitting a new piece. This is one good reason for saving a spare piece of any carpet laid in the house.

Mark out with chalk the area to be cut out, allowing a good inch or two around the burn. Then, using sharp scissors, cut from the centre of the burn out to these lines in four places; so you cut the diagonals of the chalked square. Next cut the edges, so the burnt carpet is removed in four triangular shapes. Cut a new piece of carpet to size, taking care to match the pile and shading. Cut a piece of hessian, or tapestry backing slightly larger than the carpet piece and spread glue thinly over it. Carefully slide this under the edges of the carpet on the floor, glue side up. Then insert the carpet piece and press down well. (See illustration on page 156.) Take care not to get glue from your fingers on to the carpet. Allow to dry before using.

As an alternative to glue and hessian, you could use carpet tape, placed sticky side up around the edges of the hole.

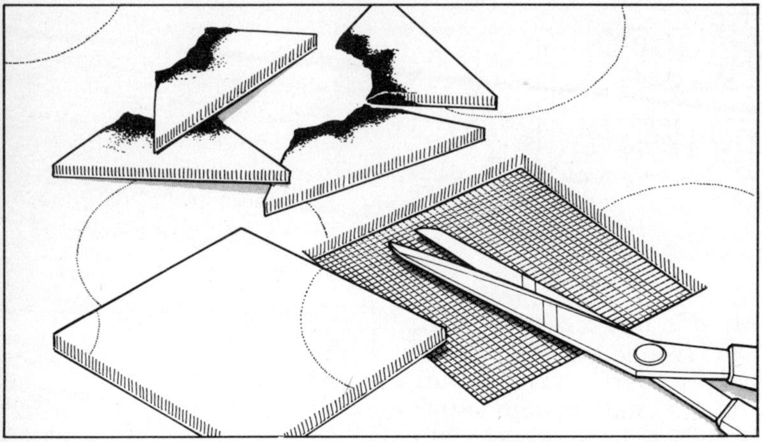

Dents on unpolished wood can sometimes be raised using heat and moisture. Wet a wad of screwed-up newspaper in hot water and lay it over the dent, leave until dry and repeat. Alternatively, use wet brown paper and carefully hold a hot iron on top of this to help the wood to swell. Take care to avoid burning the surrounding areas of wood though! Never use this method on polished or veneered wood, as it would further damage the wood. You will need the help of a professional French polisher in this instance.

Door handles which come away in your hand are particularly inconvenient. With the type where the knobs are on either end of a spindle, a temporary repair can be made by fixing a screw through the spindle on the side of the missing knob. With newer handles, you can usually relocate the handle sufficiently well to be able to turn it. If not, a pair of pliers may do the trick. Afterwards, be sure to wedge the door open until you have fixed it permanently.

Drawers that stick and do not pull out easily may be cured by rubbing a candle along the runners to lubricate them. If this does not work, mark the sides of the drawer with a little chalk before pushing it back in. Where the wood rubs, the chalk will be smudged, and this is the area to rub down with glasspaper or plane over.

Drawers that fall from a chest or cupboard when pulled open, have usually lost their stops. Fit a new one by screwing a piece of wood to the cross rail, so the drawer stops against it. If there is no room underneath the drawer, use a piece of dowel. Drill a hole in the top back edge of the drawer, put a little glue in, then put the drawer back in place. Work from above and slot the dowel into the hole, so that when the drawer is opened, the protruding piece of dowel will catch against the frame of the chest and so prevent the drawer from falling out.

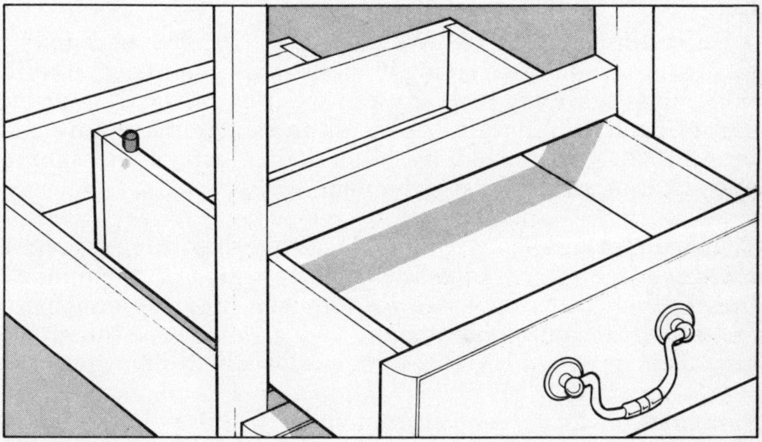

Floorboards that squeak are a nuisance, and not just to teenagers creeping in late at night! Often, sprinkling a little talcum powder or French chalk on and around the board will cure it. If not, screw the board down; insert long screws next to the nail holes.

Laminated table tops that are in poor condition are best covered over. Removing the old laminate is very difficult, and the new one will fit on top as long as the surface is smooth and free from major cracks, or grease. Clean the old surface well, wipe over with a little methylated spirit to remove any grease and lightly rub down any shiny areas with a little wet and dry paper. Dust down, then glue the new piece of laminate into place.

Light bulbs occasionally break while still in the socket. Getting the remains out can be difficult. Turn the electricity off at the consumer unit and insert a cork into the neck of the bulb. This should give enough grip to unscrew the broken bulb safely.

Net curtains sometimes develop small tears, which can be mended with a little clear nail varnish.

Removable chair seats are easy to re-cover as long as the padding underneath is sound. Remove the old cover and use as a pattern, then fix the new cover into place using upholsterers' tacks or a staple gun.

A roller blind that jams or will not roll up can often be cured by taking the blind down, laying it on the floor, completely unrolling it, then re-rolling it slowly and steadily. This will re-prime the spring. If a blind rolls up sharply and suddenly, remove and unroll it. Re-roll only half the blind then re-hang it: this should prevent it becoming over-tightened.

Saucepan lid handles sometimes break long before the saucepan is worn out. Use a cork fixed with a screw to make a temporary handle that keeps cool. New knobs can often be bought or ordered from the manufacturer, and sometimes, even if the saucepan is very old, knobs to newer pans will fit.

Scratches on some woods can often be disguised by rubbing a wax crayon of a similar colour over the scratch. On dark woods, just a little brown shoe polish applied on a cotton wool stick often does the trick. On mahogany and oak, try rubbing the scratched area with a cut Brazil nut; the natural nut oil improves the appearance.

Screws that are stuck can sometimes be shifted by putting a little vinegar on the screw head. Alternatively, try tapping them sharply with an old screwdriver and hammer.

Squeaking hinges on cupboards or doors are enough to drive anyone to distraction. Often a little washing-up liquid will silence them, or light cooking oil. If neither of these work, dry the hinge well and then try sprinkling talcum powder, or rubbing French chalk or a soft pencil over the exposed parts of the hinge.

A squeaking stair can be cured by fixing a right-angled shelf bracket to the underneath of the stair. Screw it into place to hold the wood firmly and prevent the rubbing that causes the squeaking. This can obviously only be done where the underneath of the stairs is either exposed, or can be reached through a cupboard. If you cannot get underneath, try screwing down the treads. Use two or three screws across the front at the point where the tread meets the riser.

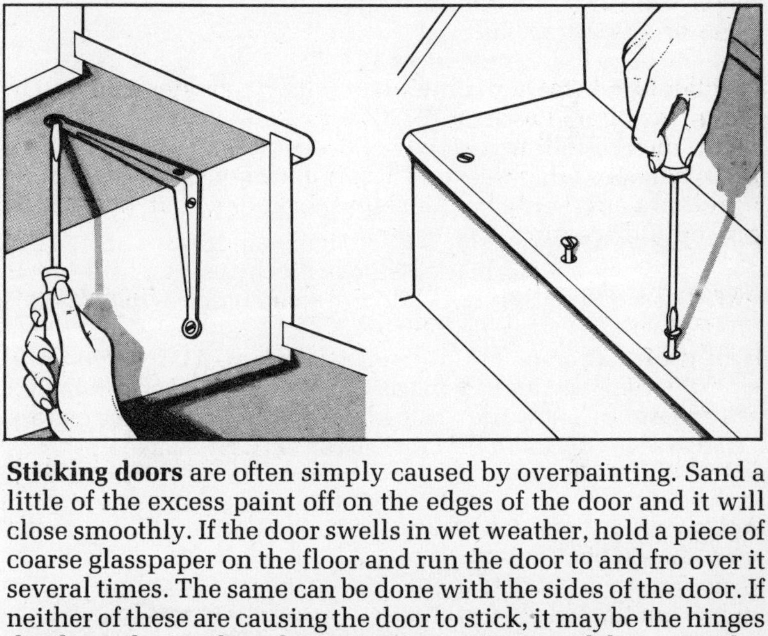

Sticking doors are often simply caused by overpainting. Sand a little of the excess paint off on the edges of the door and it will close smoothly. If the door swells in wet weather, hold a piece of coarse glasspaper on the floor and run the door to and fro over it several times. The same can be done with the sides of the door. If neither of these are causing the door to stick, it may be the hinges that have dropped, as the screws sometimes work loose. Wedge the door up while the hinge screws are replaced, using longer screws or plugging the existing hole with a matchstick first. If the hinge pin has worn, the hinges will need replacing – check by opening the door and lifting it upwards by the handle and noting how much movement there is in the hinges.

A toilet that keeps filling up and overflowing can mean that the ball float is punctured. Effect a temporary repair by unscrewing the ball, emptying any water out, then wrapping it in a plastic bag and sealing this with insulating tape.

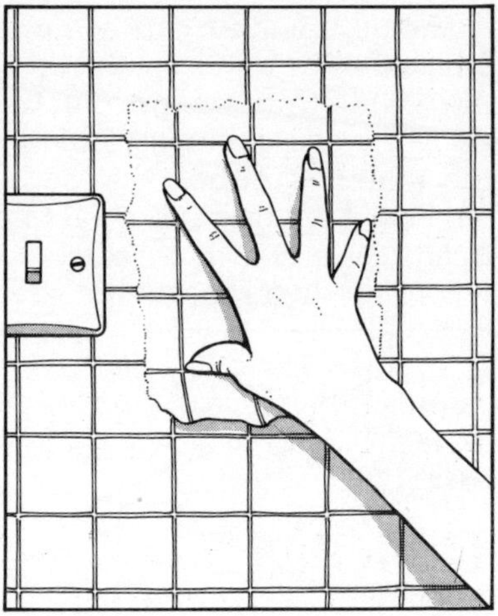

Torn wallpaper can be patched. Cut a new piece of wallpaper larger than the damaged area, taking care to match the pattern. Then tear the edges by hand, so that there are no straight lines. If the wallpaper on the wall has faded, it may be possible to fade the new piece by standing it in bright sunlight, or by brushing it with a little lemon juice and allowing it to dry. Then paste the patch as accurately as possible over the damaged area.

Vinyl floors are quite soft and dragging equipment across the floor can leave a black mark. Remove this by using a little metal polish in wadding. Work it into the scratch and wipe clean.

Wall tiles that crack are difficult to replace. They have to be carefully removed and all traces of adhesive scraped out before you can put in a new tile. Instead use self-adhesive tiles on top. Arrange several around the cracked tile or tiles to make a pattern.

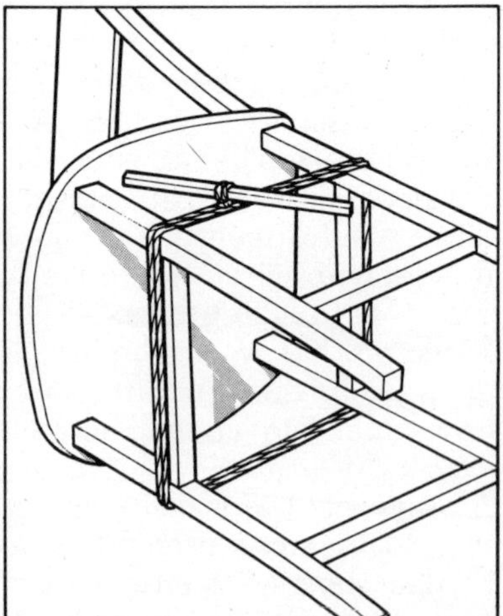

Wobbly chairs and tables are often caused by dried-up glue. Reglueing them should help. Scrape out the old glue, reglue and clamp together until dry. Chair legs that cannot be clamped can be held together with a length of string. Tie it round, then tighten by placing a length of wood in the string and turning it round several times, thus pulling the string taut. Wedge the piece of wood under the seat of the chair, so that it stays firmly in place.

GETTING MORE OUT OF IT

With a little ingenuity, ordinary household articles can be made to last longer, or serve dual purposes.

CARPETS

Fit stair carpet with an extra length folded under on the bottom stair. Then, as the carpet wears, lift it and re-lay with the extra piece on top. This will even out the wear on the tread and the upriser and so make the carpet last twice as long.

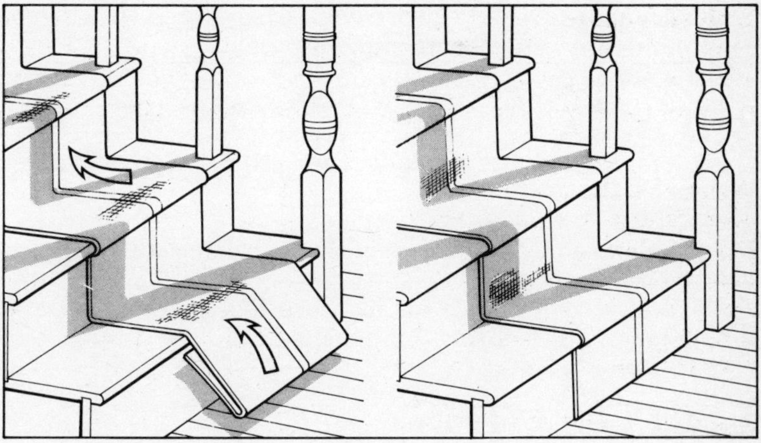

* Keep a spare piece of any carpet laid to use for checking cleaning agents on (see page 20).
* Use door mats and rugs to protect the most heavily trodden pieces of carpets.
* A good underlay helps prolong the life of the carpet. Choose

the right grade of carpet for the area of the house. Light duty carpet soon wears in a hall but lasts well in a bedroom.

SHEETS

Most sheets come in easycare, poly/cotton mixtures. These need more regular washing, since they discolour gradually in use and are then difficult to brighten up again.

* Sheets usually wear in the centre first. Cut them down the middle and turn the edges to the centre and restitch.
* Fitted sheets can be easily made from existing ones by sewing a double row of stitches in elastic thread around each corner. Sew a good 22 cm (9 inches) down from each corner.
* Old faded sheets can be easily dyed at home in the washing machine for a bright new look. Afterwards, run through the machine on its longest, hottest wash with a little bleach (but no clothes) added. The dye bottle will contain instructions.
* Cheer up old sheets and pillow cases with ribbon or lace trim.
* Sew two old sheets together on three sides and put poppers along the top to make a quilt cover. Dye or trim it with lace or appliquéd pieces of contrasting material.

SOFAS

Clean sofas regularly to avoid dust and grit damaging the fibres (see page 24).

* Turn removable cushions regularly and change them around to even the wear.
* Make slip covers for arms, or have loose covers fitted to lengthen the life of sofas and chairs.

TABLECLOTHS

Repair tablecloths as soon as they begin to thin. Avoid leaving it until holes develop. Machine darn, or cover with appliqué.

* Use an overcloth on tablecloths that have become worn or discoloured on the top, but whose sides are in good condition.
* Trim frayed edges of cloths and either resew or cut scalloped edges and oversew.

* Starch linens and cotton to improve the look of the cloth.
* Clean bad stains from white linen by using a little neat dye remover available in chemists.
* Old lace tablecloths can be cut up to make cushion covers.

TEA TOWELS

Prevent fluff coming off tea towels by lightly starching them.

* Ironing tea towels sterilizes them, making them more hygienic.
* Use clean tea towels each day, especially in the summer.
* Old, worn tea towels make good cleaning cloths.

TILES

Leftover ceramic tiles make good pot stands when fixed to a wooden base with a special wood adhesive.

* Pretty ceramic tiles can be used to re-cover an old table top.
* Individual tiles make wipe-clean plant pot stands.
* Cork tiles can be used to make a noticeboard.

TOWELS

Large bath towels that have become thin in places can be cut down into hand towels.

* Smaller towels can be used to make hand flannels. Cut one small towel lengthways, fold it in half and sew up to make a flannel that fits comfortably on the hand like a mitten. This is ideal for cleaning small children.
* Old towels make good bathwraps for children. Fold in half and sew up sides, then cut a hole for the head through folded section. Fit loops at waist height and thread through a dressing gown cord for tying.
* Badly worn towels can be cut up into towelling squares for cleaning. They give good results on silver and other metals.
* Cheer up old but not worn towels: dye them with colour-fast dyes, or trim the ends with ribbons or bias binding.
* Two or three worn hand towels can be quilted together to make a warm, absorbent bath mat.

RECYCLING

Recycle as many household products as possible to save money and make life a little easier:

CHIMNEY POTS

These are often very pretty and can be used as plant pots. Alternatively, clean the chimney pot well and use it as an umbrella stand, or set a small spotlight in the base, so that it makes an unusual garden light. To clean the pot, scrape off the excess soot with a knife or a garden trowel, then scrub with hot, soapy water.

COFFEE TINS

Large ones can be cleaned and covered with old wallpaper to make wastepaper bins. These also make pretty plant pot holders. Place the plant, in its pot, inside the decorated coffee tin. Small tins of this kind make useful holders for screws, nuts and bolts. Label the outside, or stick a screw on the outside with sticky tape, so that you can tell at a glance what is inside.

DRAWERS

Fix castors to shallow drawers and push them under beds for extra storage space. Stand drawers on their sides to make a child's height bookshelf, then fit a middle shelf. Small drawers make good doll's cots, and larger ones can be painted and used as cars or trains. The bottom drawer of a damaged chest of drawers can be salvaged and turned into a shallow trunk or seat. Cut off the bottom drawer and its casing, then fix a sheet of hardboard above the cut surfaces. Paint and add a couple of cushions to make a low seat.

EGG CARTONS

Plastic ones make useful extra ice cube trays for the freezer, and cardboard ones can be used as seedtrays. Plant out the young seedlings by tearing each egg section off, removing the base only and putting in the ground. The cardboard will rot as the seedlings grow.

PAINT TINS

These can be cleaned out and used as small buckets for carrying stones or soil when gardening or for storing large screws in the workshop. Alternatively, paint the outside and use as planters in the garden.

SINKS

An old porcelain or stone sink will make a lovely garden planter. Stand it on a couple of bricks and fill with plants. This makes a good miniature herb or alpine garden. Solid old sinks can also be used as sandpits or water play areas for children.

WALLPAPER

Pretty papers can make good wrapping paper, especially if the wrapping needs to be stronger than usual. It can also be used to cover cardboard boxes to make them both more attractive and stronger, so that they can be used for storage.

Rolls of old wallpaper make good cheap drawing paper for children and can be hung, plain side up, in a playroom or bedroom. It is also a good covering for tables under tablecloths, or for children to paint and model on. (See also page 319.)

YOGURT POTS

These, along with margarine tubs and similar containers, have many extra uses. Herbs can be grown on window ledges, poster paints mixed in them, and individual jellies left to set in them. Containers with lids make useful salad holders for packed lunches, and all sorts of pots can be used in the fridge or freezer for storing small quantities of food. Local playgroups and nursery schools usually collect plastic containers along with many other pieces of household leftovers.

CHEAP AND CHEERFUL FURNISHING IDEAS

Become a bargain hunter. Hunt out fabric remnants (for cushion covers or wall hangings), carpet off-cuts (for small rooms or extra mats), search sales for pieces of furniture or rolls of wallpaper that would look just right in your home.

Blinds of one sort or another often work out cheaper than curtains. Roman and festoon blinds are easily made with few special accessories; paper and cane blinds are inexpensive to buy. (See also 'Roller Blinds' page 171.)

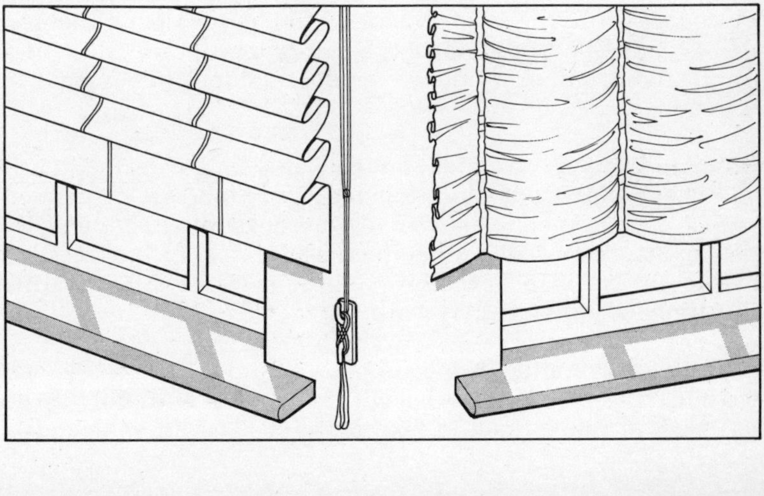

Curtain material can be expensive. One alternative way of curtaining a large window is to use curtain lining, and simply edge it with strips of brightly coloured material. Alternatively, dye old sheets with a washing machine dye and then cut to shape to make bright and cheerful curtains.

Curtains need to be generous to look really good. Don't buy the minimum amount of expensive curtain material; it is better to buy a larger amount of cheaper material, so that there are generous folds in the curtains even when they are pulled across the window (see page 203).

Floorboards can be sanded if in good condition, although this is hard work even with a sanding machine. If the boards are not good enough for sanding, consider painting them. Add stencilled shapes for colour and design, and a rug in the middle for warmth and you have an attractive finish at a fraction of the cost of a carpet.

A folding screen is a versatile piece of furniture in any flat or house. Pretty paper screens can be lit from behind to give a soft mellow look, or on a more practical level, a screen can be used to hide the kitchen area of a bedsit, the accumulated toys of several children, or simply positioned to keep the draughts out.

Garden furniture is often cheaper than ordinary furniture but can successfully be used indoors. Wooden chairs and tables, lightly varnished or stained bright colours, look perfect in a dining room, and cane and wicker does not look out of place in the lounge.

Hang up kitchen equipment on the walls. It fills a bare kitchen and keeps everything close to hand. Use pinboard, or painted chipboard and then fix cup screws or hooks into it. For a really instant hanging system, use self-adhesive hooks of varying sizes to take sieves, tin openers, knives, etc. It's a good way of covering up an unattractive wall as well.

Junk shops can often be a good place to browse round. Search out odd pieces of furniture that with a little time and effort can be restored or transformed to take pride of place in your house.

There is a wide range of easy-to-use wood strippers and renovators available now and these can turn a stained desk or old chair into a lovely piece of furniture.

Here are some other hints that may help:

* Old furniture, such as chests and desks, that are beyond stripping and varnishing, can be brightened up by repainting and adding stencils, either homemade or bought from a hobby shop. Alternatively try unusual painting techniques, such as marbling or rag rolling. A book from the library or your local craft shop will give details on how to do this and the results can be very effective.
* When buying furniture from jumble sales, junk shops and auctions take a careful look at it to assess how well it will respond to a little work. Avoid anything with structural damage, such as broken legs or cross rails, or anything with missing parts, as these could prove difficult to replace.
* Some things look much worse than they are; broken or missing beading, knobs and handles are easily replaced and there are good modern equivalents of many original handles and fittings. Poor surfaces can generally be improved with a little hard work and time. The exception here is French polished surfaces; small marks and stains can generally be removed, but larger areas of damage are best left to professionals.
* A battered tin or wooden trunk can be turned into a good piece of furniture, even if the hinges and handles are lost or damaged. Rub down, and deal with any dents, either by filling if the trunk is wooden, or by carefully tapping them out from the inside if it is made of tin. Remove damaged or broken hinges and handles, then repaint. Fix new handles, studs and hinges as required, then line the inside with ready-quilted material. Use as a linen box, blanket box or even a telephone seat.
* Old lampshades can be easily re-covered, as long as the metal frame is sound. Check that the joints are still unbroken, and the shade is not badly misshapen before buying.
* Old linen, such as tablecloths and napkins, is often sold at antique fairs and secondhand shops. Small thin patches and tears can be successfully darned by machine. Faded colours can be redyed. Odd spots and stains can be removed on white

linen by using a little neat stain remover; sold in hardware shops. Once repaired, washed and starched, an old linen tablecloth can grace your teatable and you will have a real bargain.

* Check old wooden furniture for woodworm before buying. Small round holes indicate that the furniture has been affected. Powder in the holes or nearby suggests a recent infestation. Press the wood gently with a screwdriver or small knife to check how soft it is. Badly affected wood will give. A small area, or an old infestation can be dealt with by spraying with woodworming fluids, available from shops.
* Small blisters or breaks in veneers can be dealt with by cutting the affected area out and replacing it. However, any inlay work or marquetry is more difficult to repair, so avoid this if possible.
* Most metals will clean up well with a little hard work, so brass candlesticks and silver tableware can generally be brought back to sparkling beauty, even if they do look almost black and very dingy in the junk shop.

Kitchen units can be very expensive. Buy the less expensive, plain white units and add your own touch of originality by fixing bright yellow or red plastic handles or knobs. Natural wood units can be lightly varnished if necessary with a matt varnish and dressed up with brass knobs. Alternatively, hand paint little flowers on to the wooden knobs for a really individual look.

Lighting makes a great difference to the look and feel of a new room. A single unshaded bulb is harsh and shows up every flaw in the room. Invest in good lighting; there are many good value spotlights, wall lights and lamps around, and with a little experimenting, you will soon find the best positioning and level of lighting for your room.

Make the best of a room's natural features; it may be an old fireplace that can be painted and filled with plants, or large French windows that can be made into a focal point. Even in a totally featureless room, as some modern square rooms are, you can emphasize its simplicity with low furnishing, subdued lighting and a neutral colour scheme that will give an almost oriental feel.

Plants cheer up any room; buy a few well-established ones and beg cuttings from friends and relatives. Grouped together plants make a lush green focal point in a room. Tall plants look best stood on a floor, and trailing plants can look very impressive hung on a wall, or high shelf.

Roller blinds can be hung over an alcove to make an instant wardrobe. Fit a length of dowel within the alcove to hang the clothes on and simply pull the blinds down to hide the clothes. The same principle can be used in kitchens and living rooms to cover shelves and save having to keep them tidy!

Start a collection. Almost anything can be collected from old cameras and clocks to small pieces of white china or seashells and pebbles. Arrange them on open shelves or on a small table and light them carefully for an impressive display that is sure to be a talking point.

Tables, however tatty and old, can always be made to look grand if covered with cloth. Use two cloths to good effect on side tables. The first should hang down to the floor and the second, in lace or a contrast colour should just overhang the table top. This system also makes a pretty dressing table in a bedroom and turns orange boxes into presentable coffee tables.

Trestle tables are cheap to buy and easy to store when not needed, so are useful in bedsitting rooms. On a really tight budget, buy the trestle legs and an internal door from a builders' merchants. Paint the door with several layers to ensure it is smooth, then lay this on the trestles to make a dining table. To secure, fix four wooden blocks on either side of each trestle. This will hold the trestles in place. (See illustration on page 171.)

Walls that cannot be painted can be cheered up by making a wall hanging from a pretty material, or by using posters, prints and pictures. Choose them carefully with regard to size and colour and arrange them, so they cover most of the wall. Even unusual carrier bags, advertising posters or tickets can be arranged on a piece of soft board to make a wall collage. Another good cover-up is to hang a parasol, a paper fan, a collection of hats, or a paper kite on the wall. Choose colours carefully and play around with the arrangement until you have the right effect.

Penny-Saving Ways of Keeping Warm

Blinds and curtains used together at the same window look attractive and add extra insulation, as quite a lot of heat is lost through the windows. You can also buy energy-saving curtain linings and blinds.

Central heating systems need accurate controls to make best use of them. A timer and a room thermostat are the minimum requirements and individual radiator thermostats are very useful. Try to keep the thermostat set below 23°C (70°F) as every degree above this increases the fuel bill by five per cent. Try turning the thermostat(s) down by 1°, leaving it for a while until you get used to it, then lowering the temperature by another degree, and so on, until you feel too cold. You'll probably find that you're just as comfortable at a cooler temperature as you were with the heating turned right up.

Don't, however, try using less heat where the health of sick, young or old people is at risk.

Cling film makes a cheap and easy form of secondary glazing. Fix it to the window frame with double-sided tape, taking care to overlap the sheets slightly. There are also special kits available containing tape and a large sheet of polythene for insulating windows.

Curtains, when pulled, can be almost as efficient as double glazing. Draw them across at dusk, even in unused rooms, to keep the heat in.

Door curtains cut down draughts considerably. Fit them across the front and back doors and on internal doors if there tends to be a draught from a hall or landing.

Draught-excluding strips can be fitted around doors and windows quite easily. Self-adhesive foam strips are the easiest to fit, although they need replacing every two or three years. Aluminium or plastic strips can be fitted to doors and although they take longer to fit, they also last longer. Fit a draught-excluding strip on the base of the door as well. Some of these are spring-loaded so that they can be used on an inward-opening door. Make sure, however, that there is still some ventilation in each room. It is a good idea to leave the top of the doors un-insulated. This way you get the air without the draughts!

Eat well: all those warming winter puddings and casseroles are designed to help keep body temperature high. Don't over-indulge but choose foods that are warming in addition to cold salads.

Floors can lose a great deal of heat. Carpets and underlay help keep in the heat and it may well be worth putting a layer of newspaper under the underlay as well. Even on hard floors, rugs and mats can help warm things up. Fill draughty gaps between skirting boards and floor with a mixture of papier mâché and PVA glue.

Keep moving: exercise encourages you to generate your own heat. Do the housework at top speed, and try to keep mobile. Young children who are always running around never seem to feel the cold, so take a tip from them. It will also help prevent all those winter puddings putting on unwanted pounds.

Lag the hot water tank well. Many have old thin lagging jackets around them. Fit a new one that conforms to the British Standard on top of the old one. There will still be some heat seeping out around the edges to air clothes.

Letterboxes often let in a great deal of cold air along with the bills. Fit a letter box flap to cut down the draughts and help reduce those bills!

Line curtains with heat-reflecting linings. Heavy-lined curtains are obviously better than unlined ones, but heat-reflecting linings improve the efficiency even more. These can be bought as made-up linings or by the metre. They are worth the extra cost, especially on large north-facing windows.

Loft insulation is not really cheap, but under some circumstances grants are available for putting in new insulation, so it may be well worth checking with your local council. In fact about 30% of the heat lost from a house is lost from the loft, so any savings here are worthwhile. Roll insulation is easy to lay, and even if the house has already been fitted with it, check how much. Ten cm (4 inches) is the minimum approved level but about 15 cm (6 inches) is recommended. If your house was insulated a few years ago it may well have less than this. Don't forget to insulate the pipes in your loft.

Old-fashioned ideas are often the best. Door 'dogs' were used to keep out draughts and are still a cheap and easy way to stop a cold breeze whistling around your feet.

Open fires have a great psychological benefit. Even though they may not give out a great deal of heat, they make everywhere feel warmer. Two old wives' tales that do work are to put potato peelings on the fire, and to stand a large piece of chalk on top of the fire. Both improve the amount of heat given out and as they are generally free, you get more heat for your money. The chalk can be retrieved from the cold grate and re-used.

Walls lose heat too. Radiators on external walls can be insulated by placing a sheet of kitchen foil behind the radiator. Stick it into place top and bottom and it will reflect back a great deal of the heat that usually goes through the wall. Proprietary products are also reasonably priced and very easy to fit.

Wear extra layers. Mother did know best when it comes to wrapping up warm. Thermal underwear, a vest, thick tights, or warm socks can all help you keep warm. They are particularly useful when out of the house in schools and offices where you cannot turn up the heating. Hats also keep you surprisingly warm as a lot of bodily heat is lost through the head.

When redecorating, treat external walls with universal sealant before wallpapering. This will reduce any dampness.

Window frames can often be draughty. Fill gaps with mastic sealant and make sure curtains cover the frames when drawn.

If you wish for more information on energy-saving, contact the Energy Efficiency Office at the Department of Energy, Thames House South, Millbank, London SW1P 4QJ.

1. About the House
2. Clothes Care
3. Make Amends
4. Table Talk

CREATE AN IMPRESSION

First impressions do count: an attractive table, a pleasant room, welcoming drinks will all make guests feel at home.

Arrange the table so that all guests can reach their chairs and sit comfortably. This in practice usually means that each place setting needs around 40 cm (16 inches) and there should be about 50 cm (20 inches) for the chair to stand in.

Chill white wines well. The simplest way to do this is to stand the wine in a bucket of ice and water for about one hour before serving. A pretty bucket or large bowl can be left in the dining room, otherwise keep the wine in the kitchen. Return the bottle to the bucket to keep it cool while guests are eating and remember to wipe the bottle before pouring the wine.

Decant red wines about an hour before they are needed. It looks good and slightly improves the flavour of some wines as well.

Decorating the table does not have to mean using a central flower arrangement. For a change try floating a single flower head in a shallow dish of water, or arrange a tray of small seashells in the middle of the table. A row of nightlights along the centre of the table looks attractive. Hand-painted eggs, a bowl of nuts or pine cones, can all make unusual centrepieces that attract the eye and stimulate conversation. Experiment a little with whatever is to hand or in season.

A drinks tray close to hand, with glasses, ice cubes, drinks, mixers and garnishes all prepared, will make serving pre-dinner drinks much easier and there will be no need to abandon your guests while you prepare drinks.

Eat al fresco whenever the climate will allow. Make sure there are scented candles of the kind that repel insects on the table or nearby and have a couple of spare shawls to offer in case the weather turns chilly. Move indoors for warming cups of coffee later in the evening. This is a good way of entertaining more people than you can comfortably fit indoors, but it does rely on the weather being kind, so make contingency plans for everyone having to move inside quickly if necessary.

In summer cook outdoors as well; barbecueing is simple to do and enhances most foods. Buy a portable one, or make your own from a few bricks and an oven rack. Light it about an hour before you need to cook on it; the charcoal should be greyish white when really hot. Cook sausages, chops, steaks, chicken portions or fish wrapped in foil and serve plenty of hot bread and salads. Remember everyone's appetite seems to increase when eating outdoors!

Keep entertaining simple. Cook dishes you know work well and keep numbers small at first. Try to limit the number of dishes needing last-minute attention. Simple things done well in a relaxed way will impress far more than an elaborate evening that goes wrong. Aim to make sure your guests are well fed, in comfortable surroundings, with a relaxed atmosphere and the evening will be a success.

Light an open fire if you have one whenever the weather is even slightly chilly. It looks welcoming and creates an atmosphere immediately.

Music sets the mood for the evening as well. Choose appropriate music and always take your guests' tastes into account. Never have it playing so loud that people cannot comfortably talk to each other.

Organize a sideboard in the dining room. It does not have to be very grand; a coffee table, spare desk or even a plank of wood on two boxes completely covered by a cloth will do. Arrange on it all the extra things you may need such as spare napkins, oven gloves, extra glasses, cutlery etc., so that you are not having to make countless trips to the kitchen to collect things.

Pick a colour scheme; for instance at Christmas use an all-white tablecloth and napkins, then decorate with white and gold crackers and tiny gold Christmas trees on the table. Add finishing touches with a tiny white present by each guest's place tied with gold ribbon. Or in summer, go for pretty pastels, with soft pink napkins and a centrepiece of a tray of sugared almonds or even sugar mice!

Pull the curtains in winter to keep the room feeling warm and cosy. In summer leave curtains and windows open and hang a wind chime up to move gently in the breeze.

Smells are important. Choose scented candles or fragrant flowers where you need a lingering smell but avoid too many scents conflicting with each other. Often the food or the wine will provide all the fragrance you need and flowers and candles are then best avoided.

Starch tablecloths and napkins to keep them looking good. For coloured napkins and less formal occasions use a weak starch solution. White needs quite stiff starching to look its best. Spray starches make starching quick and easy.

A theme for the evening can be fun; try cocktails and American style food, or a Valentine's day romantic meal with oysters and champagne if you are feeling extremely extravagant. Autumn harvest suppers are an inexpensive way of feeding a lot of people (serve a casserole, hot herb bread and an apple pie) and at Christmas try mulled wine and mince pies for friends and neighbours. Decorate the table and room in keeping with the theme.

Turn the lights low to make an intimate feeling but make sure there is sufficient light from candles or lamps so that everyone can see what they are eating.

Plan ahead

Good planning goes a long way to making entertaining a pleasure rather than a chore.

Balance the meal; follow a rich main course with a refreshing dessert, such as a sorbet or lemon mousse. Make sure the colours of each dish blend well with the rest; cheer up chicken with a white sauce or garnish it with red peppers or green peas and serve with stuffed tomatoes or another brightly coloured vegetable. Strong flavours from one course will linger and affect the next; so serve something sharp after curry or game.

Buffet meals make catering for large numbers much easier. Arrange the table so that guests can help themselves easily. It is easier to reach food at the back of the table if it is raised. Add height at the back using boxes or biscuit tins. Cover the table first with an old curtain or cloth to prevent the tins slipping.

Consider guests' likes and dislikes. Check if anyone has an allergy to particular foods, or is a vegetarian, when inviting people. Keep a record of who likes what and also of which dishes you served last time.

Cook extras such as home-made bread, biscuits, croûtons, and similar foods well in advance and freeze or store in the fridge or airtight tins. Breadcrumbs, pastry and gâteau bases can be made early and frozen until needed.

Find ashtrays and put them out. Many people who normally do not smoke have an occasional cigar after a meal. Also have a candle alight in the room to help disperse the smoke.

Have a dummy run for really important occasions; collect together all the plates, cutlery, glasses, dishes and tablecloths you will need and check if any need cleaning or repairing.

Individual desserts on buffet tables speed up the serving. Large quiches and gâteaux should be pre-cut or at least marked, so that guests know how much to take.

Make plenty of ice cubes in advance. Use plastic egg cartons as extra ice cube trays and once frozen tip the cubes into a large polythene bag which makes storage easier. Repeat this until there are plenty of cubes ready to be used. Freeze slices of orange, lemon and lime to add to drinks as well.

Plan the guest list with care; avoid people of opposite political views unless you enjoy the sparks that may well fly! At large gatherings prime friends to talk to newcomers at the beginning.

Plan the menu by first considering which foods are in season. These are usually the cheapest and of best quality. Think also about your cooking facilities and any special serving arrangement you might need. For instance, you may need to buy or borrow a fish kettle, if you want to serve a whole salmon, and a flambéed steak really needs some means of cooking at the table.

Prepare a coffee tray and place it in the sitting room after the guests are sitting at the table. Leave just the hot coffee to be brought in when needed.

Prevent queues at a buffet table by placing the main course in the middle and positioning plates, bread and salads on either side. This way two people can help themselves to food at the same time, thus speeding up the whole process.

A rule of one course hot, one cold and one pre-cooked is a useful one to remember when planning a meal. This spreads the work and prevents the hostess spending all her time in the kitchen keeping two or three courses hot and ready to serve.

Stock up on basics such as butter, cheese, crisps, nuts, biscuits, ground coffee (vacuum-packed) and such like a few days beforehand, so only fresh foods need to be bought nearer the time.

Try to avoid pastry in more than one course or any particular flavour occurring in too many dishes.

Wash up as you go on the day, so that by evening there is only a minimal amount to do. Stack plates and dishes as you clear the table and put cutlery straight into a jug of hot water. This way if you suddenly need an extra knife or plate you will know where to find it and washing up after the meal will be quick and easy.

Work out a 'countdown' for large scale affairs. Write down which things can be organized a week before, such as buying dry goods, washing and starching linen, etc. Then check what needs doing two or three days before, such as cooking some foods and freezing and cleaning the house. One to two days before, the fresh food shopping can be done and some fresh dishes, especially those that need to set or stand overnight, can be made. This will then leave last-minute shopping, arranging the rooms, laying the table, and the final cooking to be done on the day. Where several people are involved for, say, a family Christmas or wedding, keep lists of what dishes everyone has offered to cook and the quantities they will make and so on.

Write lists in the days before a special event of things to do and buy. Keep a note pad handy to jot things down on as they occur to you.

KEEPING FOOD HOT

A few tips on how to keep food hot for the last few minutes while guests finish their drinks or eat the first course, can make life much easier.

Custard can be made in advance and poured into a flask to keep it at just the right temperature. Alternatively, once made, float a little extra milk on the surface and replace the lid on the pan. Leave to stand for up to 15 minutes and then stir in the milk before serving.

Dishes and plates need to be hot to help keep food hot. Warm them in the oven if there is space or by stacking plates above the grill section. A dishwasher with a heated drying cycle can be used to warm all the dishes and plates needed, although this is a rather expensive method. Simply load up and turn on to a rinse and dry cycle.

Another way, if the cooker is already overcrowded, is to fill the sink with very hot water and stand the plates in it until needed. Remove and dry while they are still hot.

Fish is best served immediately it is cooked. In an emergency it can be kept hot by placing the dish over a baking tray full of boiling water. Cover with foil and leave to stand for up to ten minutes.

Hot trays and trolleys do make serving hot meals easier. Make sure they are plugged in well in advance and load foods carefully. Liquids such as soups, sauces and coffee need to be kept at a slightly higher temperature than solid foods. Often trays have a 'hot spot' for this purpose, so place jugs on this point for the best effect.

Pancakes are a popular dessert, but it is not much fun for the cook who can rarely prepare enough to keep up with the family's appetite. Instead cook them in advance, stacking them with a sheet of greaseproof paper between the pancakes. Roll them up and sprinkle with sugar. Place them in a shallow dish, cover with foil and reheat in a hot oven for 15 to 20 minutes.

Pasta is quick to cook and should really be prepared as needed. It can be kept warm for a short period by under-cooking it and leaving it to stand in the cooking water. Add a knob of butter or a little cooking oil to prevent it sticking together.

Potatoes are hard to keep hot without spoiling but mashed potatoes are easier. Cook the potatoes as usual, then drain well in a colander. Pour a little milk into the saucepan and heat, then return the potatoes to the pan and add a knob or two of butter. Place a tight fitting lid on and leave to stand for up to 15 minutes. When required, simply mash and serve. (See also 'Roast Potatoes', opposite.)

Puddings and sponges will keep quite warm, if they are left in their cooking container, covered with two or three clean tea towels.

Quiches sometimes become soggy on the base if kept warm in the oven. Instead wrap in foil and then in several layers of newspaper. This will keep in the warmth for up to an hour and is a useful way of taking a warm quiche on a picnic.

Rice for savoury dishes can be kept hot for up to half an hour in the base of a very low oven. Drain the cooked rice and rinse well with hot water then turn it into a shallow dish and cover well. Place in a low oven and turn with a fork occasionally to prevent the top layer from drying out. You can also add a knob of butter.

Roast meats actually benefit from being left to stand for a short while. Wrap in foil, with the shiny side inside, and stand on the carving dish for ten minutes. Then unwrap and carve; the slices hold their shape better after standing.

Roast potatoes should be kept hot in an oven. Remove from the roasting tin and place on the serving dish. Leave them uncovered to prevent the potatoes becoming soggy.

Sauces and custards can be kept hot in a double pan, or by standing a large bowl over a pan of hot water. For short periods, float a little extra milk or stock on the surface, put the lid on the pan and leave to stand. When required, stir and serve.

Soufflés cannot be kept hot but they can be partly prepared in advance. Make the sauce and add the egg yolks. Leave to cool. Between courses, or nearer the mealtime, whisk the egg whites and add to the sauce, turn into the prepared dish and place in the oven. So, if planning a chocolate soufflé for dessert, finish the soufflé and put it in to cook after the first course has been served (for smaller soufflés after the main course is served).

Vegetables are at their best if cooked and served immediately. However, on occasions it is necessary to keep them warm. In this case, undercook slightly, drain and turn into a very hot serving dish. Add a knob of butter and place the lid on. Leave to stand on a worktop covered with a couple of teatowels or stand in a baking tray containing hot water.

Wrap food to be kept hot in foil with the shiny side inwards.

NOT ENOUGH TO GO ROUND

We have all experienced this problem, whether as impoverished students or newly weds with one chair and no table, or as a normal family trying to cope with Christmas crowds. The answer is to improvise, and to know the telephone number of your local hire shop, which can usually provide almost anything you may need.

Food can suddenly run short as extra guests turn up or disasters occur in the kitchen. Quick thinking and a good store cupboard will save the day.

Add an extra course to the planned meal to make it go further. A good filling soup, a tinned pâté served with plenty of bread or toast or pasta shapes cooked and tossed in herb butter will fill people up, so that they eat less of the main course.

Beefburgers, chops and steaks can be stretched from four to six if necessary by cutting them into cubes and threading on skewers along with tomatoes, onions, peppers and mushrooms, to make kebabs.

Bread served with the main course will also fill people up. Most breads benefit from warming in the oven and French sticks or Vienna loaves can be sliced and filled with herb butter before wrapping in foil and cooking for ten minutes in a hot oven.

Casseroles can be padded out by adding a tin of kidney beans or baked beans. A few frozen mixed vegetables or dried mushrooms can be added as well. Alternatively, try adding a can of sweetcorn, or make some dumplings to serve along with the meat.

Chairs can usually be borrowed from neighbours, or garden furniture can be pressed into service. If not, and you don't have enough dining chairs, it may be worth abandoning the table and eating with plates on trays or laps. Give the children their meal first (often an easier way to manage anyway) or persuade them to sit at a garden or camping table near the adults' table. If only one or two chairs are needed, try using a strong coffee table with a thick sofa cushion on it. Another improvisation is to lay a plank of wood between two chairs, pad it well and stand this 'bench' against a wall, so that no-one can fall off. Push the table up against the seat and there should be room for four people on two chairs.

Crockery often runs out either because there are suddenly too many mouths to feed or because you have forgotten just how many plates have been broken!

Often a quick washing-up session in the kitchen after the first course will solve the problem. Alternatively, make plates do double duty; use sideplates for cheese and fruit for instance. Tumblers and glasses can be used to serve mousses and jellies in and many foods can be served in wicker baskets, such as bread, biscuits, baked potatoes and fresh fruit. Improvise serving plates from baking trays covered with foil. To make life easier, some courses can be served with just a napkin, for instance, cakes, fruit and biscuits.

Cutlery can be quickly washed up and re-used, or plastic spoons and forks can be used. Try serving one course that does not need cutlery, such as a dip with fresh vegetable sticks as a starter or little canapés before a meal. Individual petit fours and other little cakes make an ideal dessert that can be eaten with the fingers. A fondue meal needs little or no ordinary cutlery, so is a good choice if you are short of knives and forks.

Desserts can be accompanied by ice cream to stretch them; it is even good with hot chocolate pudding! Mousses, fools, and jellies can be more filling by serving with sweet biscuits (see page 195).

Extra vegetables will also fill plates that look rather meagre. A side salad will also help. Make one with whatever vegetables are available; finely grated or chopped with a good French dressing on top. Most vegetables, even plain ones, such as grated carrots, make a good salad.

Glasses can usually be borrowed or hired easily and plastic ones are useful for parties. Instead of serving wine or other drinks that need glasses, try offering China tea in teacups or making liqueur coffee. Mulled wine is good in coffee cups as they are easier to handle than hot glasses.

Make an instant dessert by mixing sliced fresh fruit with tinned ones in a glass bowl. Add a layer of macaroons, or crushed digestive biscuits and chopped nuts and then top with whipped cream.

Make cream go further by adding one whisked egg white to every 600 ml (1 pint) of whipped cream. Single and pouring cream can be stretched with a little natural yogurt, which also gives it a tart taste, ideal to serve with fruit.

Tablecloths can be improvised from an old (but clean) sheet, bedspread or curtain. Add a small white overcloth if the main cloth is too dark or wearing thin. Wrapping paper also makes a good table covering, small geometric prints look nice and so does gold or silver paper for festive occasions. If the table is presentable, leave it bare, covering any marks with strategically placed flowers and place mats.

HOW MUCH TO ALLOW

Working out the quantities of food to serve can be difficult and it is most embarrassing if you underestimate and wasteful if you overestimate. Here are the minimum recommended quantities for most foods. Do remember that appetites vary and if your teenage son has brought the school football team home for tea, it is quite likely they will eat far more than you expect.

Drinks; a bottle of sherry should yield 16 glasses and a bottle of spirits 32 single measures. Wine and champagne will give about 6 glasses to the bottle. 600 ml (1 pint) of milk is sufficient for 16 cups of tea and there are about 3 cups to 600 ml (1 pint) of boiled water. Fresh coffee needs 2 to 3 teaspoons of ground coffee per person and small demi-tasse cups hold only 120 ml (4 fl oz) of liquid. White coffee can be served as half black and half hot milk, although not everybody will want as much milk. If serving with cream, allow 25 ml (1 fl oz) per cup.

Fish should be bought by the number if they are to be served whole. In pieces, a rough guide would be at least 175-225 g (6-8 oz) of fish per person on the bone. Off the bone allow a minimum of 100-175 g (4-6 oz). Fish to be served in a sauce will go further and if served as a starter, less is needed.

Ice cream produces about 6 portions to the ½ litre (1 pint). Children will generally eat less and if served with another dish, portions can be smaller.

Jellies and blancmanges will generally serve 5 to 6 children from each 600 ml (1 pint).

Meat quantities will vary according to the cut and how it is to be served. Steak and chops on the bone require at least 175-225 g (6-8 oz) per person, for boneless meat the minimum should be 100-175 g (4-6 oz) per person. Meats in casseroles or made-up dishes will go further but people often have second helpings of these, so allow for this when cooking. Fatty meats that need much trimming will require more weight initially.

Rice and pasta are filling foods and swell up when cooked. Allow 50 g (2 oz) per person uncooked, except for fresh pasta when 100 g (4 oz) are needed.

Salads need to be more generous when served as a main course or lunchtime meal than when used as an accompaniment. One large lettuce will make the base of a salad for about ten people. Beans, rice and pasta-based salads are quite filling; aim to feed eight people for each ½ kilo (1 lb) of ingredients.

Sandwiches for drinks parties and buffets need to be small and dainty. Allow four to six small triangles per person. 225 g (8 oz) of butter, once creamed, will spread about two large loaves. Most loaves have 20 to 24 slices, so will produce 40 to 50 small sandwiches. When serving canapés, sausage rolls, hot sausages and the like, assume everyone will eat at least six to eight individual items.

Sauces and gravies are used quite sparingly, allow about 50 ml (2 fl oz) per person. Pouring sauces, such as white sauce, or sweet sauces including custard, need to be more generous, so allow 120 ml (4 fl oz) at least.

Soup served as a starter needs to be less generous than one served for lunch. Allow three helpings to 600 ml (1 pint). For main courses allow 300 ml (½ pint) per person.

Vegetables are not as easy to calculate, as it depends in part on how many different kinds are to be served, and also on personal likes and dislikes. As a rough guide allow 175 g (6 oz) for root vegetables, such as potatoes, parsnips, swedes and turnips. The same amount can be allowed for runner beans, peas and Brussels sprouts. Leafy green vegetables such as cabbage and spring greens lose a great deal of bulk once cooked so allow 225 g (8 oz) per person.

FINISHING TOUCHES

The presentation of a dish is almost as important as the cooking. Good, well-cooked food deserves to be properly garnished and presented. Making food look attractive does not necessarily call for anything elaborate, and many of the ideas that follow are quick and easy to prepare.

Bacon rolls look good with chicken or used as a savoury garnish on quiches, vegetable dishes or baked potatoes. De-rind slices of streaky bacon and remove the eyes. Stretch each slice by laying it on a chopping board and spreading it with a palette knife, then cut in half and roll each piece up. Thread on skewers and grill, or place in a baking tray and cook in the oven until crisp and brown.

Butter curls are worth the effort and can be made well in advance. Use the butter straight from the fridge, unwrap and dip the curler in a cup of hot water. Pull the curler along the block of butter towards you, lift the curl off and place on the serving dish. Once enough have been made, chill well until needed. Another pretty way to serve butter is to cut thin slices off the side of the block of butter and then cut shapes using small biscuit cutters or aspic cutters.

Cheer up a casserole, and add crispness to the dish, by serving it with croûtons. Cut shapes from slices of bread using biscuit cutters and fry these in a little oil. Drain well and arrange round the edge of the casserole in an overlapping pattern. Fill the centre with chopped parsley or fresh vegetables.

Chilled soups can be served with an ice cube or two in them to keep them cool.

Chocolate mousse or cakes can be decorated with chocolate curls, which are simple to make. Use a potato peeler to cut long curls from the side of a block of cooking chocolate. Make sure the chocolate is at room temperature as it will break easily if it is cold.

Crushed ice is worthwhile for serving cold fish dishes, sorbets and ices when the weather is hot. Freeze water in shallow plastic containers, turn out, cover with a tea towel and then break up with a rolling pin. Pile on to a chilled tray, then stand the fish dish or sorbet in amongst the ice. This is a particularly useful way of serving foods at buffets, where they otherwise may melt before everyone has a chance to eat.

Frost glasses for drinks and chilled desserts by dipping the rim in a little egg white, then in a dish of icing sugar or caster sugar.

Glaze fruits in flans and on cakes to make them shine. Use a couple of lemon jelly cubes melted with a little hot water or the juice from tinned fruits thickened with cornflour or arrowroot. Allow the liquid to cool slightly, then brush on to the fruit.

Home-made biscuits to accompany desserts are a special treat, but as they can be made up in advance and frozen or stored in an airtight tin they are not a nuisance on the actual day. There are many simple recipes to choose from. Anyone not keen on baking can buy brandy snaps, macaroons or other fancy biscuits to serve with mousses, ice creams and fools.

Icing sugar can be used to liven up a plain sponge. Sieve it over a paper doily placed on the cake, then carefully remove the doily. Alternatively, use a piece of paper to cover parts of the cake and sieve sugar on the rest, so lines or star shapes are made.

Individual dishes can look impressive, especially if they are small versions of dishes usually served on a large scale, such as soufflés, pizzas or even individual cottage pies.

Jelly makes an attractive decoration for sweet dishes. Set a thin layer on a sheet of greaseproof paper placed on a baking sheet. Tip the jelly off and chop finely with a wet knife. Use to decorate around the base of an ice cream bombe, or any set dessert that is turned out on to a serving platter.

Keep garnishes and decorations simple; they should complement the food rather than overpower it. The only exception is for children's food, particularly birthday cakes, where the more decoration, the more they seem to like it!

Lemon and cucumber twists can be made by thinly slicing both, then laying a slice of lemon on top of a slice of cucumber. Cut through both from one edge to the centre, then twist the cut edges apart so the lemon and cucumber pieces stand up. These look nice on fish dishes and cold savoury mousses.

Lemon wedges served with fish, salads and pancakes look good but often the pips are squeezed out on to the food as well. Wedge squeezers can be bought, or another simple method is to wrap the lemon in a small square of butter muslin, then it can be easily squeezed at the table without the pips sliding out.

Make frosted fruits to decorate sweet dishes. Lightly whisk some egg white with a fork. Dip small grapes in this mixture, then sieve icing sugar over them, to give a white frosted look.

Prevent meringue gâteau splitting when you serve it by filling at least an hour before it is to be eaten.

Puff pastry leftovers can be cut into crescents and other shapes using aspic or biscuit cutters, then baked until golden brown. Use these fleurons as a garnish on casseroles and other meat dishes. Store in an airtight tin or freeze, so there is always a store to hand.

Savoury dishes can be garnished with sieved cooked egg yolk, finely chopped egg white, and chopped parsley and cayenne pepper. Use the contrasting colours of these garnishes to make lines or to edge cold dishes, such as fish or poultry.

Serve soups with dishes of croûtons, made by lightly frying cubes of bread, and finely diced raw vegetables suitable for the type of soup.

Serving dishes are an important part of any cook's collection. Hunt out old platters and trays in secondhand shops and markets. Collect unusual shapes and sizes as you see them, so you always have a wide range available and can find something just right.

Sprinkle home-made cakes and biscuits thickly with sugar while still hot, so that it sticks to the food. Brown sugar is good on fruit and nut cakes, or use finely chopped glacé cherries and angelica.

Use up leftover egg whites to make tiny star-shaped meringues. Freeze or store in an airtight tin and serve with desserts, such as ice cream, mousse or fruit fool.

Vegetables can be brightened up simply by serving two of contrasting colour in the same dish; try carrots and peas; sweet-corn and peppers, or French beans with tiny button onions. Glaze well with a little butter to make them shiny.

RESCUE REMEDIES

Disasters in the kitchen befall us all at one time or another. Many problems can be solved by quick thinking or by changing the dish slightly.

Bread that is too fresh to slice thinly can be placed in the freezer for 30 minutes. This will firm it up enough to slice well.

Broken meringues can sometimes be repaired using cream to hold the broken pieces together. If it is beyond this kind of repair, divide the broken pieces up between individual dishes, sprinkle over fresh soft fruits, such as strawberries, raspberries, sliced peaches or kiwi fruit and top with whipped cream.

Burnt casseroles and stews can be rescued if you act fast. Do not stir the casserole, but pour off as much as possible into a clean pan. Add a raw potato cut into four or a slice of stale bread to absorb the burnt flavour. Remove after ten minutes, then season well with Worcestershire sauce and pepper. If it still tastes burnt, try adding a tin of tomatoes and a little tomato purée, or add soured cream or plain unsweetened yogurt to make a goulash, in order to mask the flavour.

Cakes that sink in the middle look very sad. Sponge cakes can simply have the hollow filled with fresh fruit and whipped cream to serve. Fruit cakes are better if the centre portion is removed to make a ring cake. Finish by decorating the top with icing, marzipan cut-out shapes or glacé cherries and nuts.

Cream that is no longer fresh enough to serve with desserts, but is not really 'off', can be used as soured cream in goulashes and stroganoff. Add 2 teaspoons of lemon juice to the carton.

Curdled custard and other sauces that are thickened with eggs can be saved if a couple of ice cubes are quickly added to the mixture, or by standing the pan in a sink of cold water and whisking rapidly to cool it down.

Curdled mayonnaise usually requires an extra egg yolk to improve matters. Remove the mayonnaise and wash the bowl or blender or processor well. Place a fresh egg yolk in the bowl or machine and gradually add the curdled mixture, whisking or beating all the time. Make sure all mayonnaise ingredients are at room temperature before starting to make it, and for really thick smooth mayonnaise, use 3 egg yolks to 300 ml (½ pint) of oil.

Heavy, textureless sponges can be sliced in thin horizontal layers. Use a bread knife and sandwich the extra layers together using cream or buttercream. Otherwise use in trifles, or cut into fingers and line a loaf tin or pudding basin with the sponge. Fill the centre with cooked, puréed fruits and stand overnight in the fridge. Cover and place a weight on top. Turn out and serve with cream as an unusual variation of summer pudding.

Lumpy sauces always seem to occur just when you are in a hurry. Either whisk the sauce while still in the pan, or pour into a blender or food processor and mix until it is smooth. Sauces can also be sieved although this takes a little longer.

Overcooked potatoes are often too wet. Drain well and heat just a little milk in the pan. Return the potatoes to the pan and beat well with a wooden spoon. Add a little butter and an egg yolk, then pipe into duchess potatoes on a baking tray. Cook for 10 to 15 minutes in a hot oven until crisp on the outside.

Overcooked rice tends to stick together, so press it into a greased ring mould and bake in the oven for about ten minutes. Turn out on to a flat plate and fill the centre with vegetables.

Overcooked vegetables can be made into a vegetable medley. Place in a casserole with a few frozen cooked vegetables and a fresh sliced tomato. Pour over a white or cheese sauce or sprinkle thickly with fresh white breadcrumbs, then brown under a hot grill for 5 to 10 minutes.

Pastry that is too sticky to handle can be chilled in the refrigerator for 30 minutes, covered with clingfilm. Then roll out between two sheets of lightly floured greaseproof paper.

Ripe fruits can be cut up to make a fresh fruit salad along with a few other not quite so ripe fruits. Add a few blanched almonds for crispness. If they are too ripe for this, make them into a purée and mix with custard and cream for a fool.

A sauce that is too thin can be quickly thickened by mixing equal quantities of butter or margarine and flour on a plate. Mix with a fork until they are well blended and then add small pieces of this to the hot sauce, stirring well. Stocks and soups that are too thin can be reduced by boiling with the lid off the pan.

Soft biscuits can be refreshed by warming them in the oven for a few minutes.

Tough meat is often improved by allowing the dish to cool and stand overnight. This is further enhanced if a little wine, cider or wine vinegar is added to it. Tough joints of meat can be minced or sliced thinly when cold.

Unripe melons and avocados will often ripen in the airing cupboard. Leave overnight, or for just a few hours depending on how hard they are.

1. About the House
2. Clothes Care
3. Make Amends
4. Table Talk
5. Talking Shop

ADVANCE PLANNING

BAGS

Be prepared and take plenty of shopping bags with you. Try not to be caught in a situation where you have to buy a plastic carrier bag from the store and provide the establishment with a nice bit of free advertising as well.

* Buy one of those expandable string bags and keep it in your pocket as an emergency measure.
* Taking a cardboard box or two with you is a good habit to get into. This saves hassle if the store has run out of its own supply and also prevents the build-up of boxes acquired afresh with each new shopping expedition.

BLACKBOARD

Instead of a notebook and pen in the kitchen to jot down food required – go for a child's blackboard, a supply of chalk and a duster or one of those wipe-clean plastic boards you can buy for the purpose.

CURTAINS

Curtains which don't quite cover the windows when they're closed aren't much good – however splendid they look when open!

* To avoid such disasters, work out how much material you'll need before you go out shopping.
* You should allow 1½ to 1¾ times the width of your window for ordinary curtains, and for net at least twice the width: more if you want them to be really full. Measure the depth remembering to start from the curtain rail and include hems.
* If you are contemplating a material with a large design on it, measure a complete pattern and calculate how many of these pattern repeats you'll need in each curtain – not forgetting to allow extra for hems. The shop assistant will generally help you with this calculation.
* If you wish to buy flame-resistant material, make sure it is labelled with the Kitemark which shows it conforms to the British Standard (BS 3120).

GOOD BUYS

Before you actually hand over your money for anything – from tights to tennis rackets or toasters, go to your local library and ask for the relevant copy of *Which?* magazine.

* You'll find that over the years the magazine has tested and done independent surveys on most items you'd buy for the household. . . . if you look at the index for a whole year's issues you can find out when the product you're interested in was tested.
* You'll also find out which special features are available, which brands have them, whether others have found them to be worthwhile or not and any points to look out for when buying. Then, suitably armed with the facts, you can assess any sales talk that may come your way!

MATERIAL SWATCHES

Make up a little 'swatch' of materials you have around the house – a piece of leftover lounge wallpaper (an inch square at the most unless it's a very large pattern!), a small piece of curtain material, a dab of any wall paint on a piece of paper, a cutting of your loose cover material or whatever else you may want to match. Then if you spot what seems like a particularly good buy – or perhaps a remnant which might be gone the next day – you will have the instant means of checking on the suitability of the colour and texture for the room you have in mind. It can save you pounds.

MEASUREMENTS

Make sure you always have a note of the family's measurements if you plan to buy a pair of slippers for your husband, shirts for sons or daughters or whatever – otherwise you might find you have simply wasted your money.

* Remember that shops have no obligation to take something back just because it's the wrong size: if they do it's a matter of goodwill on their part only.
* Jot the sizes down in your diary – and if in doubt, don't buy, unless of course you make a specific arrangement with the shop to get it exchanged.

MENUS

Anyone who cooks for a family of any size should try to take half an hour to sit down and plan out a week's menu ahead – or the main meal at least. By doing this you'll know exactly what you'll need from the shops and might get away with only one trip.

* Remember when you are making out your menus, which foods are in season, which are cheap, which will take least time to prepare (if perhaps you are going out that evening and time is at a premium or one member of the family wants to eat quickly because he or she is rushing out).

MIDWEEK SHOPPING

If you aren't out at work and have the chance to choose which days you go shopping, then always opt for midweek. Monday just might mean that some food isn't as fresh as it could be, then towards the end of the week shops are packed like sardines and food prices in street markets can rise.

* So Tuesdays, Wednesdays and Thursdays are best and try to get there fairly early to avoid the crowds and get the best bargains.

SHOPPING LISTS

Make out a 'standard' shopping list with the basic items you need to buy every week – tea, coffee, sugar, butter or whatever.

* Split these basics up according to the shop you buy them in or in the order in which they are positioned in the supermarket if you are that familiar with your regular shop.
* Keep a notebook and pencil on a kitchen unit and every time you finish, or get near to finishing, a packet of cornflakes or a jar of marmalade or whatever, write this down and encourage every member of the family to do the same or tell you so that you can write it down.
* Before you go out make a new shopping list from the regular items which need replacing, the food required for the week's meals and from the notice, hopefully pinned near the freezer, which records what is needed in the way of frozen goods.
* Work out in advance the exact quantities you'll need of the various items on your shopping list – don't just put 'mince' or 'cheese' or whatever. Think of how many you need to feed, whether extra people are coming or whether this is your week for the neighbourhood coffee morning nad so on and put down quantities accordingly.

STORECUPBOARD STOCKS

Once you have stocked up your storecupboard keep a note of anything that runs out, so that this can be added to your weekly shopping list.

* The items in your special store will depend on a number of factors: how long individual products keep on the shelf; how often you are likely to entertain unexpected guests; whether you live in a remote rural area where snow might occasionally prevent shopping trips and how much space and money you have to spare on 'standbys'.

* Basics for every storecupboard are: a few tins of cold meat, such as ham; sardines (can be turned into a snack or served as a pâté); mackerel (served as a salad or made into a quick pie); tins or packets of soup; a packet of potato powder; fruit and vegetables in tins (according to your own preference); a packet of spaghetti and one of macaroni and a packet of sauce mix to go with each; a tin of peeled tomatoes; carton of long life milk; jar of instant coffee; packet of rice; packet of whip-up cold sweet.
* Extras for the storecupboard to add the luxury touch (these can be added to the basics as and when you can afford them). Tinned pâté; packet of melba toast; tin of luxury soup; tinned cream; tin of small new potatoes; a small bottle of cooking wine or sherry; jar of peaches in brandy or similar luxury.
* If you spot luxury goods at a special price when you're out shopping, consider them for the store cupboard. Sometimes discontinued lines of items like asparagus tips are offered at low prices.

Basic Budgeting

Budgeting and some careful thinking about expenditure needn't be boring – in fact it can bring great rewards when you find you've managed to save money. It's not only the money that's marvellous, it's the virtuous feeling such an accomplishment brings.

Here are seven pointers towards a workable home budgeting scheme.

1. Work out your own income and outgoings. A basic is a notebook and in it you start doing your sums. On the left hand page work out what your income is, that is what you have left to spend after tax, national insurance stamps and any other S.A.Y.E. payments have been deducted. Next you must note on the opposite page all the essential payments, such as rates, mortgage, insurance. Electricity, gas, telephone and so on will have to be estimated from previous bills. Most of these can be put under the heading of 'Monthly outgoings'. Then you tackle the weekly spending . . . food, clothes, entertainment, papers, pets, travel and so on.

The general idea is that the expenditure side of the book should be less than the income side! If it's not, then adjustments will have to be made according to your priorities. You could cancel a paper, eat fewer convenience foods or spend less on entertainment. But whatever economies you decide on, then you must stick to the budget.

2. If you or any member contributing to the family budget earns overtime now and then, try to treat it as a bonus – something to be saved rather than something just to be absorbed into the weekly budget.

3. If regular payments on your mortgage or suchlike increase or decrease (as they do from time to time) then remember to adjust your budget – in terms of expenditure – accordingly.

4. Always allow a 'continengency fund' in your budget for all those emergencies which can crop up even in the best run households.

5. Spreading the load is a maxim which applies to bills just as much as anything else, and it certainly lessens the burden!

* Take advantage of schemes whereby regular expenditure such as fuel, rates and even insurance premiums can be split into regular instalments worked out on a basis of a year's total divided equally. This avoids finding yourself in some difficulty when faced with an unusually large quarterly bill. Spreading the load evens out seasonal variations too, because it means that there are no longer any 'heavy' periods during the winter months. Payments remain static every month, and since your income also does that, it makes a lot of sense to organize your budget this way.

6. Your bank can also help with spreading the load by means of a 'budget account'. You and your bank manager agree on what your annual expenditure on certain major items will be; the bank agrees to pay those bills as they arrive and you pay in an agreed amount every month to cover the cost. You will probably have to pay a small charge for this service, but on the other hand it does save you worrying when faced with a lot of large bills.

7. If you don't operate a budget account at your bank, but prefer to take total control of your own spending, then at the same time as you are picking up the groceries, pick up some stamps which can be used to pay electricity bills, car road fund tax, gas bills, TV licences and so on. If you budget for these items on a weekly basis you won't get such a shock when the bill comes in – or perhaps more accurately, you may still get a shock, but you'll be able to face it with a lot more confidence!

BILLS AND ACCOUNTS

BANK STATEMENTS

Check your bank statement carefully against your cheque stubs every time you get it. Mistakes have been known, most commonly when you are charged with something which should have gone against the account of a customer with a very similar, or perhaps even the same, name. Be wary too that your bank statement doesn't necessarily represent the whole truth. . . . if someone has been lazy about presenting a cheque to the bank you could be misled into thinking you have more in your account than you actually have.

* Make sure you know the exact state of your finances: enter every cheque you or your partner writes in the counterfoil of your cheque book (in which you have put the total on your last statement) and subtract the amount as you go.
* Withdrawals from obliging automatic cash dispensers must also be carefully noted and deducted.

BULLDOG CLIPS

Bulldog clips are cheap and they are a good way of keeping the various bills together.

* Screw a couple of cuphooks into the back of the kitchen door, and as bills come in put them into the clips.
* Receipts can go into another clip. At regular intervals you should transfer the receipts to a file and pay the bills.

CASH

If you pay for your groceries in cash, then only take with you a little (very little!) more than you will need, or can afford to spend. That way you put temptation firmly aside.

CHECKING OUT

Do you ever check up on charges at the checkout? Most shoppers find it such a relief to get out of the store and struggle out to the car park with their trolley full of goodies they'd never think of taking the time to check goods received against what the check-out girl has rung up on her machine. This, in spite of the fact that surveys show consistently that mistakes of both the major and the minor variety are regularly made in supermarket checkouts.

* It can be extremely tricky trying to do an on the spot check, so the alternative is to beg, borrow or buy a pocket calculator and add each item up as you take it off the shelf. If your total disagrees with the till total, then don't be afraid to say so.

CREDIT CARDS

Crafty credit card holders can get two months' free credit.

* First you need to discover when your statement is sent out (this varies from one card holder and one card company to another).
* Delay purchases if possible until just after the relevant date – the amount won't show up until your next statement which of course will be another month hence.
* When that statement does reach you, you'll have a month to pay without incurring any interest charges. So that gives you almost two months in total. Mind you – you'll still have to pay, but you will at least have had interest-free credit for as much as fifty-six days.

HIRE PURCHASE

Have a care about buying on credit or hire purchase! It's a tempting way of getting all kinds of things for the home, but if illness or redundancy strikes then payments can be hard to meet.

* Make it a rule not to take on more than two major credit commitments.
* Check your budget and your accounts every week, don't wait until the end of the month. If you have overspent – and it happens even to the best planned budgets – then it's much easier to catch up and correct a week's over-expenditure rather than a month's! If you have gone over the top one week then save the same amount on the following week's budget:

substitute a cauliflower cheese for the steak supper you'd planned, for instance.

MONTHLY BILLS

Sometimes, in small towns and rural areas, newsagents, milkmen and even some local grocers offer customers the convenience of monthly bills.

* Be wary of this system – it always seems like such a good idea, but it can have its pitfalls. You can get a nasty shock at the end of the month when the bill comes in and you've spent the money supposed to cover it. Even worse can happen with grocery bills: it's so easy to pick up a bottle of wine or a luxury item when you know you don't have to pay for it on the spot.
* It's better to deal with papers, milk, groceries and similar basics on a 'pay-as-you-go' system.

PETROL COSTS

Now that car parks are available even in the smaller local shopping precincts, many people make the trip regularly by car, even if it's only to buy a few things.

* Remember, however, that the accumulated petrol costs of such trips can be enormous and 'hidden'.
* So, get organized and arrange a rota with friends and neighbours in much the same way as you do for taking the kids to school or collecting them. If you share shopping trips you'll all save something.

RECEIPTS

Whatever you buy – whether it's clothes or electrical bits and pieces – keep your receipts, so that you have proof of purchase, should the item turn out to be defective.

* Set aside a box of some sort – or a section of a file if you are well enough organized to have such a thing – and put every receipt you get into the box the moment you get back home.
* There's no need to hang onto the receipts for very long – those relating to minor purchases might need to be kept for no longer than a couple of months, but those relating to more major ones can be kept for up to a year.

RED REMINDERS

Some people like to wait until they get red reminders before shelling out, but be wary! To cut their own costs some organizations don't bother with reminders (in certain areas of the country for example, electricity boards send you only one bill). . . . so if you don't pay but keep waiting for the reminder, you may well find that the amount due is added on to your next bill.

* Get into the habit of paying all your bills (apart from credit cards, see page 211) just as soon as you're presented with them.

SHOPPER'S BUDGET ACCOUNTS

Many shops offer credit cards or budget accounts which allow you to pay in an agreed amount and spend several times more than you put in. This can be useful if you find yourself short of cash, when some item is urgently needed, and provided you don't mind making purchases regularly in the same shop.

* Shop around in the first place because shops and stores can offer different deals on these cards. Some charge more interest than others.
* An even better bet are those which offer you interest on the money you have paid in.

CHEAPER BY THE DOZEN

Before you actually buy anything in bulk, or indeed start making plans to do it, first check your storage space. If you have barely enough cupboard accommodation to house a weekly shopping load, then work out a plan. Perhaps you have a warm, dry garage (those with heating boiler and pipes in them come into this category); can the wardrobe in the spare bedroom be used as a store cupboard; is your kitchen full of the kind of clutter that could be cleaned out to give extra cupboard space?

Bottling is a wonderful way of dealing with bulk purchases, especially if you don't have a freezer. Spiced peaches or cherries in brandy are at the luxurious end of the scale but good home chutneys can also be made using cheap fruit. Also bulk fruit and vegetables can be turned into bulk home made wine . . . which will save you even more money!

Buy in bulk only what you use regularly and like. If something seems a tremendous bargain and you're not sure whether the family will like it or not, play safe and buy a small amount of it at ordinary prices first to see if it suits. Try before you buy in bulk!

Catering sizes of all sorts of products are increasingly available in supermarkets and freezer centres. Don't be put off by the thought that you could never use five litres of soup (over a gallon) or seven pounds of cooked meat. With a bit of care, you probably could! Firstly, check just how much you will save by buying big. If it is worth your while consider the following:

Instant coffee, for instance, in a 2lb pack will normally disappear fairly fast if you drink a reasonable amount in your household and it stores beautifully in the tin.

Dried soups in five litre packs do not need to be used all at once. Just measure out the quantity of dried soup the packet tells you is needed per pint of water (kitchen scales do the measuring) and you can use the soup little by little.

Huge tins of peas and beans look as though they're intended for holiday camp consumption, but, providing your family likes these things, what you don't eat immediately can be frozen in a lidded plastic container.

Giant sized tins of peaches and fruit salad can also be snapped up when they appear (which they do from time to time in most stores) and again split up into family-sized portions and popped in suitable containers in the freezer.

Cooked meats in 7 lb sizes, which you may sometimes spot, can also be treated on the 'eat some now, freeze some for later' principle.

Co-operate with your neighbours. You will undoubtedly get the lowest prices if you can manage to form a co-operative in your neighbourhood so that you can purchase really large quantities. This sort of group takes a lot of organizing! You will need rotas for who's to collect the goods, rotas for delivering it, and rotas for working out the weekly orders and then sorting out the finances. Put the 'rules' and the rotas down in writing and make sure each member of the group has a copy.

Cost cutting is the whole point of the exercise, so check around to get the best prices before placing an order. Don't assume the local cash and carry will be your best bet. Often supermarket managers, if approached, will give excellent discounts to groups who are prepared to place a regular order.

Country dwellers can get carrots, cauliflowers and potatoes by the cartload from local farmers who invariably advertise them at enormously reduced prices. Cauliflowers will have to be blanched and popped in the freezer, but potatoes will keep perfectly well in the bag if they're in a cool dry place and carrots should also keep if they are stored in wooden boxes which are lined either with straw or with polystyrene. Carrots can, of course, also be frozen . . . but you may not have the space to freeze great quantities of different vegetables.

Electrical items like plugs, bulbs, replacement fluorescent tubes and suchlike can be bought by mail order from specialist firms at half the price you'd pay your local retailer – good quality merchandise from reputable manufacturers, not non-branded cheap items – if you are prepared to order by the dozen. In this case it is worth making an arrangement with friends and neighbours to make the occasional joint buy to be split up according to individual requirements. An added advantage is that this sort of merchandise doesn't give rise to storage problems in terms of durability or deterioration.

Farm food shops are springing up all over the place these days and they can yield useful buys like two dozen trays of eggs at special prices. Freezer centres often offer eggs in similarly large quantities at relatively reasonable cost.

Fish tends to vary in price according to the weather, but if you have a freezer it's worth looking around for a local fish firm (if you live within, say, ten miles of a port). Many of them sell a vast variety of fish; blast-frozen in individual pieces and packed in 7 lb boxes. Normally you have to take a minimum of perhaps three boxes. The cost is considerably less than shop prices, the fish will have been freshly caught and the quality excellent. Alternatively, you can get fresh fish in quantity from a fish merchant in a fishing town at a good price and freeze it.

Local butchers can prove to be a real friend. Many of them, keen to get business in bulk, will offer excellent deals to large groups they can look to for regular orders. There are advantages over buying wholesale too. Some butchers will split up individual orders so making delivery very much easier for whoever's on the collection and delivering rota . . . others will supply large quantities of individual items like chops, or liver or bacon or whatever, rather than insisting on you buying a whole or half animal. So ask around, see what's on offer and stress what your group can offer by way of cash and buying power. If you're very lucky you may find a local trader who can actually deliver the order to you and that will save on petrol and time as far as you're concerned. Another thing – complaining to a wholesaler or market isn't the easiest thing in the world – but with a local trader you can keep a better check on quality.

Look out for wool which isn't neatly split up into 50 g balls ready to use, but instead is on hanks or even cones which means that you have to wind it into balls yourself. Usually it costs a lot less this way because you're not paying for the work involved in making up the small packages. If you happen to be paying a visit to a wool mill on your holidays – or you are lucky enough to live near one – then ask if they have any bulk lots of wool like this. It's excellent value.

Marmalade oranges have a short season in the shops. They usualy appear in late January and may disappear after only a few weeks. So if you prefer home made marmalade but don't fancy a mammoth session with the jam pan all at thc one time then work out approximately how much marmalade the family eats over a year and buy sufficient fruit when it's cheap and available. Make up a quantity and put the rest of the oranges into the freezer (they can go in as they are, without blanching or other preparation), and you will then be able to thaw some out and make some more marmalade to replenish your stocks throughout the year.

Oil for central heating is always costly but if there is any possibility of you having several hundred pounds available – then it can be a very good idea to order a bulk load, say 500 gallons, and pay for it in cash, instead of taking advantage of the instalment payment system which most oil companies offer. This is because if you shop around, you'll normally find a firm which will give you a considerable discount for paying cash for a bulk load.

Pets like a good meal or biscuit type of product either mixed with meat or served on its own with gravy. Buying these things by the 7 lb bag as most households do is convenient, but it's expensive. Look locally for a shop supplying things to farmers (animal foodstuffs for instance) and you'll see 55 lb paper sacks of things like 'sheep dog mixture'. If it provides sufficient energy and goodness for a working dog you can be sure it will give your pet enough for his daily tasks too. There's no way you're going to carry that sort of load home in your shopping bag – or even on your bicycle – so you certainly need to have a car (and a strong right arm) to take advantage of this sort of bargain. These specialised shops are less likely to be found in city areas, more likely in smaller rural towns, as they are often 'branches' of big farmers' co-operatives or meal mills. One word of warning, though, some dogs can be finicky creatures and it's not uncommon for a pet to like one brand of meat or meal and refuse to touch another, so before you buy a vast amount of the one meal, try it out with Fido first and seek his or her approval!

Picking your own fruit and vegetables can be hard work but it can cut the cost of such produce by as much as half. And while

you're getting bored with bending remember that short of picking things from your own garden this is the freshest you're likely to get greengrocer's goodies and you can impose your own quality control as well as eating a few as you go!

Proprietary frozen foods can come expensive, however convenient they may be. If you do have a large freezer it's worth asking some of the large firms who make branded products whether they will give you a discount on quantity. These firms usually have depots in various parts of the country, so just look up the telephone book or Yellow Pages and get dialling.

Smoked salmon, exotic pâtés and so on can be costly in small packs, but a side of smoked salmon can, in comparative terms, work out reasonably cheaply. Here, again, you will need to get together with a group of friends to get a reasonable amount each at a very reasonable price.

Stocking is an essential skill for bulk buyers, one which fortunately doesn't require a great deal of knowledge but rather more patience and persistence. List all the products you think you'd like a lot of, then go through your existing stocks and work out just how much you use of each item – say over a three month period. Keep a check on how you actually use up those goods you do acquire in bulk and see how it compares with your original list. Any obvious 'go slowers' should be crossed off the list for next time round.

Storage life of products can vary from three months to a year, so always make sure that what you buy will last the pace. There's no merit and certainly no saving in buying things cheaply, if they are going to go mouldy or lose their flavour quickly.

Washing up liquid and disinfectant can be bought in 5 litre plastic containers and since most households use both on a regular basis you will save a considerable amount. But you'll have to hang on to an existing washing-up liquid squirt-type container and keep filling it up from the large one – and the same with the disinfectant. Pouring any liquid from a 5 litre container every time you want to wash the dishes or clean the floor can be a little tricky!

Whole carcasses, whether from your local butcher or from a market, naturally contain the bones and the fat as part of the deal. So bear this in mind when comparing the cost with your normal purchases of chops, mince and joints. Bear in mind, too, that you may only like some cuts of meat – with a bulk buy you'll get everything from liver to spare ribs. So, if you can't work out an arrangement with other members of the group, based on who likes what, then be wary . . . it's no fun, and certainly no bargain, if your freezer's full of sausages or steak or whatever. Menus can get very boring!

Wholesale fish, fruit and vegetable markets provide good pickings and super savings for bulk buyers who are prepared to get up at the crack of dawn for the best of the day's produce. Some, however, will only deal with those who have buyers' cards. To get one, go to the market superintendent's office – and try wearing your smartest clothes and a sweet smile! Whether you get a card or not depends entirely on the policy at the local level (and maybe how persuasive you are!). Billingsgate, for instance, will accept applications from those who are buying for a group of around twenty families. Remember, too, that lugging around large quantities of fresh produce may cause problems in terms of muscle power – even if you can get a porter to help at the market, you're going to have to unload it back home.

Wholesale meat doesn't always come in convenient cuts and market stallholders are not in the business of chopping up whole carcasses for you. So if you're not prepared to tackle the task yourself, then look elsewhere for your fresh meat.

Wholesale wholefoods can cut your bill by as much as half in some cases! So if you are a devotee of brown rice, honey, vegetable oil and the whole range of health foods, buying this way can keep your budget pretty healthy too. There are wholesalers in various parts of the UK, and unlike some of the cash and carry's they will happily deal with ordinary members of the public. A complete list of the firms is easily obtained from The Vegetarian Society. Most of the items for sale come into the dried category (lentils, peas, pulses, bread mixes), all of which can of course be stored in a cool dry place for a considerable time without deteriorating.

ON GUARD!

Be wary of an overloaded shop freezer. The 'load line' in a commercial freezer indicates the level to which food can be stored and remain frozen. Above this line food may not be kept cold enough to prevent the various micro-organisms which cause spoilage from multiplying.

* Products which have been stored above the load line in a freezer and become soft might eventually work their way to the bottom, be refrozen and so on and so on and so on! By the time the chicken or whatever is bought there's no telling how many thawing re-freezing cycles it's gone through.
* Avoid buying frozen food from stores which persistently stack the goods above the load line. And – if you can pluck up sufficient courage – tell the manager to toe the line in future.

A cheap product is simply a waste of money if it turns out to be poor quality – but if something you've skimped on also turns out to be unsafe the consequences can be tragic.

* Buy electrical goods – everything from plugs to domestic appliances – which come from a well known firm and which preferably have the BEAB symbol on the label which means that they have been passed as safe by the British Electrotechnical Approvals Board.

Children's feet should always be measured in the shop from which you're buying their shoes.

* This is important if you want shoes which fit properly, because different manufacturers have different sizing systems.

Curtains hang loose and as such they can be a fire risk.

* You can give yourself some protection by buying curtains (and other soft furnishing fabrics) which comply with the British Standard relating to fabric flammability. Remember, though, that laundering may remove the fire-resistant properties in the material.

Eat a good meal (or certainly a snack) before you go trolley trundling – and make sure the kids do the same.

* A hungry shopper may be an extravagant shopper!
* Avert your eyes and blindfold the kids when you get to the checkout point – because there you will undoubtedly find a display of sweets! If you allow yourself to be persuaded to spend even ten or twenty pence extra every time you reach the checkout, just consider how many pounds that will add up to over a month or a year! Keep an eye on the pence, as they say, and the pounds will take care of themselves.

However tight you like jeans to be, remember that all jeans shrink (even those marked pre-shrunk have shrunk in tests!) so always allow for that. Shrinkage can vary from virtually nothing to as much as 10% according to the composition of the fabric.

The order of the words on the label of any product can make a difference to the contents.

* Always make sure you get what you think you're paying for! 'Down and feathers' describing a duvet means a mixture of both which contains not less than 51% by weight of down. On the other hand 'feathers and down' means a mixture of both materials containing not less than 15% by weight of down. So you get 36% less down – and all because of the order of the words. But watch for this because what seems like a bargain may not be!

* Similarly with tins of food on the supermarket shelves, the order of the words gives a very important clue to the contents. If a tin is labelled 'potato and meat' pie – you could be getting mostly potatoes for your money and you'll certainly be getting more potato than meat. If on the other hand, the label says 'meat and potato pie', there should be more meat than potato.

Shop displays are just as full of persuasive sales tricks as any smooth talking salesman, so be on your guard against buying things you don't really need!

* Make out a shopping list before you leave home and stick to it, with the possible exception of special offers on goods or foods which your family use a lot of. But be wary of brands on special offer which you don't usually buy: one brand of some-

thing simple like baked beans, for instance, can taste utterly different from another. So it can be a false economy to switch just because the price is low if when you get home the only member of the family who shows an interest in your bargain buy is the dog!

* Baskets of goodies placed in the centre of the aisles so that you all but fall over them, needn't be the bargains they might seem . . . they might be the last of a line nobody liked and so getting rid of them cheaply is the only way to clear them off.

Superfluous buys are a temptation every time you get inside the supermarket doors.

* You'll probably shop wisely and spend less money if you can resist popping out to the shops every day or even twice a week. On the other hand, local shopping may mean less waste.

When you're buying a suit for any of the men in your family (or they're buying it and you go along for moral support!) then always use the checklist overleaf to make sure you're getting good quality.

1. The cloth shouldn't have any flaws in it.
2. Colour should be even throughout.
3. Seams should be uniform with no missed stitches.
4. Linings shouldn't show around the edges of the garment.
5. Buttons should be firmly attached, buttonholes neat without interlining showing through.
6. Collar should be flat and smooth.
7. Shoulders should not be lumpy.
8. Armholes should be roomy.
9. Pattern should match perfectly at lapels, pocket flaps, outbreast welt, centre back and hind arm seams. On trousers the pattern should match at outside leg and front fly.
10. Zip should be neatly hidden and firmly stitched into the material.

PENNYWISE

BP are the letters to watch out for on simple medical products like aspirins and bandages . . . and you may not find them in the supermarket, but only at the chemists. BP or BPC products are those listed in the British Pharmacopoeia or the British Pharmaceutical Codex, two reference works for doctors and chemists. Preparations with BP on them rather than well known brand names are usually quite a bit cheaper, although the essential or active ingredients are the same.

Breakfast bacon should always be the best you can afford. But compare the price of the loose bacon being sold at the counter and the wrapped equivalent . . . often the former is cheaper. if you want it for quiches or pies, then ask your butcher for ends and offcuts which are also sold cheaply.

Brown eggs are beautiful but don't be misled by that old wives' tale that they are also better than white! They are exactly the same as white eggs inside the shell so if anyone tries to charge you extra for brown – bypass them.

Bruised fruit selling off for next to nothing may not be very edible, but it can be ideal if you make your own wine.

Buy bread in weekly quantities if you only make one trip per week to the supermarket. Bread freezes well and the more bulk you have in the freezer, the cheaper it is to run.

Buy loose if you can. Some supermarkets are reverting to the old-fashioned method of selling all sorts of dried goods loose rather than prepacked. This can usually produce quite a saving on the same item neatly encased in cardboard or plastic on the shelves. And if you are at all worried about the hygiene aspect of loose goods, stick to things which will be cooked before eating – lentils, rice and so on.

Dashing into the shops just before they close for the weekend could mean you and the family spend a hungry weekend! On the other hand it could mean you get amazing bargains. Fresh food tends to be drastically reduced when it looks as though it's not going to be sold by closing time and won't keep until Monday opening time.

Filleted fish may be better value than whole fish, since you don't pay for the head and bones as well.

Long-life light bulbs may seem a sensible idea – and certainly they can last twice as long as the ordinary type. But what you must remember is that for the same amount of light the long lifers use more electricity than the ordinary ones and because of this, as careful comparisons have shown, you can in fact end up with a larger total cost when you use long lifers. However, there are now bulb-shaped fluorescent lamps which last even longer – 5 times as long as the ordinary type. They cost considerably more to buy, but should save you money because as well as lasting well, they use less electricity.

If you are on a tight budget, avoid mushroom-shaped bulbs – these look good and are smaller than the common pear-shaped ones – but they are generally more expensive to buy and yet will give no better service. Clear bulbs do, in a sense, give the best value of all, because they actually give out more light because of the clarity of the glass. A disadvantage is that they can be rather glaring in some circumstances (which is why people so often prefer pearl).

Check own brand bulbs in stores carefully before you buy. They might be what's called 'single coil' as opposed to the more traditional filament type (made by the brand name firms) and single coils give less light than the 'coiled coil'.

Maintenance contracts are usually available on any new appliance for the house. The cost of these contracts can vary quite a bit, so it's as well to make a few comparisons before making your choice of appliance. Consider, too, the possibility of choosing one of the five year extended guarantees now offered by many firms including electricity boards, instead of the traditional maintenance contract: they can usually work out far cheaper, but check what the guarantee covers.

Money off coupons which appear in magazines or get pushed through your letter box are worth having: don't turn your nose up at them. You can save as much as a pound some weeks if you save them up, then take them along with you next time you're shopping. Get together with a friend or neighbour, so that you can swap any coupons which you don't want for some that you do, and vice-versa.

Offcuts and leftovers may seem a bit offputting but they represent a perfectly good saving for the budget conscious. Glance at the cooked meats and cheese counters in supermarkets and you'll very often find little packs of bits and pieces of different cheeses selling at bargain rates or what's left of various kinds of cold meats similarly packaged and priced. The cheese is ideal for cooking and the meat can always be used for salads and sandwiches.

These offcuts are usually in the 'few pence' price bracket and there's nothing necessarily wrong with the quality – it's just that they're a bit of a mixed bag.

Pâté at a delicatessen counter is often packed in attractive large pottery bowls. Once empty, the bowl is usually available to any customer who asks for it and is prepared to pay a small price for it. Be warned though – word's got around and often there's a waiting list of customers for the bowls!

Poultry is usually cheaper if you buy a whole bird and divide it into portions yourself than if you buy small pieces. You get an extra bonus when you get the bird too: the pickings can be turned into soup.

A reduced price doesn't necessarily mean a reduction in value. Items are sometimes marked down because they are discontinued lines and sometimes (in the case of tins or packets) because the packaging has been slightly damaged although the contents are still fresh and full of goodness. So take a good look at any such items. Cosmetic counters can be a rich source of these 'bargain offers' too – lipsticks in last season's colours and so on can be sold off at less than half price. So long as the colour suits you, that's what is important and not whether it's currently fashionable.

Shelf stock of wallpaper is generally cheaper than what you have to order via the sample book. The shelf stock is sometimes bought in bulk by the retailer and he can pass on savings to customers which are as much as 30%. Another point to bear in mind is that the price quoted for patterns out of the book can sometimes increase by the time your order actually arrives in the shop from the manufacturer or the wholesaler.

Shopping around often means traipsing around and can be expensive in time and shoe leather. The pence you save may not be worth it in the end. But if you have a consumer advice centre in your neighbourhood then they can take the strain out of shopping around. They may do price comparisons on staple items and display a list in their window so that you can tell at a glance where the best buys are. Local consumer groups sometimes do price comparisons too. Take along a notebook and pencil and jot down the prices of, say, ten basic items in several shops and work out which shop provides the most bargains.

Table salt, the experts tell us, is meant to be put on the table in the salt cellar and used to sprinkle on your food, while cooking salt is used for cooking. The former also happens to be more expensive than the latter! In practice, if you use cooking salt for both purposes, no one will know the difference, though cooking salt is marginally more likely to clog your salt cellar. Incidentally, salt sold in plastic bags is cheaper than that in rigid containers, so buy the bagged salt as a refill for your container.

Take a really close look at packaging because it can sometimes give a rather misleading impression of comparative value for money between one product and another. Different shapes of jars and bottles for instance can look alike in terms of quantity, or indeed a short fat container can look as though it holds twice as much as a long thin one. Disregard the outward appearance and look at the weight.

Tempted by cheap toilet rolls? Before you buy, do a check on the amount of sheets in the rolls – that's what gives you the true value comparison. If this information is not given it may be best to give it a miss because it may cost half as much but will probably only last half as long!

Toiletries in large sizes carrying an unknown brand name – shampoos, hair conditioners and so on – will usually do the job just as well as their pricey neighbours. So don't sniff at these plainly packaged own brands on store shelves, give them a try.

Try before you buy is an excellent maxim and so, unless you always wear the same perfume, take advantage of those special trial offers of new perfumes which regularly appear in chemists shops and beauty counters. It's a much more reliable guide – being able to wear it round the clock for a spell – than the quick squirt of the counter tester! Look out too for packs containing miniatures of several different kinds of perfume – they cost very little and often have the added bonus of a voucher (for as much as £1) enclosed, which you can put towards a purchase of the perfume you like best.

Unit prices, that is, the price per pound, ounce, gram or kilogramme, give an instant and true comparison between one product and another. Look for these when shopping.

Wallpaper rolls, which you are left with because you have overestimated, can sometimes be returned to the shop where you bought them for a refund. They must be complete rolls, of course, and shop policy on this varies very much.

SALES AND SECONDS

Famous brand names sold at remarkably cheap prices on street stalls may well be counterfeits. Bear this in mind before you buy.

Remnants of material are often half the price of the same fabric on a roll. Before you buy:

Unfold the whole piece and check it for flaws.
Ask what the fabric's made of.
Ask about washing instructions.
Make sure there is sufficient for whatever you plan to make.
On printed fabrics, make sure the pattern is straight.

Search for the supposedly soiled area on 'shop soiled' appliances, such as fridges, washing machines and so on, which are being offered at a reduced price. If you can't see any evidence of soiling, ask the shop manager to show it to you. It can happen that shops buy in special lines from manufacturers and offer them as shop soiled when they are in fact brand new.

Seconds are sometimes almost as good as 'firsts' in terms of quality and represent a real bargain. Points to watch out for:

Check on clothes that the arms are both the same length – and in the case of trousers, that legs are both the same width – these are particularly frequent faults.

Blouses may have one front a few centimetres longer than the other but this may not matter if you're going to tuck them in.

Check for rips or tears, dye faults and stains.

China 'seconds' might have a slight mistake in the pattern – but who's to see once the fish and chips are on the plate!

Top quality shops have true bargains at sale time. Luxury items genuinely reduced are the value for money sale bargains.

~~1. About the House~~
~~2. Clothes Care~~
~~3. Make Amends~~
~~4. Table Talk~~
~~5. Talking Shop~~
6. Moving Moments

CHECKLIST OF THINGS TO BE DONE

Below is a handy reminder of all the things which are discussed in more detail in this chapter. Tick off all items you have dealt with, so that you can tell at a glance what still remains to be done at any time. It is worth keeping a notebook specially for the move, so that you can jot down all the relevant information in it. Consider these headings for your notebook. It's also extremely useful during the packing up process, see pages 238 and 239.

* REMOVAL FIRM: Contact several and compare costs. If you are planning a DIY move ask for details of van hire arrangements from local firms (page 235).
* LITTLE-USED ITEMS: These should be packed well in advance of the move.
* PACKING MATERIALS: Get a plentiful supply of boxes, etc. If necessary ask neighbours and friends to keep their old newspapers, as these are useful for wrapping and for making buffers between items in the one box (page 239).
* SERVICES IN NEW HOUSE: Check on things like gas, electricity and water – and how the central heating works, where the fuel's kept and so on (page 266).
* LOCAL FACILITIES: Which shops are nearby? What public transport is there? Are there good schools in the area? Ask the seller to write down a list of these for you (page 267).
* WHAT GOES WHERE: Draw up a room by room plan of the new house and decide where your furniture should best be put (page 268).
* UNWANTED ITEMS: Whether books, clothes or your old cooker – these should be listed, then given away, sold or otherwise got rid of (page 241).

* NEW FURNISHINGS: If you require curtains or similar items for your new house, measure up carefully and buy these in advance of moving day (page 269).
* TRADESMEN: Does your carpet have to be refitted or the electric cooker wired in or the washing machine plumbed in? If so make appointments for the appropriate tradesmen to do the work after you've moved into the new house (page 257).
* CHANGE OF ADDRESS: List all those who should be given a note of your new address – buy cards and send them off. In the case of some official organizations, there may be special forms to be filled in: ask about this (pages 258 to 264). Arrange, if you wish, for the Post Office to redirect your mail (page 261).
* NOTIFY SERVICES: Gas, electricity and telephone will require meter reading. Get in touch with the appropriate offices. In the case of the phone also notify British Telecom if you are taking over the number at your new address from the present subscriber, otherwise it will be cut off (page 263).
* PETS: Consider how they are to be transported – get tranquillizers from the vet if your pets are nervous travellers (pages 245 to 248).
* PACKING: Do this methodically. Put similar things in the same box where possible e.g. 'China', 'Footwear' or 'Blankets'. Either write the contents on the outside of the box

or mark it with a number or letter and identify the contents alongside the letter or number in your notebook (page 239).

* CAR CARE: Check it is in good order and filled with petrol. Any items to go in the boot or the back seat should be listed (page 256).
* TRAVEL PACK: Items for this should be planned and bought if necessary (page 255).
* INSURANCE: Arrange this to cover your possessions while in transit and on property as necessary (page 253).

THE DIY MOVE

It can work out cheaper to hire a van and do the move yourselves but it is a tiring job which takes skill, energy and a certain amount of expenditure. You need to be fit! Count up all the extras and compare them with the cost of getting a firm in to do the job for you and you may find that the saving is not sufficient to counteract the hassle. Take into account the hire charges on the van, the mileage charge, insurance, VAT and fuel. Consider, also, that you may need to make more than one trip. If you have recruited friends or relatives as 'helpers', you may have to feed and refresh them which all adds to the cost.
If you've made your calculations and have decided to hire your own van, think about the following points:

1. Book your van if possible from a company which has depots both near your old home and your new home. This saves the bother of a long return trip with an empty van.
2. Make sure that there will be somebody at the depot to book in the van when you return it, otherwise you may have to pay for lots of extra time.
3. Stipulate exactly what size and model of van you want, otherwise you may be provided with one that is far too small. As a rough guide:

* a van with 10 cubic metres (350 cubic feet) of space will take a 1 tonne (22 cwt) load.
* a vehicle with 15 cubic metres (520 cubic feet) capacity will take 1½ tonnes (31 cwt).
* a van with 26 cubic metres (920 cubic feet) will take a 4 tonne load.

4. Always hire a van with a ramp of some sort – if you've ever tried to lift a chest freezer up into the tail of a van without one, you'll know how exhausting and potentially dangerous this is.
5. Although you can legally drive a van up to 7½ tonnes (laden weight) with your ordinary driving licence, don't consider it if you are not an experienced driver. A fully loaded van with only

wing mirrors for seeing what's coming behind can be daunting, especially if you're not used to heavy vehicles.
6. If you have a choice of routes choose the one without narrow bridges or too many difficult junctions.
7. You could compromise by hiring a van with a driver and putting the furniture in the van yourself. That way you will still save money but you are relieved of the responsibility of driving the van.

And the following tips should help you with the loading:

1. Remember when you are deciding where to put what in the van that what goes on first will be off last. Heavy items should be put in first and then lighter things can be stacked on top if need be.
2. Don't move anything flammable like petrol in the van with your possessions.
3. Pack room by room if you can – it will make it a lot easier unloading at your destination.
4. Take plenty of time to do the loading, if you get flustered that's just the time when accidents happen.
5. Lift things properly if you want to reach your new home without a slipped disc or a strained back. Don't bend your back to lift something heavy, instead bend your knees, then lift with your back straight.

6. Dismantle what you can, because furniture can be much heavier than it looks by the time you've lumped it downstairs, along the garden path and into a van. If the legs come off a table for instance, take them off, take a bed frame to bits and so on. It not only makes lighter work of moving but it can help avoid damage to your furniture too.

7. At least three fit people will be needed to move the usual quota of domestic furniture (don't try to do it on your own) and if you have heavy and unwieldy items, such as Welsh dressers or large chests of drawers, then get a fourth involved for safety.

8. If you can beg, buy or borrow one of those nifty trolleys workmen use for carrying heavy loads about then do so as it will make the job of moving furniture much easier – you can put the items on it and let the wheels do the work instead of your muscles.

9. Be wary of a piano, this really is a job for a specialist, particularly if it is a valuable one. There are firms who specialise in moving pianos.

10. You can't have too many things tied down in your van to save them bumping about and damaging each other. Try to get strips of cloth or soft twine – sometimes hard string can leave marks on furniture and furnishings which can be very difficult to get rid of. Use soft things like mattresses and cushions to protect any delicate items in the van.

A-Z OF PACKING AND MOVING

Always leave a little space on top of every box on the basis that you're sure to leave something out and will need that space! The first things to be packed should be those things which you don't use on a regular basis, e.g. surplus sheets, blankets, papers and books can go into boxes, so can dinner sets and ornaments.

Make a list of the things you're most likely to forget to take with you – for instance pelmets, soap dishes and even picture hooks. Go round each room and note all such things, then put them down in your notebook so that you can do a check once everything's packed.

BOOKS

Beware of books – they can weigh a ton!

* Unless you have strong tea chests which are easily lifted, don't pack too many books into large cardboard boxes or you'll be lucky if you can even drag the box across the floor.
* If you have your books on the shelves in any particular sequence (perhaps alphabetical order, subject by subject or whatever) then pack them in approximately the same sequence splitting them into boxes and then mark the boxes A-D 'Gardening', 'Cookery' or whatever. This will make your task of unpacking them and putting them on shelves in your new home a lot easier . . . or indeed make it a matter of moments to find a particular book should you happen to need it in your new home before you've unpacked your whole library!

BOXES

Beg lots of boxes (good strong ones) from local grocers or off-licences, for packing. Some removers may be willing to sell their specialised removal cartons.

* A variety of sizes can be useful: the large ones can take blankets, duvets, sheets and even clothes, while smaller ones are ideal for packing one teaset, one set of glasses or whatever.
* Boxes, once packed, should always be sealed all round with special adhesive tape, to make sure the bottoms don't burst.
* If you are dealing with a large removal firm, they will probably be able to supply you either with cardboard cartons or tea chests but it's always wise to get a few of your own anyway, since it's difficult to estimate how many you will in fact need. Tea chests are often offered for sale in your local paper.
* Similar things should go in the same box, don't mix them all up. So ornaments, underwear, magazines, toys or whatever should all be put together and don't be tempted to push miscellaneous objects into odd corners. At the time you'll be convinced that you'll remember putting that woolly hat in with the china or your winter boots with the table lamp, but, be warned, you won't. If it means leaving a box half empty, fill up any spaces at the top with crumpled up newspaper.
* Writing the contents on each individual box is helpful but you may feel it's giving rather too much away to the neighbours and the removal men!
* The best method is to put a large number or letter (in sequence 1, 2, 3 or A, B, C, etc) on the outside of boxes using one of those thick indelible felt tip pens in a bright colour. Then keep a small notebook and list the contents of each box beside the appropriate code. This notebook method has a number of advantages over writing contents on the actual box – it allows you to put much more detail against each number or letter and it allows you to carry around the list with you. Keep the notebook by you when you move to your new house and it will be much easier to direct the removal men where you want each box put.

CARPETS

These can be the most difficult of all items to pack.

* Firstly, enlist the help of friends and move all the furniture either out of the room, or to one side.

* Be careful how you disengage the carpet from modern 'gripper' fittings.
* Roll it up loosely at this stage and manhandle the thing out into the garden or into another empty room. Put it down on the lawn, the patio or some other flat surface, then start rolling it up (rolling from the shortest side). It's best if several people can help with this if you've got a big carpet, because with only two people all that happens is the roll becomes uneven as you roll and develops a bulge in the middle.

* If you can get one of those long bamboo sticks they use in carpet shops, the job will be easier.
* Be very careful how you tie it. String can cut into the backing and leave marks around the edges too, so get something fairly soft; old rags cut into strips can be just the thing.

CLOTHING

Heavy clothes, like winter coats and capes, should be packed first, then the lighter items can go on top.

* If you can get a fairly large cardboard box, you can pack clothes with the minimum of folds. Skirts, for example, can go in completely flat and so can sweater and blouses. The British Association of Removers (Services) offer a 'Travelbox' which

is a carton with an internal liner which can be left behind with the customer.

* Have a good supply of tissue paper to hand when you are packing and 'pad' out the spaces left, so that your next layer of clothes can go on to a level surface.
* Don't be tempted to put footwear (even if it is wrapped up) in among clothes just because there's a space: the weight will leave a mark even over a short period of time.
* Use crumpled newspaper or tissue instead to fill gaps.
* Long legged boots should be stuffed with a rolled-up magazine or newspaper to keep them firm and save creasing.
* Try to pack them towards the top of a container rather than at the bottom, or if possible, pack them in a separate box inside the main box.

CLUTTER

Clear out the clutter. Moving to a new house is a splendid opportunity for sorting out all the stored up treasures.

* Go into the attic, then the garage, every cupboard, every box, every suitcase stashed under the bed and every wardrobe and – with the co-operation, however unwilling, of the rest of the family – discard all those old toys you no longer need, the pram which was last used ten years ago, the clothes you haven't worn for several seasons and all the broken bits and pieces you've been planning to mend but haven't! Be totally ruthless about it.
* You might even make a profit out of all your unwanted clutter. Hold a 'garage' sale as they call it in the States, which means that you pile all the junk in your garage and invite friends and neighbours to come and bid for it (give the proceeds to a local charity and you'll be bound to get buyers).
* Alternatively, give it to any local jumble sales, or ask your nearest charity shop if they would like it (but do bear in mind that these charities should only be given items in reasonable condition and fairly clean).
* Dr. Barnados sometimes collect clothes or bric-a-brac you don't want. In some areas they will collect bulky items such as furniture. However, they never take away gas or electrical appliances.
* If there are things you don't want to take with you, but which

are in good condition, then it's worth writing to the buyer of your house and enclosing a list of items, asking if they would like any of them.

* Bear in mind that you can, in fact, quite legally be asked to remove any junk that you've left behind.

COAT HANGERS

These can be very awkward things to pack.

* Arrange them in groups of similar shape – say half a dozen of each, then tie them together securely.

ELECTRIC BLANKETS

If at all possible, pack these in their original boxes, which were spcifically designed to hold them.

* If you've thrown them out, then treat the blankets with care just the same, folding carefully and not too many times or rolling. Then put them in a strong plastic bag.
* One thing you must avoid is to put any heavy items on top of the blankets, so put them at the top of the bed linen box.

ELECTRONICS

Stereo equipment, videos and similar pieces of electronic equipment are always best packed in the original boxes, complete with all those bits of shaped polystyrene which fit snugly round each angle of the item.

* However, unless you have hoarded all these boxes in your attic, go and have a word with your local radio and TV dealer. He may be able to supply you with a box which exactly fits your piece of equipment and, if not, he can probably give you a few tips on how best to pack them.
* Sheets of foam, old bits of carpet and polystyrene ceiling tiles can all be useful when it comes to protecting moving parts, knobs and so on from damage.

FOOTWEAR

* Shoes should be packed in plastic bags – one pair per bag. Put the shoes upper to upper and heel to toe. Any particularly

delicate ones – perhaps satin shoes, which might be liable to crushing – should have newspaper stuffed into the toes to help keep them in shape – before putting in plastic bags.

* Pack footwear altogether in one box if possible, rather than mixing it in with clothes and other items.
* Any footwear with ornamental buckles or similar decorations which might rub against other shoes and cause damage should have a wad of cotton wool put over the decorative feature before packing in their plastic bag.

FREEZERS

Refrigeration experts advise against using a freezer as a mobile refrigeration cabinet (they're not designed for this pupose); they advise they should only be transported empty and defrosted. However, if yours is a modern appliance and it is more convenient for you not to empty it, bear the following in mind:

* Make sure it's not more than half full by removal day – for the sake of the men who'll be carrying it (some firms even warn you the men won't lift a fully loaded freezer into the van). Also note if it's a freezer with shelves and front loading, if fully loaded the vibration during transportation can damage shelf fixings or, worse still, the internal insulation.
* It's as well to remember, too, that usually both the appliance and its contents will be moved *at your own risk* and will probably not be included in the removal firms insurance cover (but check this). (This can also apply to empty freezers – it's worth finding out if your own insurance covers the freezer and its contents.)
* Make sure the freezer stays plugged in until almost the moment it's ready to go in the van.
* It should be the last item to go in and the first out, so tell the foreman this.
* Put it on its fast freeze switch for twelve hours before the trip and this will make sure the contents are at a really low temperature. Before you put it on fast freeze though, fill the empty part at the top with crumpled up newspapers to help keep the contents frozen (a half empty freezer causes goods to thaw more quickly). An alternative is to wrap some blankets round the outside of the freezer when it's in the van (having first frozen the blankets wrapped in plastic in the freezer). Even

partial defrosting can impair the flavour of food and more serious defrosting and refreezing can be dangerous.

* When you reach your new house, make sure the freezer is plugged in straight away but take care! Some freezers have systems that need to 'settle' after movement and vibration. Check with a local supplier and/or the instructions.
* Take anything out you're going to need fairly soon so that it will be thawed by the time you're ready to eat.

GLASS, CHINA AND PORCELAIN

Fragile items can be successfully stashed away in the box which contains all your bed linen since this provides excellent protection and padding for them.

* However, don't forget to stick a note (which can't be easily detached) to the outside of the box, on which you have listed all the items inside.
* The packing cases should have 'HANDLE WITH CARE' or 'GLASS' or whatever's appropriate, marked on them in large red letters, so that the removal men (and members of the family) treat it accordingly.
* Write the warning on all four sides of the container just in case one side happens to be hidden by other boxes or furniture.
* The container you plan to use must be strong – a tea chest is probably ideal because it's made of wood.
* Put a layer of wood chippings, shredded paper or even a bag of polystyrene loft insulation granules on the bottom of the chest.
* Wrap each individual cup in newspaper and put a few cups inside each other (say a maximum of three); saucers, plates and other items should always be individually wrapped in newspaper too and kept in flat layers.
* Fill in the gaps between the various items with your filling material, so that there's no danger of one item damaging another. If you can't get anything else, crumpled up pieces of newspaper will do for this job.
* Don't pack too many things in the one box but don't pack too few either or you will simply waste space and packing material.
* Don't leave tea chests open – you want a good strong lid on them to protect the contents from the possibility of something

dropping on to them. If the chest doesn't already have a lid then make one from a piece of strong wood.

INFLAMMABLE LIQUIDS

Inflammable liquids, such as petrol or lighter fuel should never be packed and be very wary indeed of chemicals of any kind. They are actually all forbidden by law on removal vans, and if included might invalidate the insurance cover.

* Dispose of any leftover cleaning fluid, turps, paint remover and that sort of thing. Either give these chemicals to a neighbour (in clearly labelled bottles) or contact the local Environmental Health Department to ask for their advice on disposal.
* Drain any fuel from lawn mowers, oil heaters and so on.
* Even liquid bleach which you may use in the bathroom shouldn't be packed, because if any of it gets out of the bottle – and you can't be sure that it won't – it can cause terrible damage to everything around it. Dispose of as for cleaning fluids above.
* Nail varnish, too, can cause damage, so always seal the bottle top with lots of sticky tape, then put it in a waterproof container of some kind.

MIRRORS

These deserve a lot of care and cosseting.

* Try to get hold of some 'bubbled' polythene sheets, but failing that, use several sheets of polystyrene.
* Pack the mirrors carefully, padding out any corners with crumpled newspapers, old tights or similar.
* Tie something soft but strong (like raffia) round to keep the packaging in place.
* Stick large pieces of plain paper to the outside of the packaged mirror (on both sides) with 'MIRROR, HANDLE WITH CARE' written in large, clear letters.

PETS

Animals should never be put in the removal van: take them with you in the car. Some removers can supply cardboard pet cartons. However, before you are actually ready to go, do a trial run with cat boxes, birdcages, dogs, or even tortoises and rabbits, to work out exactly where they will be during the journey, so that you are not struggling around at the last minute trying to fit them all in. Keep pets out of the way on moving day. Most seem to dislike the upset and will either annoy you, the removal men or each other. You might try persuading a neighbour to keep them for you until take-off time. Alternatively, put them all in an empty room in the house and fasten the door securely. Put a notice on the door saying 'ANIMALS – DON'T LET OUT' or better still lock the door if you have a key to it. Make sure you shut all windows in the room, otherwise the cats may escape. Dogs could be tied up in the garden.

* Birds of all kinds should be kept in their cages with the cover on top, so that they don't become too agitated and flap about. If you haven't room to transport the cage in the car, put the bird in a box with airholes punched in it just for the trip.
* Cats can usually tell something's going on and are liable to disappear at the last minute, simply to give you even more to do! So don't leave them wandering around free on moving morning: make absolutely sure that they are where you want them to be (and that is sometimes possible with cats!). Once on the move, they should travel in an enclosed basket for their safety and yours. If the removal firm cannot supply special

boxes, the RSPCA or local vets can usually provide cheap ones.

* If your cat isn't used to being carried around in a cardboard box, being shut up inside can be a terrifying experience for him or her. So get the box well in advance and put it in the lounge. Put the cat inside it with perhaps a bit of food to tempt it (although most cats will jump straight into any box you care to leave lying around!) and shut the box for about half an hour, so that he or she becomes used to the idea. If you have a particularly nervous or obstreperous cat, it is just possible it could claw its way out of a cardboard box during transit, so a cane basket may be best.
* Dogs should be kept off the drink before the car journey to save yourself stopping every five minutes on the way! Keep food to a minimum, too, although if they are used to getting a meal round about moving time, give them a small amount – perhaps a dry biscuit – just to keep their routine going. Cats, too, can wet their box if they are nervous and upset, so keep their intake to a minimum.
* Fish must not be transported any distance in their bowls or tanks. Glass poses too high a risk to all concerned. Fish require a fairly even temperature with no rapid variations. This applies to both tropical fish and goldfish. The container used to move them should be strong and insulated; a polystyrene container which can be sealed is ideal. Place the fish in clean plastic bags filled with sufficient water, fresh or salt, according to the species. Seal the bag making sure there is enough air above the water. Do not inflate the bags too much. The bag(s) can then be placed in the polystyrene container.
* Fishes of different species should be moved in separate bags. Some species of fish with spines can be moved safely by using two polythene bags, one inside the other, with a thickness of newspaper between them.
* To prevent the water becoming too foul, don't feed the fish for 24 hours before moving them and don't keep them packed for more than 18 hours. A reputable aquarist centre may be able to offer further advice on transporting fish, so don't be afraid to ask. Prepare the fishes' new home and acclimatise the fish as though they were new.
* Packing the fish tank needs as much care as does any other

glassware. If it's small enough, pack it in a strong wooden tea chest filled with sawdust, shredded paper or something similar. Pack the filling round the outside of the tank to secure it and inside too. Clearly mark the outside 'GLASS'.

* Large tanks need special packing: ask your removal firm or local pet shop for their advice.

PLANTS

First of all, check if your insurance for the move covers the plants as well. Even though removal firms will, if asked, take plants in the van, they may well not accept any responsibility for them as with the rest of the furniture. If a removal van has to park overnight in winter, delicate plants may not survive the cold.

* Always bear in mind that in legal terms all the plants, shrubs, trees and turf in the garden are part of the fixtures and therefore should only be moved if you have come to an arrangement with the buyer regarding particular plants and shrubs. If you want to take plants with you, have it written into the contract. However, plants in pots on the patio are not fixtures, but the removal men will probably want them taken out of the pots since the pot and soil may be too heavy. Plants in boxes or pots in the greenhouse, cold frame or on the window ledges of the house are not fixtures either and can be taken with you.
* Make up your mind well in advance what plants you're taking with you and tell the estimator, so that they can be included in the price he quotes you. Otherwise you might find the men refuse to take them on the day.
* Pack as much soil as possible with plants, water well, then wrap the root ball firmly with a piece of sacking or nylon netting and put the whole plant into a strong polythene bag. If there's lots of foliage you'll do no harm to it if you 'tie' it to the main stem with a soft raffia or twine – this will prevent damage and take up less travelling space. If the foliage is too firm to tie in, put a tube of newspaper or brown paper round the pot to prevent damage.
* Pot plants travel best together. This way they're easier to handle and less likely to be damaged. You will need cardboard boxes with fairly high sides – or certainly a little higher than the plant. Line the bottom of the box with a piece of old plastic, water the plants well, then put several into a box,

packing out between the pots with folded newspaper or something similar to keep them securely in position. It's a good idea to take any plants round to your new house well before D-day, if you're not moving too far away. The occupier will probably be quite happy for you to do this and plant them out in the garden.

* Shrubs or medium-sized trees are best left behind, however fond of them you are, because they might not take to the transfer. If you're in any doubt about any plant or shrub the best thing to do is to have a word with someone at your local garden centre. Alternatively, try your local authority's parks department (see page 361); they are experts on moving plants about from one place to another and many of these departments actually run an advisory service for members of the public (it's free!)

SELF-ASSEMBLY FURNITURE

This proves its worth a second time when it comes to moving. Cupboards, cabinets, tables or whatever can simply be dismantled and packed flat for transport.

* Removal contractors may decline responsibilty when moving self-assembly furniture and may not want their staff involved in dismantling it.
* Remember to keep all the fittings (brackets, screws and so on) which are used to put the item together, in one bag or box with the furniture they relate to. Tape a plastic bag to the item.
* Mark all the pieces with their relevant positions (right, front, etc.) to help with re-assembly.

STARTER PACK

A 'starter pack' for the new house is a good idea. It might include: keys, toilet paper, light bulbs and fuses or fuse wire, first aid kit, a few tools (e.g. a screwdriver and hammer), torch, matches, washing-up liquid, all you need to make either tea or coffee (including cups to drink it from), tin opener, a plate for each of the family, kettle, saucepan, frying pan, towels and any extra bits and pieces of clothing you'll need, packed in something like a plastic bag.

STORE CUPBOARD ITEMS

Fiddly little things from the store cupboard, such as bottles of flavouring and colouring, can be tricky to pack as they break very easily.

* A biscuit tin can make a good container, as it's strong but not too large. An empty ice cream container made of rigid polythene is another alternative. The bread bin also comes in useful.
* Wrap each little bottle in newspaper and fill any gaps between them with pieces of crumpled paper.
* Any packets of things like flour should be securely fastened with sticky tape, to keep them closed. Pack these items in a strong box.
* If any of the bottles have only a little left in them it may be as well to throw them out instead of taking them with you.
* Pepper and spices in those little containers with the perforated tops can be awkward things to pack. Cut out little circles of thin card which exactly match the size and shape of the top of the containers. Attach them by putting a piece of sticky tape across the card and down either side of the container. When you're next ready to use them cut through between the card and the tape, otherwise the sticky tape will pull away some of the label.
* Maximise all that space inside saucepans by filling it up with any small and rather delicate items from the kitchen cupboards; packets of cream of tartar, which could split open, plastic coffee spoons, bars of cooking chocolate, packets of gelatine or aspic and so on. To save them rattling around, put in a couple of tea towels, a pair of oven gloves or even spare wash-up sponges just to keep things soft.

REMOVAL MEN

ACCESS

Make sure there's reasonable access to your house – ask the neighbours to keep their cars well clear. If there are parking meters they can be suspended for a fee which you will be expected to reimburse the removers if they have to pay it. Discuss any such arrangements with your removal firm in advance.

ESTIMATES

Start getting estimates at least six weeks in advance. There's no absolutely foolproof way of making the correct choice of firm, sometimes even a good one can have men off ill or on holiday, so that your furniture is handled by rather inexpert 'temps'. But ask around friends and neighbours for recommendations. Next consult the Yellow Pages and pick out at least three names. Go for

one well known national company, one large local and one smaller local (but make sure they are all registered BAR members). The British Association of Removers is always prepared to give you the names of three local members, either in writing or, preferably, over the telephone. The Association will also supply a 'hints' leaflet if you send a stamped addressed envelope to this address: BAR, 279 Gray's Inn Road, London WC1X 8SY. (Telephone 01 837 3088/9). Ask the removers if they would be available on the day you plan to move and if they'll send someone round to see what you've got to move. Also tell them where you're moving to, of course. Their price will include overnight accommodation for the men, if necessary, the distance to be covered, as well as charges covering what and how much is to be moved. Some firms supply a booklet telling you about their services, so ask about this.

* Absolute honesty is the best policy when the man comes to look over your bits and pieces. Open the garage door and let him see the array of paint tins, tools, old chairs and all the rest; unlock the garden shed and let him feast his eyes on the bicycles, the deck chairs, the wheelbarrow and the lawn mower. Don't forget the attic. This is essential, otherwise he's likely to send a van that's too small.
* Make it absolutely clear whether or not you plan to do the packing yourself or whether you're leaving it to the removal men (this will naturally cost you extra). Very often the insurance may not apply if the goods are not professionally packed, so check this. Any antiques or particularly delicate items should be drawn to the attention of the estimator, while he's in your house, so that he can't claim later that he knew nothing about them if damage results.
* Ask if their quotation will include covers to protect your mattresses, hanging wardrobes for your clothes, cartons for the linen. Do they supply you with cartons and tea chests to put things in?

* Haggle – the removal firms seem to like doing business that way, indeed some of them even advertise that they're prepared to do so. So, if the firm you really want to move your furniture (perhaps because it comes highly recommended by friends) has quoted more than you can afford, or simply much more than that of the other firms, then give them a ring and say so. Most will probably be prepared to adjust their price to accommodate you.
* If you cancel or postpone a removal at short notice you may have to pay a fee so make sure your solicitor knows this and can confirm when occupation may take place.

INSURANCE

Many a person has assumed that his goods were safe with a removal firm to the extent that any damage would be covered by the company's insurance. This is so only with a few firms, most removers expect you to purchase additional insurance. If you read the small print, you'll find that one of the standard conditions of removal firms is that they are only liable up to a limit which may still be as low as £10 for any one article lost or damaged – a sum which would hardly cover so much as a cushion these days! So if you want your things to be safe no matter what, you will have to take out insurance on them. This is usually offered by the firm – if it is, then check very carefully exactly what is covered. If the firm doesn't offer, then insist! It is your right to know before you confirm arrangements. Sometimes jewellery and similar personal items aren't covered. If in any doubt, consult an independent insurance broker.

* Your own house contents policy may offer cover of goods in transit, but it's likely to be limited. Jewellery, gold and silver are not usually covered, nor is the scratching, cracking or breaking of anything brittle (i.e. just the things you want to be insured).
* Before you breathe a sigh of relief that you're fully insured and covered for come-what-may, bear in mind that your goods and chattels are not in fact the only things at risk! Your house, the garden wall, the house next door, the house you're going to, are just a few of the items which could very easily be damaged by a removal firm's driver. Check in advance that the firm's motor insurance covers this kind of claim.

OFF PEAK TRAVEL

Unless you must move on a specific day, you can save money if you avoid the peak periods which tend to be at the end of the week, at the end of the month and in spring and summer.

PAYMENT

'Pay us before we do any work' is the policy of almost every removal firm. Many expect payment once the quotation is accepted. However, they might be open to an alternative, if you suggest paying a deposit on acceptance of the quotation and the balance when the removal is completed. That's fairer all round. If they still want you to pay all in advance, either go to another firm or offer payment by credit card.

QUOTATIONS

Before plumping for the little known firm offering the lowest quotation, check on their reputation. If it's on the British Association of Removers list (see page 252) it will be reputable.

STORAGE FACILITIES

If you are not moving into your new house right away, but want to put your goods in store, consider the container storage facilities offered by some firms. With this system your furniture is loaded into a container, which is then sealed in your presence. The container is unopened until it is delivered to your new home. This can mean there is less risk of anything being lost or damaged. Some firms load and unload their containers actually in the store and the containers themselves never leave the building. Check which policy the firm you choose adopts.

* If your things are to be in store for some time, choose a firm which offers 'valeting' as part of their package. What this means is that carpets and upholstery will be vacuumed on a regular basis and checked over for any signs of deterioration. It may cost a little more but could be worth it. Check, when you are considering particular storage facilities, whether the place is heated during the winter.

ON THE DAY

After all your preparations, you are hoping for a trouble-free day. Try to strike a balance between sitting on a packing case twiddling your thumbs and rushing frantically in and out of the house. Consider the following actions:

Look in the garden shed and garage (and even behind the garden shed in case you've left any tools there) and also look in the attic to make sure you haven't left anything. If you have one of those keyboards in the hall where you hang keys to the outhouse, garage and so on, then strip it, people have been known to set off leaving their spare set of car keys hanging in the hall.

Make sure the gas, electricity and the water are turned off. (The meters should already have been read (see page 259).) Leave any booklets or papers relevant to these services in a prominent position, so that the new owners can't miss them. Include here any instructions for central heating or other equipment in the house which is staying behind; cards or papers from gas and electricity authorities which the new owner has to fill in; a note for the new owner just mentioning that you have arranged for the mail to be redirected, that you've asked the milkman to call in should they want to order milk, that the little shop round the corner sells marvellous rolls or whatever! It's also a good idea to write down the names of the neighbours on either side of you (plus a few personal, but not TOO personal!) details. For instance 'Neighbour on right – Betty Bread – has two school age children, a dog and a cat and a husband who's the local policeman'.

Organize a 'travelling pack'. The things you're likely to need, depending on the length of your journey, could include: snacks, sandwiches, fruit, a vacuum flask with tea, coffee or soup: a damp cloth in a plastic bag for mopping sticky fingers; a big box of tissues.

Relax. . . relax. . . relax and look on it all as an adventure rather than a hassle! Try not to flutter around the removal men, and organize the various members of your family, making each responsible for some small task, then leave them to get on with it, don't fuss them.

Sort out the house keys for the new owner. Tie a label to each one and clearly write on it 'Garden Shed', 'Back Door' or whatever – use card for the labels (e.g. cut from a cornflakes carton) and punch holes in each piece for a piece of thin string to go through. Next put all the keys together in an envelope (a good strong one) and write on the outside the address of your house. Then all you have to do is hand them over to the solicitor. If you have gathered any keys which are no longer used – you may have changed the lock on a door for instance – throw them out to avoid confusing the new owners.

Start up the car while there's still time to get the local garage round should your car have decided to play up! Double check that you have sufficient petrol, water, oil and so on for the journey and that your tyres are all well inflated. If there's any slight problem you'll have enough time to nip round to the nearest service station while the furniture's being loaded on to the van.

Tell the foreman what's to go – and what's not to go. Take him round every room, into the garage and the garden shed.

Tick everything off on your list as it comes out of the van on arrival at the new house. Again, detail members of the family to go into the various rooms and do a double check that all the items have arrived. It's important to do more than glance at the furniture – now's the time to look closely and examine for scratches, gouges or breakages, not forgetting tears in upholstery. If you find any such damage it's wise to write it all down clearly (if you have a small piece of carbon paper to slip in between the pages of your notebook you'll get a copy of the list). Then take the foreman round with you, pointing out the damage, show him the list and ask him to initial it and give him a copy. Make any claim just as soon as possible, whether to the removal firm or your own insurance company.

Draw a plan of where the new property is situated. Mark in not only street names but any prominent landmarks, like a church or the Town Hall, so that the driver can recognize when he's getting near his destination. Always give the foreman the phone number of your new house or of a friend who is prepared to act as 'contact', so that if he is delayed he can ring you.

Arrange to have the cooker fixed as a priority in the new home – and if the electrician hasn't arrived at the time he said he would, don't delay, ring his firm and ask what's happened. If he has forgotten, there's just the chance they may be able to send someone else out providing you emphasise how urgent the job is. It's illegal for an unauthorised person to disconnect a gas appliance, so if you plan to take one with you arrange this in advance with the local gas region. Removal staff are not allowed to do it.

Get comfortable in your new home as soon as possible, then the move won't seem quite so much of a chore. Pick one room to get as organized as possible and ask the men to lay the carpet and set at least some of the furniture, such as chairs, into position. If at all possible hang up some curtains and don't forget to turn on the central heating or plug in an electric fire. Even when the weather's comparatively mild, it's surprising how chilly a house can feel, when it's been empty even for a short time.

WHOM TO TELL

BONDS AND STOCKS OFFICE

Lots of Premium Bonds prizes remain unclaimed and it may well be because the holders forgot to tell the office they were moving! So don't miss out – write to Bonds and Stocks Office, Lytham St Annes, Lancs FYO 1YN.

CLUBS, MAIL ORDER COMPANIES, GARDENING FIRMS

Any such organization or firm you'd like to keep in touch with should be given a note of your new address. Don't forget the AA, RAC and any newspapers and magazines you subscribe to on a regular basis.

CREDIT CARD COMPANY

To notify your credit card company, fill in the change-of-address portion on your statement and send it off when you pay.

DVLC

Your car registration document and your driving licence both have tear-off portions to be sent off to the DVLC with a change of address. It's important that you attend to this (although terribly easy just to forget to do it in all the rush) because legally these documents do require to have the correct information on them. Should you be asked to produce them by a policeman, you would technically be in breach of the law, if they still had your old address on them. Failure to notify a change of address on a driving licence could render you liable to a fine of at least £20. Not an ideal way to start off at your new address!

ELECTRICITY

Get the meter read the day before you leave – preferably in the late afternoon, so that you don't run up too much extra on the meter between then and the time you leave next day (most movers accept a few units and aren't likely to quibble about it, so don't get neurotic about using the cooker or something to get the family a hot meal after the meter's been read. The chances are there will be a little more on the meter at the house you're going to than the meter reading indicates . . . it's all a question of swings and roundabouts!). Ring the electricity showroom the day before you're due to go just to check that the meter man's coming, because it is legally the responsibility of the person moving out to have the meter read and if you don't you could be liable to pay for the electricity used until it is read! Don't leave anything to chance, moving's an expensive enough business without incurring any extras which can easily be avoided with a bit of care.

FOOTBALL POOLS

Football pools fanatics won't want to miss out on the possibility of a big win. So make sure the man with the good news knows where to call! Notify your change of address on the last coupon from the old address or give a note of it to the chap who collects the coupons in your area and ask him to make sure someone calls in the new locality.

GAS

Contact your local showroom well before you move to ask someone to come out and read the meter the afternoon before you leave. They must have at least 48 hours notice and since mistakes can happen and even gasmen can forget things, after your initial telephone call, follow it up with a letter (again to your local office). If you are moving to the same area, give the office details and ask them to make any connections necessary after you've moved. When the chap comes to read the meter be sure he affixes an official sticker to your meter – this will indicate that it has been read, note the figure, the date and have the gasman's signature alongside. Take a note of the meter reading yourself and jot it down in your 'moving notebook'. No doubt you will be given a card for the new owner of your house to fill in with all their details, so leave it in a prominent place.

GIROBANK

The Post Office can supply a special stamped addressed envelope, so that you can send a note of your new address.

GP

If you're not moving too far away you may prefer to stay with your present doctor, and in that case all you need do is hand in a note of your new address, so that records can be changed accordingly. But if you are going further afield then de-register with your doctor and find another locally. Lists of GP's are to be found in libraries but if you can't find one willing to accept you, contact the local Family Practitioners Committee and they'll let you have the name of one who does have vacancies. When you get on a new list take your family's medical cards along and your new GP will then arrange to have all the relevant records transferred to him. Ring the Family Planning Association (you will find their number in your local telephone directory) and they will tell you where your nearest Family Planning Clinic is.

INSURANCE COMPANIES

The insurance on your present property will have to be cancelled and cover taken out for your new one. So contact your insurance broker or company and ask for the relevant forms to fill in. Look over any accompanying leaflets carefully and make sure that you do insure for a sum sufficient to pay for the rebuilding of the property – don't skimp on the sum. This is a good time to review your contents insurance too and check that it has kept up with inflation. Get both index-lined to save you constantly having to review the amounts. Depending on where you move to, your car insurance may cost more or less, as there are different 'price bands' for different parts of the country and for urban and rural areas. Let your broker or firm have your new address as soon as possible and ask if a rebate might be due. If any circumstances regarding your car will change as a result of the move – for instance if your new house hasn't a garage and the car will be left in your driveway – then give the details to the company. All these things may be very important in the event of any claim you may have. Remember that, when buying a new house, you become liable for damage to the new place at exchange of contracts, so make sure you are insured from this date on. Moving house is a good time to re-assess all your insurance cover. Take this opportunity to switch your contents or car insurance to another company if they offer a better deal.

LIBRARY

Some people get sneaky about returning long overdue books to their local library when they're about to move: they leave them with friends and hope to avoid the shame! But whether you have overdue books to return or not, take the time to go along personally and let the library know you're leaving and hand in your tickets, so that they can be cancelled.

MAIL

Go along to your local Post Office for a form to fill in, so that you can arrange for your mail to be redirected to your new address. Do this at least a week beforehand. You can have this service for a month, three months or a year and you will pay a proportionate

fee. If you've been very diligent and alerted all your friends, relatives and business contacts of your new address (send out new address cards, available from most stationers (see also Telephone, page 263) before you actually move) then you may need redirection only for a short period of time. There's a leaflet available from Post Offices which gives you full details.

MONEY

See your bank manager and give him details of your move. It's very important to get his co-operation at this point because if you are opening an account in the new area and closing your existing one, you could be left with a 'cheque card gap' since these always take at least a week to be processed by the central department which deals with such matters. You don't, of course, have to change branches if you move to a new area and it might well make sense to stay with your present branch if you have a good relationship with the manager there.

POLICE

Should you be an immigrant to the UK, then let the police in your new area know you've moved in – only if you are still subject to immigration controls, of course.

RATES DEPARTMENT

Your solicitor will hopefully already have informed the local authority rates department that you are selling the house and will have passed all relevant documents over to the new owner's solicitor. But it has been known for the local authority to keep sending demands for rates to the person who has just sold the house (and since you'll have arranged for mail to be redirected they'll be sent on!) so always write independently to your Rates department informing them when you officially hand over the house and give the name of the new owners.

RENTAL COMPANIES

Rented TV's, videos and whatever can usually just be taken with you, providing you notify the local branch of the company. They will contact a branch near your new home and generally someone from the firm will visit you just to satisfy themselves that you still have the equipment and that it's in good working order. If you're reluctant to accept the responsibility of the set in transit, you could return it to your local branch and get another one locally. That might mean you are without a set for the first few days and it might also mean you will not get such a good deal on another set. Rental companies seem to operate a complicated system, whereby it isn't just a straightforward matter of getting a similar set from another branch – no, you often have to start from scratch and take on a new rental agreement! Incidentally, your household contents policy would probably cover your rented TV in transit – but check this out. Also check what cover you get from the removals firm. Don't dream of moving it unless it is insured!

You also need to tell the finance company with which you have any hire purchase agreements that you are moving.

S.A.Y.E. OFFICE

National Savings Certificate holders should give their new address to S.A.Y.E. Office, Durham, BH99 1NS giving the certificate numbers.

TELEPHONE

Look in the front of your telephone directory and you'll find details of whom to notify. Usually 7 days notice is needed. You can give the office details of the new owner, but it's as well to bear in mind that British Telecom require the person taking over the telephone to notify them personally (many a new owner has found themselves in a house without a phone and has angrily assumed the previous owner either hasn't paid the bill or has had the phone disconnected, when in fact it will be disconnected unless the new subscriber asks otherwise). So while contacting your local office about discontinuing service ask about the telephone you are taking over. If you're moving to a new telephone area, you must contact it and indicate you wish to continue the phone service at the new address. Consider very carefully when you want the meter read and the phone discontinued in your name. In some areas (particularly rural ones) no guarantee can be given that service will be discontinued at a specific time of day. Which means that if you happened to be very unlucky and the new owner phoned relatives in Australia the moment they arrived YOU could end up paying for the call! So it can be a good idea to have the service discontinued the previous afternoon and take a chance that you won't have to make any last minute calls on the morning you're moving out. Don't forget to tell people you have a new number; British Telecom often provide New address/telephone number cards for you to send out.

WATER

This won't apply in Scotland because water comes under the aegis of the local authority, but in England and Wales the Water Board should be notified at least 48 hours before you move. If you are going to a completely different part of the country, notify the Water Board there, so that water can be turned on. Incidentally, if the new owners aren't moving in straight away it's always as well to check with them whether they'd like the tanks and pipes drained – this is especially important in winter.

MOVING ABROAD

If you are moving abroad, then the organization of the packing and travel arrangements is that much more complicated. Consider the following in addition to the general hints:

1. Always choose a firm which is covered by an advance payment bond. This guarantees repayment if the firm ceases business between advance payment and final delivery. This is important because there have been instances of firms going out of business while someone's goods were still in transit, and the shipping company holding on to the goods until the firm pays them. However, if you get cover under the BAR-IMMI scheme from an overseas removal firm, the insurance will see that your possessions are delivered safely. Get a list of firms in the scheme from the British Association of Removers (send an SAE).
2. Mostly, goods will be transported to another country by ship. All experienced and reputable firms ought to be in a position to offer you excellent rates from-door-to-door if they belong to the BAR overseas group, but it's always wise to do a check on costs of both methods and see how they compare. As with UK removals, get detailed written estimates from several firms.
3. Goods in transit between countries must be well insured – and cover may be required for more than a few days. Premiums can be high so shop around but go to a well known insurance company or broker, or arrange it through the remover.
4. Although you probably don't consider moving abroad in the same light as you would holidaying abroad . . . there are certain similarities. So find out what the rules are for entry, any quarantine regulations for pets and which vaccinations may be needed, and organize all these well in advance. Most experienced removers ought to be able to help with such information, at least where the more usual countries are concerned.

THE NEW HOUSE

Checklist of things to find out about the new place:

* Where the mains water stopcocks are, inside and outside the house. If you have septic tank drainage – where is the tank situated and when was it last emptied? Who empties it and how do you make arrangements?
* Locate any gas taps, pilot lights.
* Where the fuse boxes, electricity meter and the mains switches are situated. Check on which electricity board covers your area.
* Where is the cold water storage tank and is it insulated? Locate hot water cylinders, check whether they're lagged and if they have thermostats.
* Find out how the central heating system works, if there is one. When was the boiler last serviced – is there an instruction manual for it – is it under a service contract, if so, who with and when will it run out – how does the programmer work – do the radiators have individual room thermostats – where is the entry point to fill up the oil tank – how often is oil needed – who's the cheapest supplier in the area?
* If the fuel is coal, where is it stored and who is the best supplier in the area?
* Will the plumbing fit your washing machine, dishwasher or whatever or will you have to arrange for someone to come in and do a new plumbing job?
* Refuse collection is vital and the time and quality of it can vary considerably from one area to another. So find out when collections are – do you supply your own dustbin or does the local authority supply paper or plastic sacks?
* When were the chimneys last swept? If coal's no longer used, are the chimneys sealed at the top as well as being blocked at the fireplace?

* Get the names and address of: electrician; plumber; central heating engineer; window cleaner; decorator.
* Who delivers milk in your area – how do you contact them to place an order?
* Which shop delivers morning and Sunday papers and at what times?
* How close are the essential shops: butchers, greengrocers, grocers?
* Find out which schools are in the area and make arrangements with them for your children to attend.
* Ask the new house owner who their doctor is and is he/she to be recommended?
* If you have a pet, find out the name of a reliable vet near to the new house.
* Local transport services should be checked out and bus or train timetables obtained.
* What recreational facilities are available in the area – badminton clubs, sports centres, swimming pool, etc.
* Which garage deals with your make of car and has a good name for servicing and repair work?
* If there is a telephone in the new house – will it be disconnected (see page 263)?
* If the house doesn't have a phone – where's the nearest one?
* A good hairdresser is a bonus in any area, so ask the lady of the

house if she can recommend one.

* Exactly which fixtures and fittings are being left, for example light bulbs, china door handles, curtains and curtain rails (see page 269), clothes driers (see below), TV aerial, carpets, towel rails, shelves.

ADVANCE PLANNING

Fiddling around with your furniture – on paper – can be fun, but it can also save you a lot of time, trouble and temper on removal day. Advance planning will alert you to the fact that the Welsh dresser is not going to fit into the new dining room or that the piano will get stuck if you try to push it through the lounge door.

* Take a bit of time and involve all the family in this planning exercise. Paper and patience are the main requirements. Take measurements of all the rooms in the new house (see 'Measuring Up', opposite). Draw up a floor plan of each room (transferring the measurements from your notebook) and work to a scale. Using the same scale, cut out bits of paper to represent all your furniture. By placing these pieces on the floor plan, you can try out different arrangements painlessly until you decide which looks best and where everything will fit. However, don't forget to check the height of any tall pieces of furniture or of any low beams in the new house.
* The second stage of 'pushing the furniture around' is to pick a different colour for every room. Get some coloured paper and code each piece of furniture according to which room it will be put in. Pin a large piece of matching paper to the door of each room in the new house, then it's a simple matter for the removal men to put the 'red sideboard' in the 'red' room, the 'blue' box in the 'blue' room and so on.
* It's always wise to keep your original scale plan, stick the cutouts representing the furniture down in the place you've decided they'll go, then use that as a back-up to help you get everything in its place.

CLOTHES DRIERS

Clothes poles in the back garden aren't much seen these days, instead every house has a 'whirligig' to swirl and twirl the washing in the wind. But, unlike the old sort, which were very firmly anchored to the ground, these rotary driers are normally slotted into sockets which makes them much more portable. Arguments have been known to develop between buyer and seller of a house as to whether the drier should have been left in the garden as a 'fixture'.

* Avoid such problems by coming to an agreement about the whirligig – whether it goes or stays.

COLOUR SCHEMES

If you are lucky, you will be happy with the existing colour schemes in some or all of the rooms.

* If this is the case, ask the present owner to write out a list of the brand and shade used so that you can get a match for any touching up which may be required.
* Better still, beg them to leave behind any leftover tins of paint which were used for the decor instead of throwing them out.
* If you are getting curtains with the house, ask for any leftover material, too – it could be useful for the future.

MEASURING UP

Arrange to go to the house well before you're due to move in but always check with the present owner (or with the agent, if the house is already empty) that the time is convenient.

* Take your measuring tape with you, a notebook, a pencil, and someone else to help hold the tape.
* Measure every room – taking alcoves and recesses into account. Draw a rough plan of each room and mark the measurements on it.
* Note where windows are and measure those accurately.
* Any furnishing items in your present house which are obviously not going to fit your new house should be listed now and offered to the buyer of your house (if they are not already included as part of the package). Remember, that however high the quality and price of these items, they will still be 'secondhand' to someone else, and should be offered cheaply.
* If curtain rails are not being left, measure for new ones and get them all ready to put in place when you arrive. In this context, it's as well to take a look at the surface they'll be screwed into, so that you can make provision for wallplugs if necessary.

NEWLY-BUILT PROPERTY

Always double check the entry date – delays are not uncommon – and get it in writing. Any change in date can throw out all the rest of your removal plans and may involve contacting the removal firm, electricity boards etc.

* Establish exactly what grade of central heating you are getting – there are three grades, varying from mere background heating to full heating. Ask the builder what kind of temperatures you can expect in various rooms and ask him to note it down.
* Check that gas is available if you use it – some estates can be all electric. If gas is an extra – how much will it cost?
* Is a choice in paint, wallpaper or floor finishing being offered? If so, establish in writing with the builder what your choice of such decoration is.
* Bathroom and kitchen fitments should be agreed in advance and a note of requirements given to the builder IN WRITING well ahead of the move, so that there is no undue delay in completion.
* Is double glazing and decorative glass in doors offered as an extra? Find out and agree accordingly with the builder.
* The moment you move in – do a tour of inspection, note any breakages of glass, sanitary ware or any defects (e.g. window latches missing or no insulation on the water tank). Write to the builder with details and keep a copy yourself.
* Make sure the property is covered by a National House Building Certificate and that you or your solicitor get one pertaining to your particular house, as you will need it in the case of any claim about faults later on.

OIL-FIRED CENTRAL HEATING

It's easy enough to get oil into a tank for the central heating, but very tricky trying to get it out again. If the new property has central heating it's worth asking what the position on fuel is and coming to some arrangement about buying the oil that's left in the tank.

* To save the possibility of a dispute, get it measured or 'estimated' by someone independent.
* Make sure you pay a reasonable rate for what's there. On the other hand, oil prices keep going up so you are probably getting the tank residue at less than you'd pay ordering new!

1. About the House
2. Clothes Care
3. Make Amends
4. Table Talk
5. Talking Shop
6. Moving Moments
7. Happy Holidays

BEFORE-YOU-GO CHECKLIST

TWO TO THREE MONTHS BEFORE

* Now's the time to ring up kennels and catteries to see if they're free for the weeks of your holiday. Then go and inspect them before booking (see page 307).

* Shop for any clothes you want to take with you. The best time to do this is right at the start of the summer season to get the pick of the new season's fashions. If, however, money is your main consideration, then wait until July and see what you can get at the sales.

* Check with the travel agent, if you are booking your holiday through one, that all is still well. Sometimes hotels can be overbooked and the agent somehow forgets to tell you until the last minute even if he knows in advance! Remember that in any case agents should notify you of any changes six weeks before you go. Members of the Association of British Travel Agents (ABTA) are bound by their code of conduct to tell you at once.
* Passports and visas should be looked out and renewed if necessary. Visas in particular take a long time to come through from some countries, so apply early for them.
* Vaccinations, anti-malaria tablets, all these medical matters, need to be considered at least two months in advance just in case you need a course of jabs or tablets over a long period. The DHSS have published a very helpful leaflet on 'Vaccinations Required Abroad', available free from DHSS Leaflet Service, P.O. Box 21, Stanmore, Middlesex.
* This is the time too for the animals to join in any jab sessions – you will have been given a list of which ones are necessary, when you made the booking with the kennels or cattery.
* Get the protection of the insurance companies around you. Look at the small print on any policy you're taking out along with a package holiday – make sure you have £100,000 cover at the very least for medical expenses in America (see page 287). See that you're insured against cancellation of the holiday (by you), flight delays and loss of money.
* Have a quick look through your house insurance policy too – have you sent off the renewal premium if it was due or will be while you're on holiday?
* If you plan to do a bit of touring around – either at home or abroad – start gathering together the information and maps you'll need to find out what's worth visiting. The first stop is your local library. In the 'Travel' section there's sure to be at least one book on the area or country you plan to visit – if not, ask the librarian to get one for you. Secondly, write to the national tourist board (the offices are usually in London) who will be able to supply various helpful leaflets.

  Maps can make all the difference to a holiday – they save you wasting time and temper by going off the wrong way at signposts – and a good one will let you plan your day's route properly before you set out. There are local maps for most countries (scale 1:50,000) and are fine if you get out and walk, but they cover a fairly small area and aren't so useful if you're driving. Regional maps are probably the best compromise (scale 1:200,000 or 1:500,000). You won't find footpaths or every farm marked on them but they still give details of most villages and the minor roads.

If you want to plan a route across a whole country go for a national map. Start map hunting at least a month in advance because if you can't find what you want locally, there are several specialist shops in London and the Home Counties which will be able to help and even deal by mail order. Look in the Yellow Pages for their addresses.

ONE MONTH BEFORE

* Arrange for your car to be serviced – or if you do your own – now's the time to get under the bonnet. Ask your local garage or dealer about what spares you'll need, or ask your motoring organization about their rent-a-spares-pack scheme. Apply for your green card insurance if you're going abroad.
* Get the form (E111) from the local Department of Health and Social Security Office for health care under EEC agreements, fill it in and return it.

TWO WEEKS BEFORE

* Go to the bank or travel agent and obtain or order traveller's cheques, currency or whatever.
* Look at your luggage. Repair any broken handles, straps or damage. Oil any reluctant locks. If any item is beyond repair, nip out and get a new one!
* Buy films for your camera (it will be cheaper than buying them abroad).
* Get any extras you'll need for Continental driving fitted to your car – things like yellow headlights. And even if you are motoring on home highways now's the time to look out your roof rack and fit it on.
* Cancel milk and papers. Don't just do this verbally – also send a written note to the shop giving the exact date on which you'll be going and also the date when you want deliveries resumed again. It's always wise to do cancelling at this stage

because some firms won't accept anything less than a week's notice and if you don't give it to them they're liable to charge you for the milk or papers you didn't want and didn't get.

* If you don't already have a spare set of ignition keys for the car, get them now and think of a safe place to put them while travelling.
* Have a word with neighbours, relatives, friends, or whoever you hope to persuade to keep an eye on your house while you're away and check that they know what's required of them. Include your plants, if appropriate, in the checklist.
* Clothes (the ones you plan to take on holiday) must be subjected to severe scrutiny around this time. What you're looking for is split seams, loose buttons, slight tears, stains and so on. If there are any you haven't worn since last year, it's wise to try them on to make sure they still fit! Any grubby looking items should be washed and any with special finishes which need dry cleaning should be taken to the cleaners straightaway. Shoes, last year's sandals and all the holiday footwear need to be examined for signs of wear and tear and taken to the repairers if necessary.

ONE WEEK BEFORE

* This is the time for a last minute shopping spree for anything like sunglasses or suntan lotion, paper tissues and similar items.
* Make out a list of the things to go in your cases – organizing what goes into which bag or case.
* Shoes you're taking with you must be collected from the repairers, so must clothes which are at the cleaners.
* Get all the documents you need to take with you together and put them into one bag. These will include passports, visas, health form for cover in the EEC, insurance cover, driving licence, green card, registration document (if needed in the country you're going to), currency, tickets, vouchers and so on (but see pages 284 and 286 for what to do with documents when travelling).
* Check that you've paid the 'phone bill and any other bills and do one more check with paper and milk providers that they will cancel as requested.
* Decide what clothes you will wear for the trip and similarly

for the rest of the family. Now's the time to get all the arguments over and done with! But keep it casual (the clothes)! If you haven't got one of those foldaway plastic macs – get one . . . even abroad you get sudden, fierce thunderstorms.

* Organize the washing of the family's holiday clothes.

THE DAY BEFORE

* Take pets to kennels, catteries or friends.
* Take a look in the fridge and make sure you haven't left something that's likely to go off or go hard while you're away.
* Water all the plants and perform any similar chores outside in the garden or patio.
* If you're going by car (the whole distance or just to station or airport) put the packed suitcases and bags in the boot. Book a taxi to take you to station or airport if required.
* Gather any reading material you're taking with you and if you need extra comics or paperbacks go out and buy them.
* If you are taking a packed lunch or a meal of any kind with you, plan it and prepare it.
* Your handbag should be turned out, cleaned, then packed ready for your holiday. If you are taking a large handbag, you may want to put things like spare tights, travel sickness pills and other medicines, moistened tissues, aspirins and so on into it as well as what you'd usually have. On a long trip a toothbrush is also handy to keep with you.
* Don't go overboard, but it is a good idea to give the whole house a quick clean and tidy (it doesn't look so depressing when you get back from all that splendid sea and sunshine!).

THE DAY YOU SET OFF

* Get up in good time – don't eat anything heavy or fatty for breakfast – stick to something light.
* Fill vacuum flasks if you're taking them.
* Leave any last minute instructions with neighbours or friends.
* Wash up any dishes – don't leave them lying in the sink.
* Make sure you have left the freezer switched on and, unless it is on a separate circuit, don't turn off the electricity.
* Go round all windows and doors and see that they are secure.

BOOKINGS

Basics like food, drink and entertainment vary in cost according to the country you're considering for your holiday and this can obviously make a difference to your budget, especially if it's a bit tight. Check on the cost of petrol, too, because it can vary a lot. Skimping on basics during a holiday is never a good idea, it's far better to settle for your second choice of resort or country and not have to keep an eye on the pence.

Before you book your airline ticket – compare costs by train. Today the rail journey can actually be competitive in terms of price and if you don't want to get to your holiday destination in the quickest possible time or you want to see some of the country as you go, this can provide a highly acceptable alternative. You can buy an international timetable to plan routes in advance.

Beware of brochures which feature all sorts of special offers: if you book a little further down the page you'll usually find that these 'specials' are only available at certain times of the season (maybe April when you wouldn't want to go on holiday), or they are not all available at the same time – you can actually only choose one, contrary to the impression given. Always double check that you get these cut price offers when the bill comes in!

Children are sometimes given special terms, so look out for firms offering such a saving. This may mean you taking your holiday at a specific time (perhaps early or later in the season) to get the reductions, so that must be put in the balance when deciding.

Compare the prices from as wide a selection of brochures as possible. Many a holidaymaker has had their holiday quite spoiled by the fact that they discover, while in Ibiza or Corfu, that someone staying in the same hotel and enjoying exactly the same facilities is paying considerably less for the privilege! It happens fairly frequently in fact that different tour operators

charge more or less for the same holiday. The 'more' or 'less' can be as much as £50 and with a family of four that adds up to a cool £200. There's only one way to avoid it happening to you. Get a lot of brochures. When you've dediced where you want to holiday – make a game out of comparing prices. Divide the brochures between the various members of your family and get one person to act as note-taker. What you do is call out in turn the price each operator is charging for the same duration of holiday at the same hotel and the note-taker jots down the cheapest.

It may sound a bit dull but once you've done a few comparisons and discovered just how much you could save by playing the game, enthusiasm will grow! When doing comparisons remember to compare like with like – package holidays starting midweek should be compared with others starting at the same time – compare the same dates, too, because charges vary with the season – and full board holidays with full board.

Cross Channel ferry crossings involve several considerations. In fact, there's an art to travelling this way and it can pay – both in money and comfort – to learn that art!

* Don't assume that charges will be the same with every company and on every route. The size of car can make a difference for instance. Many ferry operators divide them into three groups and the longer your chassis the higher the cost, but

there's at least one operator who treats a Mini exactly as he would a Rolls Royce.

* There's a right time of day and a right time of week to travel too. Costs could be cut by as much as a third if you're prepared to make the trip very early morning (like 1 a.m. or 5 a.m. – each operator has his own idea of 'early') and could be cut if you pick a weekday rather than a weekend to head for the Continent. And if you want a little comfort, a cabin can be cheaper at night on short crossings than it is during the day, but cheaper during the day than at night on longer crossings. So if Dad's a night shift worker a day cabin might be ideal!
* Remember – the more you save on the journey, the more you can spend when you get there.

Cut price holiday bargains advertised by little known companies should be treated with caution. Go for an established firm which is a member of the Association of British Travel Agents (ABTA) or the Bus and Coach Council, because these organizations give a guarantee that, if disasters happen, they will help out holidaymakers by getting them home again or whatever. If you have paid by credit card, the credit card company will be liable, with certain provisos.

To check on a company's credentials, contact ABTA (at 55-57 Newman Street, London, W1A 4AH) in the case of an agent and the Department of Transport in the case of a coach company.

Early booking nearly always means you can get a 'no surcharges' guarantee with many holiday firms. This can be a worthwhile saving since the surcharge can be 10% of the total or more. Read the brochures carefully for dates in this context, because there's a wide variation – sometimes you have to book as early as the end of January to get this special surcharge concession, sometimes as far on in the season as the end of March.

Elderly and handicapped people included in your party will need certain extra facts. Ask about any steep slopes near the hotel you fancy, which can prove awkward to negotiate.

Get extra booking conditions, such as babysitting services, a ground floor room, no single supplement, special diet (e.g. Kosher cooking) requests, in writing from your agent. It may not avoid disasters but it will certainly make them easier to put right, if you have written evidence to back up your claim.

Glossy pictures of fantastic beaches and hotels can sometimes tell only half the tale: there can be a factory just out of camera range, or the beach can turn out to be miles away. So how does one avoid disappointment?

Ask the travel agent if he'll let you have a look at a 'trade only' publication called 'Agents' Hotel Gazetteer'. That will give you plain and accurate information about both the resort and the hotel you think might suit you. The guide generally doesn't pull punches. There are guides covering most European countries and America. Incidentally, if the agent denies all knowledge of such a publication or says he can't let customers see a copy, then go to an agent who will.

Hotels in Britain can sometimes seem remarkably cheap when you 'phone or write to ask for their charges. But it may not be quite so cheap as you think, because some have a habit of quoting the price exclusive of VAT, service charges etc. So get the inclusive figures in writing every time before you make a booking, then you won't get a nasty shock when the bill is presented to you.

An international reply coupon can often speed things up considerably if you're making your own accommodation arrangements abroad. This is the equivalent of sending someone a stamped addressed envelope in the UK. The coupons are available from the Post Office. And it's worth remembering that whoever you are writing to may not speak English at all – or may have only a very limited grasp of it – so keep your letter simple and clear. If you want to be quite sure your letter will be understood, why not find out whether a teacher at your children's school is qualified to draft out a letter for you.

Phone bookings should always be followed up by a written one. Receptionists can leave, fall ill or simply have their attention diverted in that moment before they write down what you've just said to them on the phone, then forget to do it at all. Always include a phone number with your booking letter, so that if there is any change of plan you can be told about it just as quickly as possible.

Nip down to your local library or railway station and take a photocopy of your letter, just in case there are any suggestions that it might have been lost in the post!

Points to check before signing on the dotted line:

* Is the flight during the day or at night?
* Do you get meals on the journey or do you have to provide your own?
* Is transport arranged from airport to your hotel?
* Is the kind of room you want – single, double or with balcony, actually available on the holiday you want?
* Are there extra charges for a single room?
* Are there extras like taxes to pay at your destination?
* Does the price quoted include travel from Glasgow, Edinburgh, Newcastle, Manchester or wherever . . . or does it simply apply to the London take-off point?

Standby seats aren't always worth the saving they represent. It has to be weighed against the risk of not getting a seat at all and losing a day or so of your holiday as a result. During the high season the risk is naturally higher than if you're going out of season.

When is a double room not a double-bedded room? Quite often these days, when twin beds are much in fashion due to the flexibility they give the hotelier. So if you want a double bed, then you'll have to do better than simply book 'a double room': you'll have to specify a double bed.

Youngsters and students in the family can often get cut price fares on airlines and on trains. Check this well in advance of making firm bookings because you may, in the case of students, require a letter or other confirmation from a college or university about the full time study.

Customs

Avoid arguments over the origin of expensive-looking cameras, radios, binoculars and similar things you may have actually bought in the UK to take on holiday with you but which the eagle-eyed customs man is convinced came from the Costa Brava. Take the receipts for these items from UK shops with you. Otherwise you might find they are confiscated and you will be involved in a long drawn-out hassle trying to prove you aren't due to pay duty on them.

Children – if you've got a large family – can't be relied on to get you increased duty free allowances. While under-seventeens are allowed to bring some items in without the imposition of duty, what they can't bring in is tobacco and alcohol.

Make a list of all the items you've acquired abroad on the boat or the plane trip home and have it ready to reel off when you go through customs. It's easy to forget the things you've bought which must be declared at customs, so don't be caught out with a bottle of brandy in your case when you have blandly informed the gentleman in the peaked cap 'Nothing to declare'.

Plants are best left where they are. If you're the kind of person who goes around begging strangers as well as friends for cuttings of this and that from their garden, then curb your collective instincts while abroad! Restrictions and rules regarding the 'import' of plants (and that can literally mean one cutting) are very strict indeed. Some flowers and plants of the wild variety need a licence from the Ministry of Agriculture and they have to inspect them even if they do let you bring them in! Even bulbs from Holland can't simply be put into your suitcase: they must be inspected first by a plant health officer in the country where you buy them. The point about that procedure is that if the bulbs are passed, you'll get a Phyto-sanitary certificate (yes, really you will!) which must be handed to the customs officer back home.

If you are utterly determined to bring some floral fancy back from your holiday – perhaps you found an edelweiss on the Alps – there is a way you can get the plant through customs without difficulty. You can bring it back cut (that's the flower not the whole plant complete with roots) or you can dry it or press it or settle for a few seeds.

Remember that there are two separate categories of duty free allowances. One is for goods you buy in a normal retail shop in an EEC country on which you have paid duty or VAT to that country – and another is for goods obtained duty and tax free in the EEC or goods bought outside the EEC. In the main, the amount of cigarettes, alcohol, perfume, toilet water and so on, which you're allowed without duty being payable is more generous from countries within the EEC than outside it.

Save your blushes if you are unlucky and are asked to turn out your suitcases by the customs officer, by carefully placing your purchases right at the top of the suitcase.

Vegetables are just as much protected from tourists as plants are. Even if you want to bring in a bag of potatoes, you may well require that same certificate (see 'Plants', opposite) issued by the country of origin.

EMERGENCIES

Always make a note of your passport number, date and place of issue and put it in a safe place separate from the passport. If you lose it when you're abroad, don't panic (or at least panic as little as possible) because you won't be stuck in the Sahara or whichever exotic holiday spot you've picked for the foreseeable future. You can get back! First report the loss to the local police, then go to the nearest British Embassy or High Commission where they should be able to issue you with the required documents.

Cash is the easiest thing to lose and if this particular disaster strikes you in foreign climes, then the first thing you must do is report it to the local police. This is not because there is any great hope of them catching the thieves but because most insurance companies require police confirmation of a theft when it comes to a claim. Having told the police, contact your insurance company. They like to be told within 24 hours and will want written confirmation from the police that you reported the theft.

Continentals can be odd about accidents – so if you're travelling by car stop, however minor the mishap. In some countries, any kind of accident involving a car should be reported to the police as a matter of law. You can check out the policy in regard to this, of any particular country, through your motoring organization or a tourist office before you go. It's not a bad idea to keep your camera at the ready when you're motoring abroad, so that you can take a quick pic to have handy as evidence. Don't forget to take a note of the names and addresses of any witnesses to the incident, too.

Crimes against a foreign country's laws may not always be obvious. In Spain, for example, they consider the wearing of a bikini a crime in certain areas – you could be arrested. Keep your cool, even in the Mediterranean heat, and ask the police to let you contact the British Consul. Hopefully he will arrange to have a local lawyer assist you. If you're on a package holiday, let the local representative know what's going on (by whatever means you can). They may be able to get you out of gaol.

Cutting short your holiday because of an emergency at home is unfortunately something which is necessary on occasions. So what do you do if the same thing happens to you when you're on holiday abroad? If you're on a package holiday, the local rep is your best source of help in getting back home as quickly as possible. If you're travelling on an independent basis get down to the airline office as quickly as you can, or 'phone them. Ordinary tickets can normally be exchanged to allow you to get on the next available flight at no extra cost. If your ticket happens to be related to one flight time only, then you might find you have to pay a little extra to get things rearranged but in emergency situations most airlines are understanding and will do all they can to help get you back home just as quickly as they can.

Emergency services aren't at the end of a 999 call but it could just be a 110 call, as in West Germany. Most European countries do, in fact, have their emergency services listed in the 'phone directory just as we do in the UK. So if someone falls ill or is injured and you want to call an ambulance, head for the nearest 'phone box. If you have to contact someone back home concerning the illness, then the best place to ask for help is the British Embassy.

Fires in hotels happen, so be prepared. Before you go, ask your travel agent what arrangements there are in the hotel in the event of fire. And when you reach your hotel, double check there on fire escapes, fire drills and so on. Insist on getting the information when you sign the register and settle in, particularly if your room is above the first floor.

Medical treatment can be difficult to organize if you can't speak the particular language. If you've arranged insurance with the right company before you left home, you need have no worries on this score. Some tour operators have a Europe Assistance service, normally arranged through an insurance policy. You telephone them at their London number and they will contact doctors and hospitals in your holiday country. They will arrange a cash deposit if you need one, guarantee payment of bills and even arrange an air ambulance if that's required. The service operates on a 24 hour basis.

Strikes at the ferry terminal can be expensive as well as boring. You will need a meal and may need somewhere to sleep. So before you go on holiday, take out insurance with a motoring organization. You will then receive vouchers to pay for meals, accommodation and so on – as part of a family policy.

Suitcases which end up in Boston while you're in Bordeaux, considerably reduce the possibility of a pleasurable break. However, cheer yourself up with this statistic: Bagtrac, a computer which searches for lost luggage which most of the main airlines use, can claim to find 80% of what's lost within 24 hours.

To set Bagtrac in motion, you report the loss straightaway to the baggage superintendent's office and tell him all you can about it, such as the distinctive labels it has, the scratch on the lid of the suitcase and other such endearing details. Leave a note of your address and if your luggage hasn't turned up within that 24 hours ask for some money to buy a toothbrush and so on. If the computer and the staff fail to produce your case within seven days, make a claim in writing. The address to write to should be given on your insurance policy. Obviously you're going to need something to wear in the meantime nad some cash to buy it with – here's where, if you're on a package tour, you put on your most woebegone expression and go to the local tour representative. Provided that you're insured with the tour operator's scheme, they are likely to lend you at least £50. Some insurance policies include cover for delayed buggage.

Travellers' cheques save trouble – or so many people believe, but if you lose them you may not get the instant refund you imagined you would. Before you buy them back home, ask what arrangements are available in the area you're spending your holidays in, should you lose them. Sometimes sterling cheques from a bank can mean you have to notify the branch in the UK and go through all sorts of complicated procedures, while you are left without cash to cover the cost of your next meal. Before you go on holiday make sure you take with you, in a safe place, the receipt given to you when you bought the cheques. Keep it somewhere separate from the cheques.

HEALTH

America, and most countries outside the EEC do not have an arrangement for medical expenses. To ensure you don't have to take out a mortgage to pay for your treatment, take out adequate insurance instead (see page 273). There are lots of policies on offer and indeed some package holiday companies insist on you paying for the policy they provide as part of the package. If you're in any doubt, it always pays to take out additional cover. The policy recommended by the Association of British Travel Agents (ABTA) for instance, provides cover for an unlimited amount in terms of medical expenses, for up to 12 months' treatment.

Be prepared – take with you on holiday alongside any other personal papers, a note of medical information which might be relevant if you were ill or in hospital. Blood group; any allergies to drugs; a prescription for glasses or contact lenses; and if you are diabetic or suffer from epilepsy, note that too.

Chronic illness of any sort need not cut out your chances of getting insurance for your holiday. It's just a matter of travelling with a tour operator which offers insurance to suit your circumstances or taking out cover independently with an insurance company which caters for such problems.

Common Market membership does entitle EEC nationals who are resident in the UK to immediately necessary treatment while on holiday in other EEC countries. In some countries the treatment is free, in others you may have to pay a percentage of the costs and repatriation is never covered. You will need a certificate of entitlement (Form E111) unless you are visiting Denmark or Ireland. Leaflet SA30 (available from local offices of the Department of Health and Social Security) explains how to get one. Apply for the certificate at least a month before you leave. The procedure to be followed in each country is explained in Leaflet SA36 which will be sent to you with your form E111. This tells you with which countries the UK has some form of agreement covering medical expenses. Not every country has the same procedure so check this out – some will require only the production of your passport, others want to see your NHS medical card. This doesn't give you the kind of comprehensive medical treatment you'll get at home for free nor does it cover repatriation expenses, but you could regard it as a useful extra to any insurance you may have taken out privately.

Diabetics need to be wary of time zones. If you fly across them, so that the day is prolonged by more than four hours, you'll usually be offered an extra meal. Take it by all means, but also adjust insulin intake to cope. The British Diabetic Association have a booklet called 'Holidays and Travel for Diabetics'.

Exclusion clauses should be carefully noted in holiday cover. The kind of thing you could find you're not covered for are: 'dangerous' sports such as hill climbing or skin diving; driving or riding pillion on a motor cycle you've hired while on holiday; dental treatment; venereal diseases.

Check that if you have to be flown back home for specialist treatment the policy will pay out, will also cover the cost of someone travelling back with you and any extra hotel bills you run up as a result of the illness or accident.

Healthy holidays may mean a course of injections before you go. Usually a good tour operator or travel agent will advise you exactly what is necessary for where but make your own enquiries too and thus save any last minute hitches. The DHSS has a leaflet called 'Protect Your Health Abroad' (SA35) which gives full details of exactly what jabs are advisable for particular countries, which are compulsory and also tells you where you can get them. Some jabs have to be done as much as eight weeks in advance, so get the leaflet in plenty of time. It's available from DHSS International Relations Division, Alexander Fleming House, London SE1 6BY. If you are taking pills or medicine on a regular basis, this may be affected by crossing time zones. Always have a word with your G.P. before you go, tell him where you are holidaying and ask him whether any adjustments in the times you take the medicine will be required.

Heat – which is what everyone wants on holiday – can bring as many problems as benefits, so treat it with respect and take precautions.

* Drink more water or soft drinks than you would normally.
* Take extra salt either on your food or in the form of tablets.
* White clothes rather than dark can cut down by half the heat absorbed by your body.
* Don't sunbathe for very long on your first day on the beach: ten minutes is quite enough.
* Wear a hat and use plenty of suntan lotion for protection.
* Choose a cream or oil which has a very high 'protection factor' in it. The maximum rating on suntan cream is 15, so check it out before you buy. If you have children with you this is even more important because their skin can be particularly delicate and subject to severe sunburn.

Malaria is still prevalent in some places – and if you venture to one of these you're going to need a course of anti-malaria tablets from your doctor. The course will begin before your holiday does (and will continue after you return), so have a word with your local G.P. about it and see what he advises.

Pregnancy is no bar to a happy holiday but it may restrict your travel arrangements.

* Airlines for instance demand a medical certificate after 28

weeks declaring that you are in fact quite fit to fly. After 36 weeks they won't allow you to travel at all.

* Boats have their own rules regarding pregnant passengers in spite of the fact that most cruise ships have their own doctor on board all the time. Those rules vary from one cruise company to another, so you must always check, but after seven months you'll probably have great difficulty persuading them to let you up the gangplank.
* Package holidays where air or boat travel is part of it are slightly more flexible in their approach to pregnancy. Most tour operators will leave holidaymakers to make up their own minds.

Seawater can be quite good for hands and nails, however dry and stringy it can make your hair look. However, it can take out some moisture, so take a large jar or tube of your favourite hand cream with you and use it regularly while you're on holiday.

Spiny creatures, sea urchins and jellyfish, can be real holiday hazards on some Mediterranean beaches! If you step on them they'll almost certainly sting you, but they might produce a state of shock too in some people (and that's quite apart from the shock you get standing on them). Take precautions. Rubber or plastic shoes may not be the best fashion accessory for a swimsuit but they will provide protection from these nuisances – so let people laugh and play safe.

Sunglasses are essential for sunny holidays. Get a really good pair before you go. Don't be tempted to buy a cheap pair, which turn out to be little more than coloured glass, as they will not cut out harmful radiations from the sun, they will merely slightly reduce the intensity of the light. So buy the best you can afford and keep them in their case or in a soft pouch because once lenses become scratched they aren't so effective.

Traveller's tummy may be the stuff of music hall humour but it can make a holiday something less than a joke to the person afflicted by this misery. So take precautions where possible when you're abroad. The cause can range from an infection in some Middle East countries to unfamiliar cooking methods or just eating more than normal. Kaolin and morphine which are available in liquid and tablet form can minimize some of the effects but try these avoiding tactics:

* Don't eat anything unless you're sure it's thoroughly cooked.
* Any fresh fruit and vegetables, even simple things like tomatoes, are better peeled before eating or washed first in bottled water.
* The local freshly made ice cream may be very tempting but it can sometimes present a health hazard. So stick to well known brands which come already wrapped.
* Steer clear of salads and shellfish.
* Water for drinking should be boiled in any country where you're not certain how high the hygiene standards are. You can take sterilization tablets with you and add these to the water. Alternatively, buy and drink only mineral waters which are commercially bottled and are likely to be safe.
* Clean your teeth using bottled water.
* Milk – if it's not pasteurized or sterilized – should always be boiled before drinking.

HOME SECURITY

Burglar alarms act as deterrents not only while you're off on your annual holiday but all the year round, too, but they sometimes go off on a false alarm in the middle of the night.

* So if you get one installed, make sure you leave instructions with a neighbour as to how it can be turned off, otherwise you might find you've lost all your friends when you get back.
* A 'mock' alarm fixed to the outside wall can be useful if you are short of money.

A dark house, even on light late summer evenings, will be bound to attract the attention of potential burglars. You have two options here.

* Ask a neighbour to go in regularly every evening, draw the curtains, put on the lights, then do the reverse at the appropriate time.
* Alternatively, fix a time switch which will do the light switching on and off automatically (and some will operate the curtains as well). These switches aren't difficult to install and some will switch on a radio as well as lights which is another good deterrent.

Don't advertise your absence!

* Cancel the milk and the papers.
* Don't talk loudly in local pubs or shops saying you and the family are off for a fortnight in sunny Spain or whatever, you never know who might be listening for just such information.

Insurance doesn't always give you the kind of protection you think it does. When you come to make a claim you could find all sorts of things in the small print you weren't aware of. So, even if your house and contents are thoroughly insured don't feel too smug around holidaytime: get out that policy and check that there are no hidden clauses.

* If you are going off for more than, say, three weeks, check that your policy will still cover you, because some don't pay out if the house is left empty for a certain period. It may be that you are expected to inform the police, turn off the water and so on.
* Look up what the limit is on any single item (it can be 5% of the total contents insurance) and if you feel there's an extra risk because you'll be away, contact your insurance company or broker and ask if you can take out extra cover.

Ladders, steps and similar means of access should be locked securely away in the garage or the garden shed. Leaving them lying out in the garden or by the side of the house is extending an open invitation to any passing burglar.

Lawns should be cut just before you go and perhaps a neighbour will do it again while you are away, so that your absence isn't advertised by knee-high grass.

Lock up both front and back doors as securely as possible – two locks are always better than one, so, if possible, use a mortice and a slam-style lock (Mortice locks can be fitted only on doors which are at least 45 mm (1¾ inches) thick.)

* On the back door put bolts on the inside too – this can pay off, because back doors are probably used more often as means of access than front doors – particularly if you live in a street with other houses where neighbours would notice an intruder at the front.

Mail may or may not be a problem – it all depends on how much of it you get. We've all probably seen bigger pieces of mail stuck halfway through someone's letterbox and it is equally true (although no doubt the Post Office would frown on it) that postmen leave things like mail order catalogues and telephone directories sitting outside the door if they get no answer from the doorbell. This habit has often proved a source of complaint because it can draw attention to the fact that there's no one in the house.

* Ask a neighbour to pop in from time to time just to make sure all your mail is inside the front door and not halfway through it or scattered on the front step.

Small valuables like jewellery, stamp collections, precious coins and so on could be taken to your bank for safe custody.

* There will be a small charge depending on how many valuables you have but some banks are sympathetic to regular clients and give the protection of their strongroom free.

* Alternatively, if you have a safe deposit box already, put your precious things in it while you're away.
* Safes installed in your own home will also provide protection, although not necessarily against professional burglars.

Trying to imagine breaking into your own house may seem daft – but it's a very good way of finding out just how secure it is!

* Imagine that you've lost your key, then think about how you would find your way in without it. If, for example, it would be very easy to smash a pane of glass in the kitchen door and gain entry that way or slip a knife blade between sash window frames to open the catch, then you'll know that any burglar could do the same.
* Find out the weak points and strengthen them.

Videos, Hi-fis and other pieces of easily portable electronic equipment should be moved well out of sight from prying eyes: they are top of the takeaways for modern burglars. You can put such items up in the attic for safe keeping, especially if it is only accessible by a ladder, which you put out of the way. The chances are that, unless your thief is very professional or very determined, he's unlikely to risk being seen carrying a ladder into the house just to get into the attic. So it's worth a try – but don't put too many items away or you will arouse suspicion and the thief may start looking around for them. Moderation, as always, is the best policy.

Windows need locks, too, wherever possible and certainly any which are easy to get at. That means on the ground floor or above a flat roof of an extension or a garage building.

* All windows can be secured from the inside with simple and not too expensive D.I.Y. devices. Go along to your local iron-mongers to see what's in stock.
* Don't leave a small window open for the cat – that's exactly the kind of thing a thief will spot and take advantage of. Have a proper cat flap fitted to the back door. One thing though – get it fitted well in advance of the holiday and make sure your pet becomes familiar with this means of access to the house. Don't fit one at the last minute – or the poor cat will still be expecting to get in and out the window and may not be able to get out of the house.

PACKING

Checklist of basics:

Toiletries:	Face cloth or sponge Toothbrush and paste Razor and blades Talcum powder Cologne/aftershave Deodorant Nailbrush Shampoo Soap Suntan preparations After-sun preparations
Cosmetics:	Packed in small plastic bottles or tubes – things like cleanser, moisturiser and so on. Plus your usual lip and eye make-up.
Medical:	Whatever essentials you have decided to take (see page 303) – things like aspirins, TCP, elastoplast etc.
Extras:	Needle and thread and safety pins for running repairs. Small torch. Sunglasses. Packaway umbrella. Tin opener. Writing paper and envelopes (a few of each). Books to read. Maps and guide books. Address book. Travel and insurance documents. Travelling iron. Hair curler (if it adapts to voltage abroad).
Accessories:	Belts; shoes; tights; socks for all the family; scarves; a spare handbag; gloves; jewellery; ties.
Clothes:	How much you take will depend on the individual – but don't take too much – fashion everywhere is so casual these days that it's quite possible for every member of the family to get by quite happily with mainly separates which can be changed around to give different looks.

Jeans – for every member of the family take 2 pairs.
Tops – a selection of T-shirts, blouses or shirts and a heavier sweater or cardigan for everyone in case it gets colder. Shirts and blouses should of course be drip dry where possible.
Swimming things.
Underwear.
Two dresses for the females in the family – but preferably something loose and kaftan-like which can be worn during the day, on the beach even, and for a night out.
Bathing wraps or bath robes which can double up as dressing gowns.
Towels.
Jacket for the menfolk – of a lightweight (and preferably fairly uncrushable) material.
Foldaway raincoats for everyone.

Notes

* Don't take hats on holiday – they are awkward to pack and are usually very cheap to buy in the various resorts.
* Do try to make things do double duty where possilbe – an extra foldaway shopper for instance can be used as a beach bag. Alternatively, save even more space and money by simply using large plastic bags for taking towels and things to the beach and carrying wet swimwear back to the hotel (gather together shop carrier bags before you go and put several in your suitcase).
* Try to take shoes which pack flat – sandals, canvas number and so on – they save space and travel better.

ACCIDENTS

Avoid accidents in the air by NOT packing the following items:

* Camera film, which may suffer damage if you are subjected to any kind of security checks with X-ray type machines.
* Aerosols of anything from suntan lotion to hairspray which seem absolutely leakproof at ground level (and for just that reason may seem to be the ideal packaging) can develop leaks at high altitude.

* Lighter fuel is absolutely forbidden, so leave it at home and use matches instead if your lighter runs out while in flight.

BAGGAGE ALLOWANCE

Packing too much means paying for it, because both planes and trains allow passengers to take only a certain amount of baggage free.

* Ask at the airline or station what that allowance is and try to stick to it. The amount can vary according to whether you're on an international or a European and domestic flight or even on a package holiday and whether you're travelling first or second class.
* If, on the other hand, you prefer to travel with everything including the kitchen sink, then there are a couple of ways you can do so at less cost. The first is merely dependent on asking to send it freight, the second takes a lot more nerve, since it involves hanging around at the check-in point until you hear someone's baggage allowance being called out which is well within the amount permitted. What you do then – and this is where the nerve comes in – is suggest that your extras be counted in with their 'free'.
* If you want to keep an eye on the weight of your luggage before you get to the station or airport either buy luggage scales (not too pricey and can be used for weighing other things throughout the year) or rely on the bathroom scales instead.
* If you plan to send luggage separately and in advance of your own travel date, make sure you allow enough time for it to reach your holiday destination.
* Sending by rail can take over a week's notice and delivery and collection facilities by van from your home may only be possible in certain areas.
* Lively labels can help you spot your luggage as it hurtles along the conveyor belt at the airport. Make your own from brightly coloured pieces of paper stuck on to the surface – use those indelible pens (the kind you use to label freezer packs) for your name on the label. Don't put your address on the outside, as this is a give-away for opportunist burglars.
* Try a couple of tie-ons too, then inside the lid of the case put another stick-on label with full details of your name, address and phone number, so that, if lost it can be returned.

* A note of your holiday name and address (and the dates you'll actually be there) is useful, too, so that if the case is found in time it can perhaps be re-routed to you there.

BETTER SAFE THAN SORRY

A strong strap's a good buy for giving a little extra security to your holiday holdalls or suitcases.

* A strong lock is also a good thing but these can tend to go a bit wonky over the years, so check them from time to time and add a drop of oil as required.
* An extra set of keys may well prevent you having to break into your own suitcase, so get them cut well in advance of your travel date and keep them separate from the original set (but not inside the case).

CAR BOOTS

If you're travelling by car do a trial run with your luggage in the boot. It's only when you try to fit it all in that you may suddenly realise just what awkward shapes your cases are.

* If you can't afford a whole new set of suitcases, a roof rack for the car is an alternative to think about.

CLOTHES' BAGS

Wardrobe bags, hanging bags and similar inventions seem like such a good idea but check with friends, who have actually used them, before you buy.

* They don't always keep your clothes as uncrushed as one might hope and if your family goes in for easy-to-care-for clothes in synthetic fabrics, such bags are an unnecessary expense.

CONTENTS

The contents of your suitcase somehow always seem to swell in that summer sun, so that by the time it comes to pack up again for the return journey, even several strong men sitting on the lid of the case don't get it closed! It's all those 'extras' we buy, of course, that cause the problem.

* Avoid strain to yourself and your suitcases by taking some kind of packaway, fold-up bag with you. There are several types to choose from. One which takes up very little space indeed and can even be popped into your handbag, is a fabric type which zips up into a flat compact rectangle measuring only a few inches either way.
* There are times when two suitcases or bags are better than one and going on holiday is one of those times. If you pack everything into one large case and it ends up in Tangiers while you and your partner are having a couple of days in Paris, both of you will be without clothes. So each should take his or her own case but in it pack some of the partner's more essential items, that way you'll both have at least a change of clothes in the event of only one case being lost.
* Another good reason for two suitcases rather than one is that two small are far easier to carry than one large.

ELECTRICAL ITEMS

Try to take as many washable, uncrushable items in your suitcases as possible. But if you pack a small iron you can be quite sure of making an unruffled appearance at all times.

* Don't just take any old iron or you'll probably find it tricky to plug it into the electricity supplies in some countries. Buy one

designed for the job which operates on two voltages, and if necessary buy adaptors which will cope with several different fittings. Don't ever guess – ask a reliable electrical shop to advise on which particular iron and adaptor you're likely to need for whatever country you're visiting.

* Be very wary of buying an iron or any other gadget abroad. Rice cookers of a classy Continental make and design which look as though they'd be just the thing to take the trouble out of cooking the stuff in a British kitchen, have all too often turned out to be useless since they couldn't be used with UK electricity supplies.

HAND LUGGAGE

Large handbags come into their own at holiday time – since ladies are allowed to take a handbag on to the plane with them, as well as a 'carry bag', as personal luggage.

* Pack just as much as you can into your handbag. Items like toilet equipment and spare pairs of tights for instance can become hand luggage.

INSIDE THE SUITCASE

Everyone has their own special way of packing and some are more expert at it than others – but if you haven't worked out your own formula yet, try these basic rules for best results.

* Put awkward little things into the bottom of the case and 'level them off' with soft flexible items like tights or undies which can be rolled up or folded as you like without any problem about creasing. If you get uneven layers you'll get things all out of shape.
* Put heavier garments nearer the bottom of the case, so that they don't crush the lighter ones.
* Separate each layer with a piece of tissue paper folded to fit the dimensions of the case or large plastic bags (these could be useful for all sorts of things when you're on holiday).
* If you want to be really organized make a note of the items in the various layers and put it right at the top – that way if you are looking for something you can find it without unpacking the lot.
* Shoes should be wrapped in plastic bags – but they needn't

always be packed in pairs. Often one can be squeezed down into a corner of a case while the other can be put in elsewhere and give much more space than if you insisted on putting them in pair by pair.

* Sandals and casual styles with uppers which pack flat do tend to take up the least space.
* Don't take slippers unless you absolutely must, instead use a pair of beach mules to double up or choose a pair of those flat packs which literally fold up into a plastic envelope.
* Pleated skirts should be carefully rolled up longways and pulled through the leg of an old pair of nylon tights (or stocking) and they will stay crease-free in your case.
* Skirts with small kick pleats should have these stitched into place (a few large tacking type stitches will do the trick) to keep them in place while in transit.
* Two tips to keep things crease-free: first fold them crossways and not lengthways, so that when you take them out and hang them up the creases will hopefully drop out more more easily. And to prevent really firm creases forming at folds, you can make little 'rolls' out of face tissues (or toilet paper, it's probably cheaper), then put the 'roll' on the inside of the fold.

LAUNDERING

Do you want to leave all thoughts of ironing at home? Then choose cotton jersey, cheesecloth, terylene and as many drip dry shirts and blouses as you can muster.

* Evening tops should be simple and uncrushable.
* Jeans of course are also OK – they can probably last out the holiday without laundering and shouldn't need ironing. If you do wash them, slightly wrinkled jeans are acceptable.
* The minimum to take, if you wish to take anything at all, would be some washing powder in a small, securely sealed container, a travelling iron (with voltage adaptor if necessary) and a couple of fold-up hangers.

MAKE-UP

Pretty summertime faces don't need a maximum of make-up, so don't overload your case with too many beauty items.

* Invest in one of those little flat boxes with a selection of face

paints, which will cover everything from your eyes to your lips, each in a small portion on the palette.
* Do take plenty of moisturizer to counteract the drying effect of the sun.

MEDICINE

No one wants to anticipate trouble – but it's a good idea just the same to pack a few basic items for the medicine cabinet. It's not much fun standing in a chemist's shop hopping about on one foot in utter agony and trying to explain in non-existent French that you've just been stung by a wasp and can you please have something to soothe the pain!
* Stick to some aspirin or whatever painkiller your family prefers; travel sickness tablets; something for tummy upsets; sticking plaster; insect repellant; a small tube of sting ointment; antiseptic cream; indigestion tablets; some TCP and calamine lotion.
* Take them in small sizes and in non-breakable packs – either plastic containers or tubes.
* If in any doubt about what you should take for any particular country, have a word with your local chemist and take his advice.

SUITCASES

Spare a thought for your suitcase: not what to put in it, but what kind of case is best for your particular purpose and is also reasonably priced.
* Leather was once the traditional choice and is still around, but although it looks good and lasts a lifetime, it can weigh a ton – even without your clothes and holiday souvenirs inside!
* Soft-sided models look smart, modern and – simply because they are flexible – can be easier to pack.
* If you like to travel light, holdalls have a whole lot going for them. For a start, you can take one with you on a plane as hand baggage, so you've no worries about it being lost.
* Check out the size allowed by the airline before you buy one of these bags.
* Castors are what every weak and weary traveller needs! They'll help you beat the queues too. Cases with their own

integral wheels can be a little limiting but a separate set you can attach to any case, then fold away neatly when not required, is just what you need. Incidentally, make sure you're fully insured for third party damage – these 'wheelies' can do a lot of damage if you're a learner driver!

TOILETRIES

It's temping to bundle all your toilet items into one big bag – but in the first place it will be difficult to pack, and in the second place you'll simply end up with a clutter of bits and bobs and find it very difficult to lay your hands on anything.

* Split them up into groups and pack them separately (don't go to a lot of expense, ordinary household plastic bags will do and they have the distinct advantage of being see-through). The products you use for your hair can go in one bag, for nails and feet into another, bath things into yet another and so on.
* Avoid taking standard sizes of all these toiletries, instead get some small plastic bottles and put just enough into them to last the week or the fortnight.
* For face washing, the item which takes up the least possible space is a sort of magic cloth. You can buy them as very small cylinders which look rather like large sweets and appear to be made of compressed paper, they're usually packed two or three in their own plastic bag. However, the 'magic' comes in when you pop the little round object into water. It turns itself into a proper facecloth made of material very similar to terry towelling.

PASSPORTS

Without a passport you won't be allowed to enter a foreign country, so if you're planning a holiday abroad you must apply for one well before you go. Consider the following:

* Get an application form and send it to your area office at least a month before your departure date. There are passport offices in London; Liverpool, Glasgow, Peterborough and Newport (Gwent) and Belfast and you can take your application there in person or send it by post.
* A visitor's passport sounds a lot less trouble and is cheaper than the standard one. But consider its disadvantages and be sure that it will actually suit your purpose, before you apply. It can only be used for leisure – not for business travel. It's only valid for a year and it can only be used in certain Western European countries, Canada, and some other specified countries. But, if you have forgotten to get your standard one in time or you are desperately short of cash, then certainly the visitor's version can be issued to you more or less on the spot

at a main Post Office. You'll need two photographs and some proof of identity such as a birth certificate, NHS medical card or pension book.

* For 1½ times the cost of an individual passport you can get a family passport which includes husband, wife and children. The disadvantage is that whichever of the couple is 'included' rather than being the holder, can't use it independently. So unless you can be certain you won't travel abroad on your own during the ten year duration of the passport, don't risk it. Incidentally you can't have it both ways – have your own passport and be on the family one too.
* You don't always need a passport to go across the Channel – some firms offer air or ferry trips for up to forty-eight hours duration to allow holidaymakers to nip across to the Continent briefly. Instead you get an identity card supplied at the point of departure by the organizers of the excursion.
* Any child can have his or her own passport and there's a special application form for this purpose. A child over the age of sixteen doesn't have any option but to have his or her own. Under sixteens can be included on a family passport but they then have to travel only with the parent who is the passport holder. However, if parents each have their own passport, then children can in fact be named on both parents' passports. Children can also be included on the passport of a relative such as an aunt or grandparent, providing a letter of consent is given by the parent.
* Photos for passports must be signed by someone 'responsible' according to the regulations. If you're not a church goer, don't know any local magistrates and don't speak to your bank manager, then you have a problem. Try the Citizens' Advice Bureau or your local library for advice on getting someone to sign, or contact the Passport Office.
* Ask your travel agent if you'll need a visa for the country you're going to. The United States, Eastern European, Middle Eastern, Far Eastern and African countries generally want one, so make enquiries well in advance of your holiday.
* Change your passport to your married name, if appropriate. Your passport is a document of identity and airlines, especially, check passports against the passenger list and require that the names are consistent. Also, remember to include new babies on your passport.

PETS AND PLANTS

Bag your houseplants! If you're only off for a week you can put small foliage plants in plastic bags to keep them comfortable and moist. Water the plants thoroughly, then put each pot into a bag – big enough for it to fit inside with ease – trap as much air as you can inside the bag and secure with a rubber band to make the whole thing airtight. If the plant has been well watered before being bagged it should stay moist – but remember not for more than a week. Other plants that are being left for no longer than one week should be watered well, then put in a shady area.

Boarding out any animal – dog or cat – needs careful consideration and a good deal of research in advance. Don't ever make a last minute decision and just ring any kennels or cattery which happens to be nearby. Check around with neighbours and friends for recommendations, ask your vet perhaps, then visit the kennels for yourself. You may have to book as much as two months in advance – so be prepared for this. Be prepared for the price too – it could cost as much as £50 for a fortnight for a dog. Practically all kennels these days will want your dog to have the normal vaccinations – so will catteries – and they will demand evidence. So check on this before you book to avoid any last minute snags.

Cats, goldfish, rabbits, budgies and similar pets may well be best left at home in familiar surroundings and with a friend of yours ready to pop in on a regular basis to feed them. If this is what you decide on, be sure to give the pet minder precise instructions as to what and when they all get fed, otherwise you may find the goldfish on the same diet as the budgie! Buy in sufficient food to last the holiday period. Leave a note of your regular vet's phone number just in case of any emergencies.

Cats will settle down well in a rented cottage but they shouldn't be taken to hotels. Dogs can go to hotels on the other hand, but only if they are actually welcomed and that's something you should find out in advance. Never just arrive with an animal, however cute, not unless you're prepared to end up in the dog house yourself! There are many books and brochures published which give details of thousands of hotels, inns and guest houses in the UK which welcome pets.

Certain breeds of dogs are inclined to be car sick. So pay a visit to the vet and get some pills for the dog. If yours isn't a regular pill popper be sure it actually eats them by concealing the pill in a small portion of food and hopefully the dog will gobble it down without looking. But don't under any circumstances give dogs a large meal before setting off on a car journey. And although one doesn't want to get any animal hooked on pills there is simply no point in it fretting and getting nervous in a car and making its owners equally anxious. Instead, ask the vet for mild tranquillizers for your pet and you'll all travel better.

Dogs definitely cannot be left in the house – even if there are plenty of local volunteers to pop in and see them – they can pine, get restless and even cause damage by chewing and tearing things! They either need to go to a helpful friend or to a reputable kennels.

In dry weather new plants need plenty of care. If you have to leave something newly planted while you're on holiday, try this: Take the bottom off a plastic squash bottle. Push the bottomless bottle into the soil neck down. Fill the upturned bottle with water. The water should slowly soak down into the soil and to the roots of your plant provided you've placed the bottle near it.

Large indoor plants like palms or cheese plants will need water while you're away on holiday, so if you can't prevail upon a kindly neighbour to do the job, get a self-watering device.

Plants which need regular watering should first be given a good soaking by standing in their pots in a sink of water. After that they can be positioned on a tray filled with a layer of moist gravel.

Play safe and move your plants away from windowsills where they might be subject to a dose of direct sunlight and give them an alternative spot in some cool but not too dark area. Whatever you do, don't put them in the shade.

Protect your plants in garden and greenhouse from drought while you are away during good weather by enlisting the help of a neighbour. Ask him or her to pop in perhaps once a week to do the watering, paying special attention to anything you have in growbags because these are particularly susceptible to water shortage and do need regular watering. If you have no obliging neighbours and your plants are precious, your only alternative is to purchase one of the automatic watering systems available for greenhouses.

Self-watering containers are useful all year round, especially for those who tend to be absent-minded about plant care. They are particularly helpful at holiday time. The containers are made with a tank in the bottom so that water gets through regularly to the soil. There's also a gauge to show when the tank needs to be refilled. The water in the tank will usually last about a month – which will give you time to have a nice long holiday!

Take a few simple precautions before you go and you may save yourself coming back to an overgrown jungle!

* Mow the lawn.
* Cut any hedges.
* Weed the flowerbeds.
* Put nets over soft fruit bushes to prevent the birds getting the pick of the crop.
* If vegetables are ready to pick – do so, then eat, freeze or give away the produce.
* Any plants you have on a patio should be moved to a shady spot.
* Open vents in the greenhouse and shade the glass with one of the special preparations available for precisely that purpose.

TRAVEL TIPS

Checklist if you're travelling by car:

* Take a basic tool kit with you and some spares (your local garage will advise on which ones if you're not sure and may even be able to provide a kit for your car on a sale or return basis). A list of spares for touring at home might include: a set of contact breaker points; a distributor rotor; a fan belt; top and bottom radiator hoses; insulating tape; a torch; a fire extinguisher and a tow rope. For travel in remote areas and abroad take these as well: a set of lamp bulbs and fuses; at least two sparking plugs; a windscreen wiper blade; an inner tube; a length of HT lead; a length of wire; a tin of gasket compound and a tin of radiator seal.
* Carry a First Aid kit in the car.
* Remember you must display a GB nationality plate. Since we switch road sides for driving on the Continent headlights must be realigned or converted to take account of this.
* Buy a brochure or booklet which gives full details of the law relating to motorists in the various countries. This should only cost a few pence and could save you pounds in fines or even prevent you spending a night in a foreign jail. Be prepared for the fact that the Continentals do have a quite different attitude to law-breaking motorists on occasion. In fact if you are going to Spain it's absolutely essential that you get what's called a 'bail bond' from your insurance company to pay any fines you might incur and get you out from behind those prison bars if need be!
* Registration documents and all other motoring papers should be taken with you – but do keep them in a safe place, not somewhere a pickpocket can reach them for instance. Should you be taking your firm's car with you, it's as well to get your boss to put it in writing that you have authority to do so.

* In France, Norway, Spain and Yugoslavia it is a legal requirement that spare bulbs should be carried in cars – and that applies to foreign tourists too. Some EEC countries, such as Austria, insist on drivers taking a First Aid kit.
* Take one of those red warning triangles with you in case of breakdown – again it's a matter of law in many countries that you must use one.
* Get a 'Green Card' from your insurance company, so that you have adequate cover abroad just as you do at home.
* Most countries accept a UK driving licence but in some an International Driving Permit is required. Find out about this from your nearest AA office.

Airlines may not be overfond of pregnant ladies as passengers (see page 289), but they seem to dote on babies, judging by the amount of special facilities which are provided for this age group! Providing you give them some warning, special food, nappies and even a cot can be provided. If you want to take your own cot on board, check with the airline first. They do allow cots but only within certain dimensions and a certain weight limit.

Arriving at the airport in good time but not with loads of time to spare is something of an art. There are various ways to manage this. If you're taking your own car you can do a 'trial run' of the trip in advance, then add on a little extra in case there's a traffic jam the day you go, due to roadworks, a Royal visit or something similar. Alternatively, book a taxi and ask the firm to call in plenty of time to cover the journey. They will be well used to ferrying passengers to the local airport and will know, probably to the minute, just what time it takes. Alternatively, get an airport bus, having found out from the bus company beforehand which one will get there in time for your flight.

Big airports like Heathrow have nurseries staffed by trained children's nurses. Babies can be fed and changed and the under eights can use the play area which will keep them from under the feet of other passengers – and their parents. Services are normally all free of charge. Another bonus at big airports is a nursing mothers' room which passengers can retire to for a little privacy when baby starts bawling. Often there are no staff in attendance which makes it even more private.

Check on charges before you think of leaving your car in the airport car park while you're away. Some airports let you leave your car absolutely free, others can charge almost £10 for only 24 hours. For a week's parking for instance there is a considerable price variation. Two UK airports make no charge, some charge from £3 to £10 and one major airport will produce a bill for over £50! Alternatively, ask around local garages where you could get cheaper terms. Whatever you do, don't ever just turn up in your car assuming that you can park it with the airport.

Never leave your car unattended outside an airport terminal: the police are quite likely to tow it away after an interval.

Coaches these days are equipped to luxury level but even so this can be a very tedious and tiring way to travel with a toddler or baby. There isn't much seat room for nappy changing and you cannot get up to walk the baby up and down, which is a great disadvantage.

Cushions can increase your comfort on a long coach trip. Forget the inflatable kind, they may be portable but they can get rather hard. Plump instead for one of foam rubber or the aerated kind invalids like. Make it a small cushion – not a sag bag.

Don't be diverted by all the shops, food and facilities available to tempt travellers at airports. Concentrate on your flight number and keep an ear on the announcements and an eye on the departure board.

Fear of flying is quite common amongst airline passengers. However, don't be afraid of telling the airline in advance that you are frightened. At least one airline will put the words 'nervous passenger' alongside your name on the passenger list and you may be given a seat near to the cabin staff, who will keep a check on how you are feeling.

Hired cars on holiday are best booked before you go through one of the big hire firms – you stand a better chance of getting exactly what you want, when you want.

Jet lag is a nuisance if you are travelling through several time zones. The best thing is to give in to it! Just get to bed as soon as you can and the next couple of nights go to bed at least an hour before you normally would and you'll soon get back into your old routine again. An alternative method, which is not quite so painless, is to stay awake until you can go to bed at the time when everybody else does in the new time zone.

Off-peak travel on trains can win you friends and make life a lot easier all round. If your kids are inclined to be noisy (and you can bring yourself to admit the fact) they will obviously be less annoying on a less crowded train! The buffet can be an endless source of amusement (as well as sticky buns) and you may be able to get some hot water there to help with baby feeding. Most importantly, off-peak travel is usually cheaper.

On the midnight express to Moscow – or even just to Paris – in a sleeper, remember to lock your door from the inside. There are burglars even on trains these days.

Smelly socks can put yor travelling companions off, so lots of talcum powder to dust inside your shoes and socks, moistened tissues and a large size of deodorant are necessities. A large bottle of toilet water or cologne with a fresh fragrance will be a bonus for you and those sitting around you!

To relieve pressure on your ears, particularly during take off or landing try swallowing, pinching your nostrils, blowing your nose, or sucking a boiled sweet. Incidentally on some long flights your legs can swell, but it's not something to panic about as the symptoms will go when you get back on the ground again.

Toddlers on a cross Channel ferry, or any boat, should be kept on a tight rein when up on deck. Rails which are usually all that's between them and the water won't keep an inquisitve little person from harm, so don't let young children wander around on their own. If you are breast-feeding and would like some privacy during a day trip, book a cabin, but remember to book early.

Travel sickness can ruin the start of a holiday. So if anyone in your family is prone to it, then the day before you go off, try to keep to plain foods – nothing too fatty, too rich or too sweet. Get travel sickness tablets and take them as instructed. But do be sure not to take them too far in advance or the effects may have worn off by the time the plane takes off or the boat sets sail. For children in cars it will be worsened if they jump about and look around in all directions; encourage them to sit quietly and look ahead instead. Keep a window open and try to keep the person interested; sometimes a car radio can be a help here.

Always be ready for the worst by taking along some plastic bags, tissues and possibly a damp cloth in a plastic container.

Window seats on coach tours and train journeys may seem to be the ideal, but that's only in the cool of the morning! When the sun beats mercilessly down from the sky you may get a grand view of the countryside but you may also get a headache or eyestrain.

Young children in cars should be firmly secured in the back seat and babies need carrycots firmly restrained.

1. About the House
2. Clothes Care
3. Make Amends
4. Table Talk
5. Talking Shop
6. Moving Moments
7. Happy Holidays
8. Children and Pets

SURVIVING CHILDREN

Cotton reels and an old boot lace make a good threading game for babies aged eighteen months onwards. You can increase the fun and make it last longer, if you allow them to paint or decorate the reels first.

Early risers in the family can be a nuisance until they are old enough to play by themselves. Try to encourage small children to play happily in their bedrooms by putting together a playtray. On an old tray place a drink, something to eat and a few tempting toys. You can also make a cassette of their favourite stories, and let them turn this on when they wake. It may only gain you another ten minutes in bed but if your child wakes regularly at dawn, every minute counts!

Empty cartons and boxes from the kitchen can be collected together to stock a play shop. Stick the lids down so that the last dregs of custard or sugar are not spilt on the carpet and arrange along a shelf or windowledge, with a coffee table as a counter.

Encourage children to hang their own coats and hats up by placing a row of hooks at child height. Make pretty wooden ones in the shapes of animals, or use shop bought ones and fix pictures of coats and hats next to them.

A feelie box is great fun at parties or for wet afternoons. Cut a hole in one end of a cardboard box, just large enough for a child's hand. Place an object, such as a toy, a piece of fruit, or a balloon in the box, while the child covers his eyes, then let him guess what is in the box by feel alone. This goes down well with 3 to 5 year olds.

Hair washing can be a difficult time. Make it fun by propping a plastic baby mirror at one end of the bath and encouraging children to make horns and other shapes with their own soapy hair. Smear a band of petroleum jelly on their foreheads to stop soap running into their eyes and use a gentle baby shampoo. Rinse their hair so that the water falls backwards

Join the local library: most have children's sections, with a wide range of books and often cassette tapes as well. Even three year olds can look forward to a trip to the library and the chance to choose new books.

Labelling children's clothes and shoes clearly often helps them get dressed by themselves. Use a colour coding system for those too young to read, so all the clothes belonging to one child have a yellow tag, and those of another a red tag. Teach them a way of remembering how clothes go on; the label always goes at the back, the buttons usually go at the front, etc. Once they can identify their own clothes and get themselves dressed, life is much easier, especially in the mornings when there is often much to do anyway.

Large cardboard boxes of the type household equipment is delivered in make versatile playthings. Once the children have exhausted the possibilities of climbing into it, over it and carrying it around, suggest they decorate it as a Wendy house, a post office or a space rocket. Use poster paints, or cut-out pictures and stick them on. Older children may even like to wallpaper the inside with a little adult help.

Measuring and pouring fascinates most 2 to 4 year olds. On sunny days send them out into the garden with a plastic jug of water and a collection of yogurt pots, margarine tubs and plastic cups. Grains of rice will serve the same function in winter and makes less mess indoors. Provide a large tray with a lip, to contain most of the rice.

Open-wire undershelves, of the kind sold for larders, will fit on shelves in a child's bedroom and hold a great number of small toys. Fix them low enough for the child to be able to reach them.

Paint an area of wall with blackboard paint, or fix a large piece of wood to the wall and paint this. Add a box of chalks and a couple of cloths for cleaning, and you have a good sized play area for very little cost. Make sure the children understand that their designs must be confined to this area. Chalking will keep even school age children amused as well as toddlers and chalks do less damage to carpets and furnishings than crayons.

Plastic laundry baskets of varying sizes make good cheap toy boxes that are light enough to be moved around as necessary. Solid plastic vegetable racks can also be used and are ideal for small toys and puzzle pieces.

Puzzles often become muddled up and it is such a nuisance having to sort through to find out which piece belongs in which box. Make a habit of numbering the backs of puzzles as they are bought; so the first puzzle a child has gets number 1 written on the back of each piece and the second has number 2 written on it. This way it is easy to sort them out.

Rainy days are usually the worst with small children in the house. Keep a rainy day box and gradually fill it with games and ideas about things to make and do on rainy days. Hide a few Christmas and birthday presents that did not seem very interesting at the time plus odds and ends like yogurt pots, cotton reels, coloured tape and glue. A packet cake mix needs little adult help to prepare even for quite small children and making 'rainy day cakes' is one good way to pass the afternoon.

Save old catalogues and magazines for cutting up and sticking games. Buy safe round-bladed metal scissors and sticks of glue, cover the table with newspaper and let 2 to 5 year olds loose making pictures, calendars and covering boxes.

Use local facilities: there is often a story reading at a local library, or a tufty club (Road Safety for under 5s), or a mother-and-toddler club to join. If you have a local indoor shopping centre, this can be a good venue for a winter time picnic. A train ride is a great adventure for most children, even if it is only one stop along the line. Local exhibitions and open days are a good, cheap way to spend an afternoon keeping the children amused. Check your local paper for nearby activities and consult the library notice boards.

Wallpaper rolls make good drawing and painting paper. Cut a roll up into large squares or unroll about half the roll and rewind around a piece of wood or plastic, so that the white side shows. Hang this from a shelf or wall, then your children can unroll and tear off as much as they need.

A Wellington rack, made of pieces of dowel set in a flat plank of wood will help keep a whole family's Wellies in order, as well as encouraging the children to put their own away.

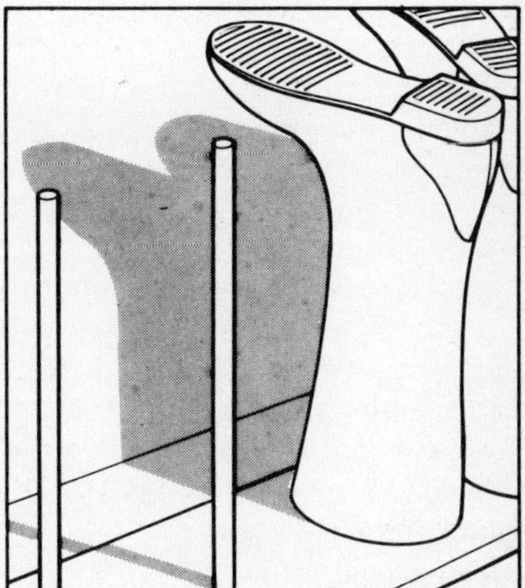

MAKING CHILDREN'S CLOTHES LAST

Cover odd stains and marks with sew-on braid, appliquéed fabric shapes, or pretty buttons. A large stain can often be covered with a pocket made of contrasting material. For instance, on a little girl's dress cut out the shape of a doll's pram in a brightly coloured cotton and sew on, fixing it round the base of the pram and the hood. Pop the smallest of her dolls inside the new pocket and the dress is sure to be very popular again.

Dungarees are usually good value for both boys and girls, but it is a nuisance to keep having to move the buttons as they grow. Instead sew the buttons on to a small piece of wide elastic. This way they give as the child moves and there will be far less need to adjust the positioning.

Fix a length of elastic with poppers at each end to mittens and gloves. Sew another popper to the inside of coat sleeves and fix the gloves/mittens into place as you dress the child. This will prevent gloves becoming lost quite so easily.

Girls' dresses often become too short before they are worn out. Turn them into a blouse by trimming the hem off and then gathering the base with elasticated thread. If the style does not lend itself to this, sew a length of pretty cotton lace on to the hem to make it longer and add matching lace to the neck and cuffs.

Look for detachable collars and cuffs on girls' party dresses as often these areas get dirty after one wear, but the main dress remains clean. This is especially useful on velvet.

Odd socks are the plague of any mother's life. After buying six matching pairs you can only ever find six odd ones, when searching in the sock drawer. Make life a little easier for yourself by buying all the same colour socks, so that any two socks will make a pair.

Patches on knees and elbows can look very stylish. Patch new clothes and remove them as they become worn rather than trying to patch old worn material. When hand knitting, knit extra patches, to sew on to the finished garment.

Pyjamas often wear out at the knee. Use the long sleeves to cut patches from, then turn the top into a short sleeved one. It is worth buying pyjamas in complementary colours, so that different tops and trousers can be worn together. This solves the problem of half of each pair being in the wash because of 'accidents' during the night.

Seams are often the first area to go on shop bought garments. Prevent this by reinforcing them while the garment is new. Sew over crutch and sleeve seams with a zig zag stitch or a hand blanket stitch. For very active children overstitch where straps are fixed to waistbands as well.

Smocks are a pretty and practical way to get more mileage out of little girls' clothes. They are easy to make as well, and are ideal when out for the day; as the smock gets gradually dirty it can be removed and there is a clean dress underneath.

Socks, T-shirts and underwear are often handed down the line in large families but they do tend to look a little worse for wear by the time the youngest inherits them. Brighten them up by dyeing them in cheerful primary colours. This is cheap and easy to do in the washing machine or by hand and the latest types of dyes mean that almost all fibres including polyester can be successfully dyed.

Thick winter socks usually wear on the heels and toes. If they are brightly coloured they can often have the foot section cut out completely and be used as leg warmers. Sew a hem on the cut section or edge with braid to prevent it unravelling.

Tie a large wooden toggle on to the end of a small child's zip to make it easier for him to pull up. This also protects the zip, since uneven tugging often makes it catch on the lining material.

Torn or very worn jumper sleeves can be removed and the armhole and neckline edged with braid to make a sleeveless top. When an anorak sleeve is torn beyond repair the garment can be reused. Remove both sleeves and the hood. Bind the edges with wide bias binding or braid and use as a padded waistcoat.

Trousers that are worn and thin in the legs can often be cut off to make good play shorts.

When hems have been let down, the previous hem often shows as a faded line. Disguise this with several rows of satin ribbon in different colours, or hand stitch rows of embroidery thread in a pattern around the hem of a skirt or dress.

Worn necklines and cuffs on young children's dresses, blouses and jumpers can be covered with a lacy collar and turn-back cuffs to match. Sew more lace across the yokeline or down the front to give a completely new look to the garment. For boys, sew braid around collars and cuffs. Use the same braid to sew his name or initials on the front.

A BABY IN THE HOUSE

Life with a new baby often takes some organizing. However, things gradually sort themselves out and some kind of routine evolves. The following hints should provide some ideas to help you cope.

Baby lotion and a packet of tissues make a cheaper and more versatile alternative to the special dampened tissues in a plastic tub, usually sold for babies.

Bedwetting is a common problem in young children. Protect the mattress with a plastic sheet, or a thick old blanket. This then makes the job of dealing with a wet bed much easier. Remove sheets and blanket and put them in the washing machine or leave to soak in the bath until morning, when they can be washed as usual. (See page 44 for how to deal with a wet mattress.) A waterproof mattress or sheet can be topped with an acrylic blanket which can be washed and dried in no time.

A changing mat can easily be made from a piece of PVC of the kind sold for tablecloths. Place an old towel underneath to make it more comfortable for the baby to lie on.

Choose clothes carefully for babies and toddlers. Pretty dresses and suits are often given as presents. Day-to-day clothes should be soft and warm, machine washable and non-iron. New parents are unlikely to have the time or the inclination to handwash and iron clothes.

Cupboards fascinate crawling children. To avoid repeatedly having to turn them out of the china cupboard, put all the plastic boxes and containers in one cupboard for the child to play with and put safety locks on the rest. Take particular care to lock cupboards containing detergents and bleaches.

Electric sockets at floor level are very tempting to small children. Even with modern shuttered sockets, it is still worthwhile to fit socket covers both for your own peace of mind and to remove the temptation from the child's sight. Socket covers are available from most High Street baby stores.

Fireguards are important and indeed a legal necessity when there are small children in the house. BS3140 is the British Standard that applies to fireguards and it is worth checking that any guard you buy is made to this standard. A full size nursery guard, firmly fixed to the wall offers good protection to a baby.

(Note that it is a Trading Standard requirement that all girls' nightdresses should be flame-resistant, but this Standard does not apply to pyjamas.)

Fit and use stair gates as soon as your baby starts to crawl. The first you may know of the new-found ability to climb stairs may well be when you find your child half way up! For much used stairways a gate that swings up to one side is very useful. Movable stair gates that fit into a doorway are also practical when you need to keep a child away from a potentially dangerous area, for instance out of the kitchen or away from a chaotic redecorating session.

Fix a mirror or a musical mobile above the changing mat to occupy the baby while he or she is being changed.

Fold nappies ready to use next time. This way you are not struggling to get it into the right shape while holding a wriggling baby.

Have everything ready to hand for nappy changing. In the early days you may have to change the baby's nappy eight or nine times a day, so it is worth setting up a particular nappy changing area, or arranging evrything in a basket to move around as needed. You could even have a nappy changing area upstairs and one downstairs.

Have two nappy buckets; this way you can have one batch sterilizing and one being rinsed. Make up a fresh sterilizing solution one day and put the dirty nappies in it. Next day, drain that bucket and add rinsing water and fill the other bucket with sterilizing solution ready for use. Two nappy buckets full of nappies make an average automatic washing machine load.

Large ice cream tubs make useful sterilizing containers as they hold several bottles. They are also useful when travelling as clean sterilized bottles can be carried in them. (Wrap them first if they happen to be glass.)

Leads and flexes from electric appliances should not be left trailing over the edge of a worktop. A small child can pull on the lead and hurt himself.

Mobile babies are forever getting into mischief. It is often worth going round the house and moving up anything low down that is likely to be damaged or dangerous to a crawling baby. Do this the first day the baby crawls, then check again as he or she becomes more mobile and begins to stand or climb.

Pram and crib sheets have a very limited use as the baby outgrows both so quickly. Use larger cot sheets and blankets folded in two instead.

Small babies often get bored laying in their prams with nothing to occupy them. If they can see something moving, it will occupy them long enough to allow them to drift off to sleep, or keep them amused for a short period while you get on. Try placing the pram so that the baby can see washing blowing in the breeze or a tree moving. The baby will accept these as pretty things to look at just as much as toys hung over the pram.

A soft sided freezer bag makes an ideal carry-all for baby equipment, nappies and spare clothes when out visiting. It is quite cheap and light to carry and can be used for frozen food when no longer necessary for the baby.

Sterilizing fluid made up for bottles is the ideal place to clean teething rings, rattles and drinking cups.

Store medicines and cleaners in a locked cupboard well out of the reach of a child. *Never* leave tablets or medicine around. Even cupboards containing glass and china can be dangerous for very small children. Fit childproof catches which allow adults in but fox most children. Alternatively, tie two adjoining handles together with a short length of string.

A string bag, particularly the plastic type, is ideal for holding all the bathroom toys for a small baby. Hang the bag over the bath taps when not in use and it can easily be removed when adults want to use the bath.

Tissues and cotton wool seem to be constantly needed with small children around. Leave some in each room to save having to collect one box all the time.

Use a pram parasol to hang collections of small toys on for a small baby to look at. This keeps them easily in view and can be moved from cot to pram quickly. The toys can be securely pinned on and changed from time to time as the baby becomes bored.

MESSY MEALTIMES

Food and children inevitably mean a certain degree of mess. Small babies just starting solids seem to take a long time to realise that food is supposed to go only in the mouth, and not smeared on every surface within reach. Toddlers never seem to sit still throughout a whole meal, and often a trail of crumbs, or pieces of bread seem to be laid around the house after tea. We do survive this messy phase, but a few things can make life a little easier.

Cook quantities of suitable baby food, then purée. This can then be frozen in ice cube trays and once solid tipped into a polythene bag. Use as required which will eliminate the need to purée small quantities daily with all the accompanying washing up that that involves.

Finger foods fulfil a baby's desire to feed himself with the minimum of mess. Toast soldiers, coarsely grated cheese, miniature squares of bread and butter, minced, cooked chicken or strips of ham, seedless grapes cut up, or slices of apple or carrot can all be placed on to the high chair tray and are much easier to cope with than puréed food.

Make a stick down plate using a rubber soap pad placed on the tray and a plastic plate or dish on top.

Older children may well enjoy kitchen picnics; place a plastic cloth on the floor and all sit round to eat. This is ideal for when several small children descend on you at once. Another way, especially useful for parties, is to give everyone their very own 'tuck box'. Use cardboard baker's boxes (available from a friendly baker) and fill with food that is easy to eat with the fingers. In the summer, children can be sent out with these boxes to eat in the garden or tree house.

Place a baby's high chair on a plastic tablecloth or sheets of newspaper to catch the food. They are then easily cleared up at the end of the meal.

A plastic bib with a turned up section at the bottom collects all the oddments of food that otherwise find their way on to the floor. It is also easy to wipe clean or wash after use.

Shaped spoons and forks that fit a toddler's hand easily make independent eating so much easier and hence keep the mess to a minimum.

Use a little cunning to persuade school age children to try foods they say they do not like; cabbage may be boring but savoy is suddenly an interesting new vegetable. One family calls baked jam pudding 'Journey to the Centre of the Earth', because it has a crisp top and a hot jammy centre, and it is the most popular pudding of the week!

BABY EQUIPMENT

With babies and small children in the house, a whole range of equipment is needed. Many items can be bought secondhand and renovated or cleaned up. Items infrequently used can need a quick wash and brush up after being stored in the loft or garage.

BATH AND STAND

This is useful while the baby is young and the stand can often be used as a carrycot stand as well.

* Plastic baths can simply be washed with hot soapy water.
* Scratches will often improve if you rub them with a cream cleanser or a little dry bicarbonate of soda on a damp cloth.
* Badly scratched areas may respond to a little metal polish used on wadding to smooth the surface. Wash well before use.
* The stand can be washed or polished with a spray polish.
* Oil the hinges or loosen sticking hinges with an aerosol lubricant, of the kind used for cars.
* Chrome stands can be cleaned with a little paraffin or with a special chrome cleaner sold in car accessory shops.
* Aluminium frames that are slightly corroded can be washed with warm soapy water to which a little borax has been added. Dry and rub down lightly with steel wool, working along the length of the frame to restore the shine.
* Baby baths are often good value secondhand and can be used later as outdoor sand and water tubs for toddlers to play with.

CARRYCOT AND STAND

These are useful while a baby is tiny but are soon outgrown. Some have separate wheels, so they can be used to move the baby around as well.

* Check that the carrycot section is well balanced and the

carrying handles are firmly fixed to the body of the cot.

* Wash the inside of the carrycot with warm soapy water, if it is plastic lined.
* Fabric linings can be brushed or vacuumed to clean them.
* Any greasy marks can be removed with an aerosol solvent. Brush and air well before use.
* Vinyl outer coverings can also be washed with a damp cloth and warm soapy water.
* Cord or fabric outers are best brushed or vacuumed. If very dirty they can be cleaned using pure soap flakes in warm water. Dip the cloth in the liquid, squeeze out the excess water and use to wipe over the cord. Rinse with a cloth dipped in clean water, then dry with a soft cloth to take up any excess moisture. Allow to dry naturally with the apron on and the hood up. Before cleaning the whole carrycot, do a test to make sure that the colour is not affected.
* Oil the hinges on the stand or transporter if necessary and check that the plastic anti-slip feet are still in place.

COTS

Again these are good value secondhand.

* Check the width between the bars. It should be no more than 6 cm (2¼ inches) and no less than 2.5 cm (1 inch), so that the baby cannot become stuck or slip through.
* Check that the cot is sturdy and the mattress is low enough, so that the baby cannot climb out, and that the mattress fits the base well.
* Make sure there are childproof catches on the sliding side.
* Check that there are no projections for clothing to catch on.
* Clean it well before use, whether it is secondhand or has been in the loft for a year or two. Take the cot to pieces and wash well in hot soapy water. This is easiest to do outside if the weather is mild. Dry, then check that the paintwork is intact and that there are no flaky areas.
* It may be worth repainting it in which case make sure that a suitable paint is used. Mention, when buying the paint, that it is for a baby's cot.
* Check any metal parts for signs of rust and rub them down well with fine sandpaper. Brush off, then smear a little petroleum jelly over the metal parts to prevent further rusting.

This is also a good idea if you are dismantling a cot to store it.

* Mattresses are usually covered in plastic and can simply be washed with warm soapy water. Any stubborn marks can be removed with a cream cleanser, or a little dry bicarbonate of soda on a damp cloth.
* Fabric mattresses can be vacuumed or brushed to remove dust, and aired if at all damp.
* If the mattress is old and worn, you should buy a new one. Check the dimensions carefully, so that it fits the cot well. If too large, the turned up edges may provide a foothold for an adventurous toddler to climb out. If it is too small, a baby may slip down the gap between the mattress and cot side.

HIGHCHAIRS

These need to be strong and stable as they are often in use for up to two years and during this time the baby is very active.

* To clean the highchair, first remove any tray, seat cover and straps, then wash well using hot soapy water and a cloth, or a nail brush for scrubbing very dirty areas. Obviously this is best done outside or on sheets of newspaper.
* Don't forget to clean under the seat, as small sticky hands often leave their trademark there.
* The tray and straps can be washed in the sink and dried well before fixing back on to the chair.
* The straps may need scrubbing with a nail brush as well to clean them.
* Plastic seat covers usually clean up well with warm soapy water but you may need to loosen dirt accumulated around stitch lines with an old toothbrush.
* Once in daily use, a highchair should be wiped regularly after use and cleaned weekly.

PRAMS

These are often stored in the loft or garage between babies. Any pram that has not been used for some time should be serviced, either by your local specialist baby equipment shop or by you.

* Check the wheels, the brakes and any folding devices.
* Spare parts can usually be ordered through local specialist shops or direct from the manufacturers.

* Replace any worn parts and renew straps, mattresses, etc., if necessary.
* Small tears in vinyl hoods can be mended by using a piece of sticking plaster. Fix this to the inside of the hood and press the torn vinyl on to it.
* Clean the inside of the pram by wiping it out with hot soapy water. Fabric inners need vacuuming or brushing well. Greasy marks can be cleaned with a grease solvent.

PUSHCHAIRS

These are generally used daily for two or three years and often become very dirty in use. Food tends to find its way on to the seat of the pushchair and drinks are often spilt as well. Add to this the worst of winter rain and mud and the pushchair can end up looking rather the worse for wear after just one year.

* Most pushchair seats are made of a coated material which prevents spills penetrating the fibre. This kind can be wiped over with a damp cloth and even scrubbed with a small brush dipped in warm soapy water.
* Cord seating is better cleaned with a cloth which has been dipped in a warm solution of pure soap flakes. Rinse with a clean damp cloth and remove excess moisture with a soft dry cloth. Leave to dry naturally.
* Remove hoods, covers and straps and clean separately.
* Clean the metal frame with a spray or cream furniture polish.
* Wash the wheels using a long bristled brush dipped in warm soapy water.
* Balloon wheels, in particular, can trap dirt in between the wheels, so a soft brush, such as a hand brush, will get into the gaps and clean them.
* Occasionally children are sick: a mixture of one teaspoon of bicarbonate of soda in 250 ml (½ pint) of warm water will clean the pushchairs and help remove the smell. If the soiling is extensive, try putting this mixture into a small, hand-held garden spray. Remove as much of the deposit as possible, then spray. Scrub with a nail brush, spray again and leave to dry outside. This is also a useful method to use when children have been sick in the car.
* While cleaning, take this opportunity to check for any missing or damaged parts and fit new ones immediately.

FIRST AID FOR FURNISHINGS

Upholstery and carpets take a great deal of punishment when children are small. Sticky fingerprints, spilt drinks and over-enthusiastic games on the sofa soon take their toll. Take preventive action wherever possible; rugs will help even out the wear and tear on carpets, and confining food to the kitchen or dining room whenever possible will help, too.

Make sure you are ready to tackle spills and stains as they occur and know in advance what cleaners are safe to use on your particular furnishings. Put together a stains box; collect a good carpet shampoo, an aerosol grease solvent, a small bottle of clear methylated spirit or white spirit, a nail brush and an old toothbrush, and plenty of white rags. Keep this near to hand but out of reach of small children, so that you are equipped to cope with most accidents.

Treat stains quickly; most will come off if still fresh, dried stains are much harder to tackle and may well need professional help.

Carpets and upholstery can now be treated at home with a stain repellant, available in an aerosol form. It is worth treating arms and seats of sofas and chairs, and possibly light coloured carpets with this system to prevent stains soaking in.

Biro and felt tip inks need quick treatment or they become permanent. Use methylated spirit applied on a piece of white cotton, or a cotton bud. Take care not to spread the stain by constantly turning the cloth to ensure a clean piece is being used, or use fresh cotton buds.

Chocolate is a grease-based stain and it is often possible to track the passage of small children simply by the sticky chocolate fingerprints left around the house. On carpets and upholstery scrape up as much as possible, then use a carpet shampoo. Finally treat the area with a grease solvent or upholstery cleaner. Check on a test area first. On vinyl wallpaper and paintwork it can usually be washed off using a cloth dipped in warm water and a little washing-up liquid. On other wallpaper, try a soft artist's putty rubber, or a piece of old bread.

Coffee and tea usually contain milk, so there are really two stains to remove; the coloured stain of the drink and the grease-based stain the milk leaves. On carpets, blot up the excess quickly using kitchen roll, tissues or even tea towels. Cover the stain and press on the cloth or stand on it to help absorb the liquid. See Chapter 1, page 35 for the rest of the cleaning hints.

On upholstery, blot up excess tea or coffee, then sponge with clear water. Use carpet shampoo or apply the foam only from a mixture of washing up liquid and warm water; once dry brush or vacuum off. A grease solvent can usually be used on upholstery but check first by doing a test area. For old stains, equal parts glycerine and warm water spread over and allowed to stand for about one hour may help. Wipe off with a cloth wrung out in warm water.

Crayons are generally wax-based, so a grease solvent will usually remove the stain. If there is a large amount, scrape up the excess first.

Food is generally a mixture of different types of stain. Upturned plates call for quick scraping up of the debris, followed by the use of a carpet shampoo. Once dry, remove any lingering grease-based stains with a grease solvent.

Vinyl wallpaper will usually wipe clean along with paintwork. On other types of wallpaper, sponge lightly to remove surface soiling. Do a test area first though, in case the colour is affected.

Fruit drinks stain badly if left untreated, since many children's drinks are quite vibrant colours. Act fast, mop up the excess and treat the area with a carpet shampoo. Alternatively, mix a little washing-up liquid with warm water and apply the foam only on a small brush; work in and allow to dry, then brush or vacuum off. Remove any traces of colour left behind by rubbing lightly with a little white spirit on a white cloth. Do a test area first to make sure that the white spirit will not affect the colour.

Glues should always be used carefully and any marks treated immediately while wet. Clear and contact glues will generally respond to a non-oily nail varnish remover. Use with care, though, as this may cause the dye to run and will damage acetates. Do a test area first. Alternatively, try lighter fuel, but still do a test area. Some glues are almost impossible to remove wihout a special solvent, available on request from some manufacturers. Always check on the instruction leaflet for information on this.

Grass stains appear as if by magic in the summer and cuttings are often walked on to carpets or sofas and chairs. See page 35 for carpet care. And the same instructions apply to upholstery.

Milk is often spilt over carpets and sofas and while trainer beakers help prevent major spills most toddlers seem to delight in watching the sprinkling effect, when they are turned upside down! On carpets, flush the area with warm water and blot up. Do this thoroughly as even small areas untreated can smell terribly for some time afterwards. Rather than overwet the carpet, rinse and blot the area several times before using a grease solvent. On upholstery, blot well, then wash the area well with a damp cloth dipped in warm water. Rinse the cloth and repeat the washing several times to draw out the milk. Finally treat with a grease solvent. Do a test area first to check if the colour is affected. On Dralon, a weak biological washing powder solution can be used; mix one teaspoon of powder with ½ litre (1 pint) of warm water and sprinkle over the affected area, or apply on a sponge. Rinse and blot well. Lingering smells can be treated with a carpet deodorant, or by sponging with warm water and bicarbonate of soda. Use one teaspoon to ½ litre (1 pint).

Muddy feet on carpets or, even worse, clambering over the sofa, are enough to make most mothers lose their temper. This is, in fact, one stain where it is better not to act immediately, except perhaps to tell the children off! Instead, allow the mud to dry, then brush off with a stiff brush. Any remaining stain can be treated with a carpet shampoo, or a washing-up liquid mixture.

Poster paints are water-soluble and can, therefore, generally be easily washed out of clothes and fabrics. On upholstery and carpets, sponge well with warm water, blotting as you go, to prevent overwetting.

Urine is acidic and will weaken fibres if left untreated. When in the throes of potty training, some accidents are inevitable, so prepare in advance. Use the nappies you are no longer putting on the baby as a supply of absorbent material for quick mopping up. Cover the stain with the nappy and press down well or stand on it to help absorb the moisture. Then use a carpet shampoo and finally rinse well with warm water plus a little disinfectant.

PETS

Pets need a certain amount of housekeeping done for them. A few tips to save time, money or effort are worth passing on.

Bath a small dog in a baby bath (which is no longer used for your child). This can be placed outside if the weather is warm, or in the garage in cooler weather to prevent a mess indoors.

A bitch on heat can attract dogs from miles around. Chemists sell concentrated chlorophyll tablets, which will help get rid of the smell and discourage 'suitors'.

Cats left in the house all day will find a cat flap useful. Sternly discourage other cats from even coming near the door when you are around in the house, so that they don't get the idea of coming in and eating your cat's food.

Garden produce or grass clippings which have been sprayed with chemicals, such as weed killer, should not be given to pets as they may be harmful.

Gerbils and guinea pigs are good pets for small children. They have a reasonable life span and can withstand some handling. Since guinea pigs can be kept in a cage outside, the children can be supervised when helping to feed, clean or play with them; they will not interfere much with day-to-day life in the house.

Grass clippings, once dried, make a good cheap base for rabbit hutches and it smells sweet too.

Leave cat and dog food out on a plastic mat or sheets of newspaper. If there is space in an enclosed porch or hall, leave the food there, rather than in the kitchen, where the smell will linger while you are cooking. The food should always be given in dishes kept specially for that purpose. Take care to wash them separately from other plates and dishes. Store dry food away from human food and remember to wash the tin opener after use, or keep a separate one for tins of dog and cat food.

Line a bird's cage with folded newspaper to make cleaning easy.

Make sure to take a newly bought puppy or kitten to the vet for an overall check up and to sort out what injections it may need.

Mice should not be fed cheese: it makes them smell strongly.

Most pet owners eventually run up against the problem of fleas. Your vet can prescribe an effective spray that will clear the house of any fleas, and another type which will treat the animal.

Rabbits are quite hardy and able to survive the cold if they have a well built hutch. Make sure they are dry and draught-free. Very young rabbits may need extra shelter in a shed or porch. Use straw or hay as bedding and sawdust as flooring. Check the sawdust is not made from wood containing a preservative.

Remove cat and dog hairs from carpets by using a damp cloth. Wipe small areas with the cloth, rinsing the hairs off as you go.

Rub chair and table legs with a little oil of cloves to prevent puppies chewing them.

A scratching post, made by tying a piece of old carpet round a chair leg or stair rail, may well prevent cats scratching anywhere else. Every time you find your cat scratching your wallpaper or carpet, take it to the scratching post and gently make scratching motions with the paw in the right place.

Train a young puppy, starting in the garden, where everything is familiar and with just one member of the family giving the orders at first. Do a little training every day and gradually build up to training when out in the street.

Young dogs that are lonely at night can sometimes be comforted by placing a ticking clock next to their basket.

~~1. About the House~~
~~2. Clothes Care~~
~~3. Make Amends~~
~~4. Table Talk~~
~~5. Talking Shop~~
~~6. Moving Moments~~
~~7. Happy Holidays~~
~~8. Children and Pets~~
9. Outside the House

WEAR AND TEAR

Wear and tear on the outside of the house tends to be gradual and often goes unnoticed until it becomes a major problem. Spring is a good time to take stock, assess the damage caused by the worst of the winter's rain and snow and do some routine chores.

This section gives some ideas and tips on minor maintenance jobs, such as redecorating, and deals with small scale renovations. Obviously for larger jobs you should consult a professional. Make sure you get at least two, and preferably three, proper quotations for the work to be done. Beware of estimates. A quotation is legally binding, an estimate is not, so with the latter you could end up paying far more than you expect.

Airbricks sometimes become blocked with general garden debris, or by plants growing up against them. Beware of storing sand or ballast against a wall as this too may block up an airbrick. Go round and clear the airbricks by cutting back growth, or sweeping away dirt. Clean out the holes in the airbricks.

Brickwork occasionally has a whitish deposit called 'efflorescence' forming on it. This is quite common with new bricks and is caused by salts within the brick coming to the surface. Do not wash it off with water as this only increases the problem. Instead, brush lightly with a stiff brush from time to time. Gradually this whiteness will disappear; the occasional brushing will help it on its way.

Clean windows that have accumulated grime and dust from traffic fumes and general weather conditions with hot soapy water. Wash well, then rinse off with warm water and a little vinegar. Use one teaspoon to 250 ml (½ pint) of warm water. Finally dry with crumpled-up newspaper to make the windows shine.

Creosote only needs reapplying every three or four years. Brush down the fence with a stiff brush to remove any dust or algae growth before repainting. Take care to wear thick rubber gloves and a long-sleeved coverall. Anyone particularly sensitive to creosote may find that smearing petroleum jelly over the face will give some protection from splashes.

Gutters need checking in the spring for damage and blockages. Clear any dead leaves or birds' nests out and check that they are still firmly fixed and that there are no gaps between sections. Cast iron guttering can be cleaned with a wire brush to remove loose rust, treated with metal primer, then painted. Use leftover paint mixed together and strained through a stocking. If bituminous paint was previously used, either apply the same or treat with a sealer then apply ordinary gloss paint. Cover the gutters with chicken wire to prevent the leaves falling inside and blocking them.

Logs should never be stacked against a wall as they will hold moisture and make a damp patch. Logs are best stacked and partially covered with a tarpaulin which will prevent them becoming wet, but will also allow them to weather naturally.

Oil on paths is slippery and dangerous. Remove by warming some builders' sand in a roasting tin in the oven. Once hot, sprinkle over the oil and allow to stand for five to ten minutes.

Then brush the sand over the oily patch with a stiff brush, so that it picks up as much oil as possible. Repeat with fresh warm sand if necessary, then wash the area with hot soapy water, or use a proprietary cleaner.

Paths that become covered in lichen and moss can be dangerous. Remove as much growth as possible with a spade, then wash the path using a proprietary moss killer or a solution of about one eggcup of bleach to each bucket of warm water.

Shed roofs that have become leaky can be refelted. This is reasonably quick and easy to do, and most sheds are low enough to work on safely with a standard ladder.

Unblocking drains is a messy job. Remove any obvious debris such as fallen leaves, then lift off the grid. An old ladle or unbent coat hanger will pull up some or all of the blockage, although you may have to resort to putting your hand down to remove the last of the rubbish. An old pair of stout rubber gloves is essential here. Finally clean with a spray from a garden hose. Replace the grid and, if necessary, make a drain hole cover from wood or metal to prevent rubbish accumulating around the drain hole. This also discourages small children from playing with it.

Use an old pair of sunglasses as makeshift goggles when doing any messy outside job such as brushing down brickwork, or removing a broken pane of glass. Goggles are obviously tougher and should be used for major jobs like breaking up areas of concrete.

Wooden window ledges that show signs of cracking can be filled with wood or general-purpose filler or by using a mixture of glue and sawdust. Once dry, repaint immediately to prevent the cracks becoming damp and reappearing.

Wrought iron gates need repainting every few years. Clean down well with a wire brush followed by emery paper to remove flaking paint and rust, then give the gates a coat of metal primer then repaint with undercoat and two coats of gloss.

DECORATING THE OUTSIDE

External decoration does not usually need doing every year but will need regular tackling to keep woodwork in good condition. Don't allow paintwork to deteriorate to the point where the underlying wood is badly affected by damp, or the repair job will be a major one.

Cold weather means that paint takes that much longer to dry, so remember to allow for this when planning to paint over an undercoat.

Cover bushes or shrubs that are near the house with an old cloth or blanket to prevent them becoming splattered with paint. Do the same when rubbing paintwork down or when using a chemical paint stripper.

Do not paint in direct sunlight; the paint will dry too quickly and will probably crack and blister, making it necessary to do the job all over again.

Hang a bucket on to a ladder using an S-hook, available from DIY stores. This is a useful device, particularly when cleaning gutters, so that any rubbish can be placed straight into the bucket.

In late summer and autumn, finish painting about two hours before sunset to allow the paint to dry. Otherwise condensation will cause a pitted finish.

Ladders should not be leant against guttering, whether metal or plastic: it will not support the weight (see also page 344 for ladder safety).

Never paint in high winds. Dust will be throw up on to the wet paint. It is also very dangerous working on a ladder in windy weather.

On soft ground stand the ladder on a piece of strong board. Nail a timber batten to the board to wedge the ladder against to prevent it from slipping.

Paint splashes on glass can be removed when dry, using a special blade tool in a holder available from DIY stores.

Take care with ladders. Make sure that the base of the ladder is a quarter of its height up the wall away from the house to prevent it slipping or overbalancing. Ladders should be secured at the top and the bottom. Never lean out from a ladder: your hips should not move beyond the sides of the ladder. If you can't reach comfortably, climb down and move the ladder along. For security, store a ladder padlocked to a fixed braket. When not in use for short periods, tie a board to the rungs at the base of the ladder to prevent children climbing it.

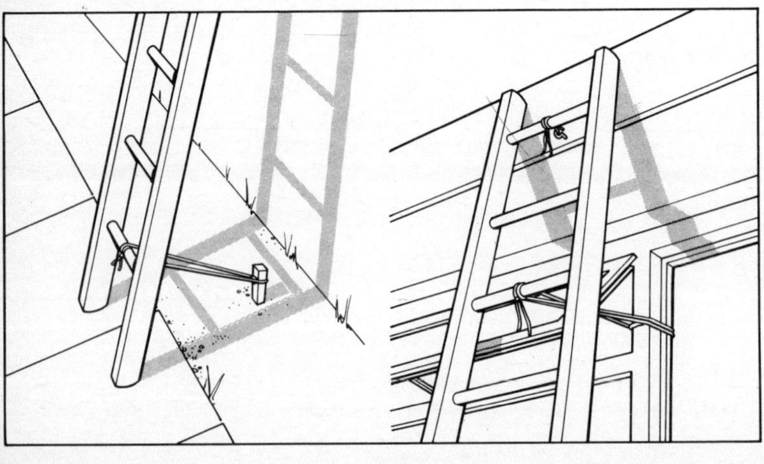

Treat brickwork and other absorbent surfaces with a proprietary stabilizing solution before painting. Apply one coat with a paintbrush and allow to dry. This takes roughly 24 hours.

When painting a wall, wrap the drainpipe with pieces of newspaper to prevent paint being spilt on to the drainpipe.

When painting the downpipes, hold a piece of card behind the pipe to prevent paint splashing on to the wall.

GARAGES

Most people's garages contain everything except the car! We tend to use them as extra storage areas, as workshops and hobby rooms. A little order in the chaos will sometimes help create more space.

Adequate lighting is essential if any work is to be done in a garage. Strip lighting gives good overall light, but an extra directional lamp is useful for woodworking and other hobbies. For car maintenance, a guarded light on a flex, that can be taken under the car if necessary, is ideal.

Bicycles can be stored on a hoist, so that they are completely out of the way when not needed. Alternatively, fix stout brackets to the wall so that they can be lifted up and hung on the wall when not in use.

Ceiling joists that are exposed can be fixed with hooks so that ladders can be hung on them to keep them securely out of the way. If the joists are not exposed, strong wall brackets are a much better idea.

Deck chairs and other garden furniture can also be hung on the wall to keep the garage floor clear. Fix several small brackets, so that chairs can be hung up individually. This will also prevent them slipping down and becoming damp on the garage floor and so keep them in better condition.

Duckboards made from an old pallet, or made to measure, will allow people to work in the garage even when it is cold, without having to stand on a cold concrete floor. They are also easy to lift and sweep under. For non-messy hobbies an old piece of carpeting will also insulate the floor.

Empty coffee jars make handy storage for screws, nails, nuts and bolts. Fix the lid securely to the underneath of a shelf, then screw the jars into place. This will keep the screws tidy and you can see at a glance which screws are where.

Freezers, especially the chest type, are often conveniently stored in a garage. However, to ensure that it is not accidentally unplugged, cover the socket with sticky tape or fit a switched fused connection unit, which can't be unplugged. Since it is possible for a freezer to break down in a garage without anyone noticing until the food has completely thawed, it may be well worth fitting a freezer alarm. These sound an audible warning if the temperature of the cabinet rises. It is far more likely to be heard, than a warning light is to be seen.

Paraffin, petrol and other highly flammable liquids should not be stored in the garage. Store in a shed or outhouse which is not attached to the main house. This also applies to emergency heating such as paraffin heaters, which may well have some paraffin left in them.

A shadow board for tools keeps them all tidy and within reach. Buy a sheet of peg board, fix hooks where needed and paint in the shapes of tools in the best storage position.

Sharp tools, such as chisels, for which you have lost the special blade protectors, are best stored on a rack fronted with clear plastic, so that you can see which tools are in the rack, but cannot accidentally cut yourself as you reach for a tool.

Store chemicals such as cleaners or solvents in a lockable cupboard. Make sure each bottle or container is clearly marked, and avoid decanting one chemical into anther bottle, so that you are no longer clear about which is which.

Store large toys, such as bikes and go-karts on wall brackets, or hanging from the ceiling. Alternatively, storage nets are available to suspend from the ceiling which will hold toys like these and offcuts of wood.

Tools, both electric and non-electric, will suffer from the effects of damp, so check that the garage is reasonably dry and not prone to damp. Deal with leaks quickly, as they will damage the structure of the building as well as the contents of the garage.

PATIOS AND GARDENS

Most of us use our gardens as an extension of our homes, at least when the weather is warm enough. Small children rather take over the garden, with climbing frames, swings, sandpits and the like, and any paved area makes a good outdoor eating area. Keen entertainers often find a simple barbecue worthwhile as well.

Build a simple temporary barbecue using bricks and an old baking grid or oven rack. Stack the bricks round in a semicircle until they are a convenient height. Then place a sheet of metal to hold the charcoal, and add another layer of bricks before placing the grid on top. A final layer of bricks will protect the cooking food from the wind. At the end of the summer the bricks can be stacked in a corner ready for next year.

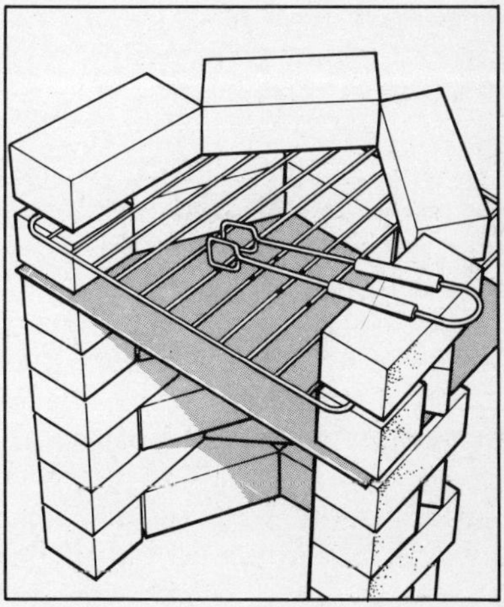

Camouflage bare walls and harsh angles of outbuildings by growing suitable plants up the wall, or even training a fruit tree against it. Many plants and some trees can even be grown in tubs on patios and paths.

Check climbing frames annually for rust spots, sharp corners or loose bolts. Ideally they should be dismantled each autumn and put up again in the spring to lengthen the life of the frame.

Wooden frames in particular need protecting from rain and damp conditions; check the area where the frame meets the ground as this is where rot sets in.

Dustbin powder helps keep smells at bay in hot weather. All foodstuffs should be well wrapped in layers of newspaper before putting them in the dustbin to prevent stray animals being attracted to the bin. Stand the dustbin in a cool shaded place and wedge it in the upright position so that it can't be knocked over, if local animals are a nuisance. Often a brick on the lid is enough to discourage cats.

Dustbins benefit from the occasional wash with a weak bleach solution (see page 31). Wash first with hot soapy water to remove any food debris, then rinse with weak bleach solution to make sure any germs are killed off. Use an old brush to clean the dustbin with and wear old rubber gloves. Dry well and leave to air in the open for two to three hours with the lid off before bringing into use again.

Good lighting is essential for safety and security. Light steps and paths, doorways and porches. Patios with outside lighting can be used all evening in the summer and by adding a couple of insect repelling candles.

Hide drainpipes and other pipes which have an ugly appearance down near the ground by arranging one large or a group of small potted plants in front of them.

Old chimney pots and discarded sinks make attractive planters for use on paths and patios (see pages 164 and 165).

An outside tap makes life easier in summer, whether for filling the children's paddling pool or watering the garden. However, if it does not have a stopcock for isolating it, make sure it is well insulated in winter.

Paint cheap plastic pots and troughs bright red or terracotta to make them look more attractive. Once they are arranged in groups and the plants in them are established, they look remarkably realistic.

A planting trough can be built from bricks. Make sure there is ample drainage. One easy way to do this is to use offcuts of garden hose and fit these pieces in between the bricks as the trough is built. They will squash easily between the bricks and allow excess water to drain off. Do not build the trough against a house wall, as this will bridge the damp-proof course and render it ineffective.

Rain barrels should always have a lid to prevent dirt and leaves falling in and spoiling the water. In winter, weight the lid with bricks to prevent high winds blowing it off.

Re-cover old deck chairs rather than throw them away. New canvas can be bought from stores with good fabric departments. Use the old chair canvas as a pattern to cut round and make sure the new canvas is securely fixed and doubled round each wooden bar so that it cannot be pulled out when in use.

Sandpits are an ideal play area for young children. Place a sandpit away from the house, so that not too much sand is walked in. Choose one with a lid to keep the sand dry and cats out. Empty and clean during the winter.

Screen dustbins and rubbish sacks with a small fence and plants or shrubs, especially if they must sit on or near the patio.

Softwoods often used for garden seating or climbing frames need two or three coats of wood preservative applied regularly to help protect them from rotting.

Steps should not be allowed to become overgrown or they will be slippery when wet. Moss and lichen on steps also makes them slippery, so clean off as described on page 342.

Swings can be hung from a sturdy tree or on a frame. Check for worn ropes or split seats. Metal frames may rust if left out over the winter, so check them carefully before use next spring.

Treehouses are great fun and amuse children of most ages. Check that they are not causing damage to the tree and that any parts in contact with the trees are well padded. Also check each year that they can withstand the ever increasing weight of your children. Consider safety too, and make sure access steps or ropes are repaired or renewed if necessary.

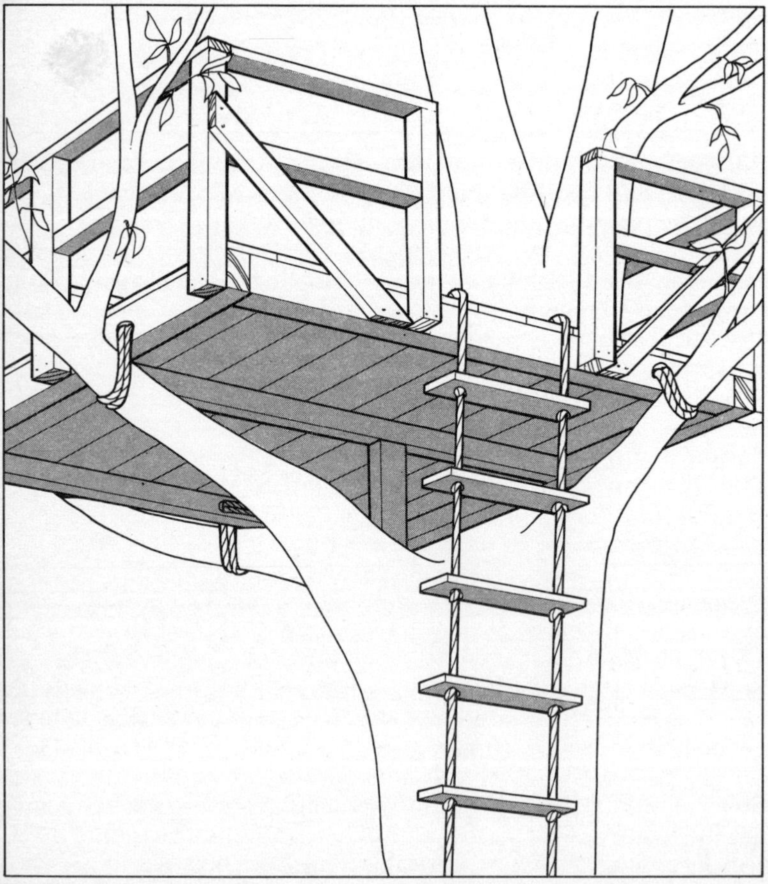

HANDYMAN'S HINTS

Most of us have to be handymen or women at some time. Nearly half the women in the country do the decorating and many more change lightbulbs, rewire plugs and get on with general day to day household repairs. Here are some tips for easing your way with minor jobs.

A candle rubbed along a plane before use will help it run more smoothly. This is also a good remedy for a saw that sticks.

Cover up mistakes and screw holes in wood by filling with a mixture of sawdust and adhesive.

Drill a hole in the handle of a paintbrush, so that a skewer or stick can be pushed through it. Use this to suspend the brush in cleaning fluid and so avoid bending the bristles. It also means that it can be hung on a nail for storage.

Drill chuck keys should be taped to the drill lead about 7 cm (2½ inches) from the drill head, so that they are always to hand and cannot be lost.

Ensure that ceiling paper is straight by using a string and chalk to mark the first line across the length of the room. Keep a good length of string in a tin with some powdered chalk. Measure and mark the width of the wallpaper at either end of the ceiling. With one person at either end, hold the chalked string taut across the ceiling between these two marks. Tweak the string gently and it will leave a chalk mark neatly across the ceiling. Paste the paper, fold and hold the excess paper with a full roll of wallpaper. Then place against the chalk line and press down with a smoothing brush.

Hold tacks or short nails by pushing them through a piece of card, or a polystyrene ceiling tile. The card can be cut away once the tack is fixed.

A little soap applied to the end of a screw will make it easier to turn so that you can get a nice tight fit.

Paint tins can be stood on large paper plates when in use. They will absorb more paint than newspaper and are easy to carry around with the tin.

Place a strip of tape around a chisel to measure the depth of cut needed. So if you need to chisel out a piece of wood 2 cm (¾ inch) deep, measure this distance on the chisel and place the edge of the tape in position. Then, when chiselling, you will know when you have cut deep enough.

Plywood can splinter when sawn, so stick a line of sticky tape on to the wood, then saw through the tape.

Remove nails without damaging the surface of the wood by using a small block of wood next to the nail. Pull the nail with the pincers and make sure that the pincer head sits on the block of wood.

Strain old paint through muslin or old tights to get rid of any lumps before using. If you have spilt a large quantity of paint, try to retrieve as much as possible using a clean plastic dustpan. Strain into the tin before using.

Tie a cord across a paint or paste bucket, so that the brush can be wiped across the cord to remove any excess.

Use power tools safely: make sure you are not wearing any loose clothing such as a tie which could catch in the tool. Work with the lead over the shoulder and always carry tools by the handles *never* the lead.

When painting large areas, a roller is one of the quickest ways. Start off with criss-cross strokes, then finish with straight strokes to make sure no lines remain when the paint is dry.

1. About the House
2. Clothes Care
3. Make Amends
4. Table Talk
5. Talking Shop
6. Moving Moments
7. Happy Holidays
8. Children and Pets
9. Outside the House
10. Services

ASBESTOS

This substance is often used on ironing boards and for oven linings, oven door seals or some gutters. If it starts to disintegrate or flake, it can be a health hazard. Don't attempt to remove the asbestos yourself but contact the local Environmental Health Department, who will advise you on the best way to deal with the problem. The advice is free.

BUILDING

Building regulations can restrict you in terms of what you want to do to your home, even if you do own it! They can be to your advantage too – in the sense that they can prevent your next door neighbour making your life a misery by indulging in all sorts of nightmarish building projects.

* Your local Town Hall Building Control Department will be happy to give you, free of charge, advice as to what you can and cannot do if you are planning to improve, change or extend your house in some way.
* Apart from Building Regulations approval (which ensures that work is carried out safely and to certain standards), you may need planning permission for your new playroom, verandah, swimming pool or sauna, which governs the appearance of the structure on the environment. Check with the Planning Department (at the local borough or district council offices). They will also be happy to provide free advice.
* Are you looking for some impartial advice on your building plans? The Building Centre in London at 26 Store Street, WC1 (and in Scotland at 3 Claremont Terrace, Glasgow G3) is just the place to go. They can put you wise about everything from the sort of bricks you might use to the best way to ventilate the chimney. They can also put you in touch with other people and other organizations for any information they don't have on hand at the centre. No charge is made. If you don't live near London or Glasgow, you can always telephone your query to the centre nearest you and it will only cost you the price of the phone call.
* While the various fuel suppliers will advise about heating systems (and probably each claim theirs is the best), you can

get impartial advice by writing to the Heating Centre, (The Institute of Domestic Heating Engineers), 77 New Bond Street, London W1Y 9DB. The centre does charge for this though, so check on this first.

CRIME PREVENTION

Free professional advice is available to every householder about how best to keep the burglars away.

* All police forces have a crime prevention officer who specializes in this field. Ring the station or call in personally and you will be able to arrange a time for the officer to call. He or she will go round your house and advise you how best to protect it and its contents. Usually there are leaflets they can leave with you too.
* Good neighbour schemes operate in some areas and as part of the scheme someone could check your house regularly if you're away from home. No charge would be made. Your local police station is the place to ask for details of any such scheme which may be in your area.

* Police can't physically protect your property if you're away from home – they just don't have the manpower to do it. However, if your house is to be empty for long periods, leave a note about this at your local station and if it's possible they will ask the local beat bobby to make a spot check now and then to see if all's safe and well. Again, no charge.
* If you need greater protection, then a private security firm should be contacted. They'll charge for their services of course.

ELECTRICITY AND GAS

Normally the electricity and gas supplies to our homes operate smoothly without our having to give them a second thought. Which seems to make it all the harder when things go wrong.

* If your electricity supply falters and you establish first that there's no general power cut in the area, and secondly that all your fuses are intact, then call your local electricity board to send someone out. In a rural area particularly, there can sometimes be a fault at the point where the overhead line brings the supply into your property. The service to mend a fault in the supply will be free, but if your domestic wiring is at fault, a charge will be made.
* Would you like to know how many units the toaster or the TV uses? Your local electricity board showroom will be able to tell you and also supply you with leaflets which detail the consumption of every sort of appliance from blenders to battery chargers. Leaflets on the running costs of gas appliances and central heating are also available at gas region showrooms.
* Is the electricity or gas meter whizzing round at an alarming rate? It could of course be because you are using power at an alarming rate! But if you think there might be something wrong with the meter itself, call your local electricity board or gas region and they will arrange to have it checked out. There may be a charge.
* When you move into a new house or leave your old one, the local electricity board and local gas region will send someone out to read the meter. No charge will be made.
* The moment you think there's a gas leak, turn off all

appliances and the meter, extinguish all cigarettes and naked flames, and open doors and windows. Don't turn any electric switches on or off. Then call your gas emergency number – it's in the directory under 'GAS' – who will send someone out as soon as they can. No charge for the first 30 minutes' work including parts up to the value of £1.

* Those who are elderly or handicapped and find difficulty operating domestic appliances using gas or electricity can get in touch with the gas regions or electricity boards in their area (look under 'Gas' and 'Electricity' in the telephone directory) and a home economist will visit them and advise about ways in which operation of the appliances might be made easier. No charge is made.

FIRE

When there's any fire about – whether it's straw burning in a nearby field which looks as though it might spread to houses or you set the chip pan alight – call the Fire Brigade by dialling 999. They will come out and deal with the fire, free of charge.

* If you have worries about how safe your house would be in the event of a fire – for instance if you have a property several storeys high with inadequate escape facilities – give your local Fire Prevention Office a ring and ask for advice. An officer will normally be pleased to help. If you have any worries about fire precautions, such as which type of extinguisher to buy and so on, again the local Fire Brigade will usually advise you. All extinguishers should comply with British Standard 4547 or be included in the 'List of Approved Portable Fire Extinguishing Appliances' published by the Fire Offices' Committee (such extingishers are marked to that effect).
* Emergencies in the home, such as young Timmy sticking his head in the garden railings or the cat getting stuck up a twenty foot tree, will also be dealt with by the Fire Brigade, probably free of charge. The policy does vary from one area to another. The brigade can, in fact, make a charge for any service other than putting out fires but most don't usually do where life and limb is threatened – for instance if a youngster gets his head jammed in railings. However, some brigades have been

known to refer cat-in-tree cases to the RSPCA if there's a local office and will only shin up a ladder at the RSPCA's request. You will be told in advance of any such charge.

IMPROVEMENT GRANTS

Local authorities can provide various grants to householders – for the improvement of the property in some way or another. The conditions attached to the grants can vary, according to its purpose, the authority's attitude and also government decisions. Some grants are given at the local authority's discretion while others are mandatory. For complete details always contact your local council offices. The following are the main grants currently available.

* Standard Amenities Grant: This one is mandatory and covers such things as the installation of a bathroom, kitchen sink and larder facilities.
* Improvement Grant: Discretionary. Given for improving existing houses or for converting existing houses or other buildings.
* Improvement Grants for Houses in Housing Action Areas: These are given in an area where the council has decided that some houses must be demolished and others need to be brought up to a specified standard.
* Repairs Grant: For houses requiring repairs which, if neglected, would threaten the future life of a house and the cost of which would cause the owner hardship.
* Insulation Grant: Where you have no insulation at all in the attic or round water pipes, the local authority will pay a proportion of the cost.
* Replacement of Lead Plumbing Grant: This is for replacing certain lead pipes which carry drinking water – sometimes only given if there is a high percentage of lead in the water – sometimes given automatically, depending on the council.
* Leaflets are available from all council offices giving details.

IN THE GARDEN

Most local authority offices will be more than willing to give you free advice on all sorts of gardening problems.

* They can advise you which varieties of flowers and shrubs are best suited to the local soil; how to cope with everything from greenfly to grubs; how to perk up your soil. The actual service varies from one authority to another and indeed even the department which gives it can vary. It could be the Parks Department, it could be the Leisure and Recreation Department or it could even come under Amenities, so check locally. You're likely to get the best services in urban areas, incidentally.
* Often there are what are called 'demonstration gardens', where local authority gardeners show you how to do all sorts of tasks from pruning roses to propagating pansies: all for free. Usually these demonstrations are held regularly throughout the year and are advertised in local papers.
* Other authorities have a number you can phone to get answers to your garden queries, and if you are very lucky, and your local authority has a special interest in gardening, you might even get someone coming along to your garden to advise you. Again, at no charge.
* Tree trouble? First port of call should be your local council. Many of them will help you identify pests which happen to be attacking your favourite beech (or any other type) and quite a number actually have arboricultural officers who will visit your garden and tell you whether trees are dangerous or not, whether they need pruning, and so on. And even those authorities which don't run to that, will at least be able to give you a list of local contractors who will prune or, if necessary, fell trees.

LAW

If you have any queries on how the law affects your family, your property, tenants rights or which benefits or social services are available, the local Citizens' Advice Bureau is the place to go for help. If they cannot provide the answer, they will certainly point you in the direction of someone who can. If there is no CAB near enough to your home for you to call in personally, you can telephone with your query. Citizens' Advice Bureaux offer free, confidential, impartial and independent advice and information on any subject. Your local library is another source of information. Facilities do vary, but many have at least a small reference section and the librarian will be able to tell you where to look for answers to your query.

PESTS

Since the 1981 Countryside Act came in it's been illegal to get rid of or block the access of bats.

* The law doesn't mean, though, that you are likely to be stuck with the bats for ever or until they decide to move on. What you do is contact your nearest branch of the Nature Conservancy Council. They will send someone along and, when they consider the time to be right, will move (not destroy) the furry creatures. You may have to wait some months, if it's the breeding season for instance. Look for the Council in your local phone book and if there doesn't seem to be a nearby branch, contact their headquarters at 19-20 Belgrave Square, London SW1. They do not make a charge.
* Woodworm and dry rot can literally leave you without a roof over your head! There's no free service available to get rid of these beetles or prevent them attacking your timbers in the future but you will be able to get a free quotation from professional firms who deal with this problem. And, since it is free, get as many estimates from different firms as you can. There can be a quite amazing difference between what one charges and another. Shop around and do choose one which gives you a twenty year guarantee. This can be useful, not just for your own peace of mind, but when you sell the house you can proudly display your certificate.

Rats and mice can often be dealt with by the householder but a positive plague of them can be hard to handle.

* Environmental health departments of local authorities are usually prepared to give you advice on how to get rid of pests and they may do it for you (but this is purely a matter for their discretion, you can't demand this service as a ratepayer). The attitude varies throughout the country and also according to how busy the department is when you call.
* Your other option is to pay for the professionals to do the job. The British Pest Control Association at Alembic House, 93

Albert Embankment, London SE1 will give you a list of local firms. Always ask for a quotation before you book them.

* Wasps' nests should be left to the experts, unless you have specialized knowledge yourself. Most local authorities do have facilities for dealing with wasps' nests but they are likely to make a charge for the work. Pest control firms will also deal with nests.
* Cockroaches, fleas and lice may not do any real damage to the fabric of a property but they can make life a misery. If DIY treatment doesn't seem to be having much effect, you'll find a sympathetic ear at your local council offices. Depending on where you live – you could get advice or someone to treat the problem, and often no charge will be made.
* Honey bees can often escape from hives and swarm all around somone else's house or garden; they may even like the idea of setting up home in it and build a nest. These are not strictly speaking pests, just a nuisance. If you find yourself in the middle of a swarm, don't start swatting, contact a local bee keeper. If you don't know any, then ask the police or the local authority who may keep a list of names for emergencies such as yours. No charge.

REFUSE

Local borough or district councils are responsible for the collection of rubbish. There's no direct charge for this regular service, it's paid for through the rates, is a statutory duty, but the local authority can, and often does, set down certain rules and conditions.

* Put out your rubbish in a cardboard box or a dustbin and you may find the binmen walk past it. Although the local authority agrees to pick up your empty tins and household leftovers they can insist that you put them in a particular type of container: it could be a bin, a bag or whatever. If they require you, for instance, to use paper or plastic sacks, they can decide how many free sacks each household is entitled to and that you must buy any extra you need.
* If someone else's rubbish is causing a genuine obstruction in front of your house, the police should be contacted.
* The authority can also dictate where you leave your rubbish for collection – i.e. at the front of the house, at the back, by the kerbside or whatever.
* Remote areas could have problems with rubbish, so bear this in mind before you move to the top of a mountain! Councils don't have a statutory duty to collect remote rubbish. However, if they prove stubborn on the point, contact the Secretary of State for Environment, he can require the local authority to provide a service.
* You could, in theory anyway, charge the local authority if they don't relieve you of refuse! Once they have agreed to collect it, they must do so regularly and you are perfectly entitled to charge them 25p for each day they don't collect it. The snag is that if they have a 'reasonable' excuse for failing in their duty to you, you've no claim! And only a court would decide on a definition of 'reasonable'. This doesn't apply in Scotland, incidentally.
* Any old bedsteads and suchlike – even your old cars – can be disposed of free of charge at local depots or 'tips', which local authorities have a duty to provide. Of course they don't have a duty to provide one near you, they will be located at a suitable site, and that might be many miles away. Your local Town Hall will give details of where such depots are.
* Alternatively, if facilities for 'medium size' household rub-

bish are few and far between, get together with a group of neighbours and ask your council if they could provide a skip in your area. Watch out, though: skips can bring a lot of mess and broken bottles and litter all over the place! Another point to bear in mind about skips is that, if you don't have space to put one inside your own boundaries, you will have to ask the local planning department for permission to site it on the pavement or roadway and it must be well lit at night.

* If someone parks their old banger near your house and the local vandals start stripping off the wheels and then the doors and then the kids start playing in it and you get angrier and angrier because it's proving such an eyesore, get in touch with your local environmental health department. They are usually quite sympathetic to the abandoned car problem and will probably try to find the owner of the car or remove it themselves.
* Getting a new fridge or washing machine or whatever is lovely but what do you do with the old one? In spite of the fact that some people seem to think the only thing you can do is dump them on the nearest bit of open countryside, there is a simple answer! Once again, your local environmental health department will come to the rescue. Almost all of them, wherever you live, will call and collect these larger household items but you may have to wait until the regular collection day in your area, so be patient. Usually this service is free, but it may vary and some authorities may make a small charge, especially if they have to make a special trip.
* Rubble can ruin your garden – you can't expect the refuse collectors to take it away and if you were simply to slip a shovelful of it at a time into your bin or bag it would probably take years to clear the stuff! There are two alternatives. Some local authorities (roughly half) will take it away for you free. The alternative is to hire a skip (see above).
* Many local councils have set up 'bottle banks' in car parks or near to large stores and all you have to do is pop in your empties. The bottle bank service is quite free to the public and in fact it can even help to plough money back into the community because the scheme is usually operated in conjunction with one of the large glass companies and they pay for the glass they get from the banks. Ring your district council to check whether there's one in your area.

TELEPHONE

* Repairing faults on your line is a free service from British Telecom. And if the fault isn't repaired two days after it has been reported, you can apply to the Customer Service division of your local telephone area for a pro rata rebate, which is standard procedure now.
* If you want to check up on how much you've spent on phone calls and the bill's not due for a bit you can have a special meter reading. Contact your local area telephone office and ask for it. There will be a charge for this service though, it's normally around £2.
* You can in fact rent a meter for an annual charge (check the current charge with your local Telecom office). However, it's claimed that there are possible line conditions which could interfere with the operation of your home based meter, so it won't necessarily compare exactly with the meter used to calculate your bill. But there shouldn't be huge discrepancies and it would certainly make a worthwhile comparison point if you feel your bills are always too high.
* If you are constantly getting calls for the local pub because the number's similar, you can get your number changed – at the price of a few pounds.
* When you move to a new house and a new phone number, there may still be some people trying to get in touch with you at your previous number. While the old number is covered by rental you have already paid, the operator will tell callers your new number for no charge. But that's likely to be a very limited time – after that you can arrange for an 'interception on a ceased line' service from British Telecom but you'll have to pay for it.
* Disabled subscribers can rent extra equipment to make phone calls easier. There's an amplifying handset with a volume control on the earpiece and a faint speech amplifier, so that people you call can hear you more clearly – rental charge is made for both.
* No-phone neighbours can't use yours when you're off on holiday and leave the keys of the house with them, if you arrange for a temporary cessation of service. There's a small charge for this service and you still have to pay rental during the period. Alternatively, you could buy a lock for your telephone.

WATER/DRAINAGE

* If you live in a rural area and rely on a cesspool or septic tank to provide a foul water service to your property, these receptacles will need to be emptied from time to time. Some local authorities offer a free emptying service, or may subsidise it, but others make a full charge for it. There are different rates of charge, for example, it could be according to whether you have it done on a once a year rota basis or call the local authority to make a special one-off trip out. If your local authority does not provide this service, then the other option is to have the tank emptied by a private firm – names will be found in the Yellow Pages.
* Those who live near a river bank may find themselves flooded out of their houses in severe weather conditions. There are several sources of help in such circumstances. The local authority may provide sandbags and help with building barriers, while the fire brigade and police are the people to deal with any rescue which may be required.

* For help on dealing with the aftermath of major flooding, see page 151.
* Blocked drains not only cause a nuisance, they could also be a health hazard. First call your local authority. In some areas they may be prepared to clear it for you without charge, but

they are entitled to make some charge if they are convinced that the blockage is in some way due to your neglect. You would, of course, only call the local authority in the case of underground, outside drains. If your sink is blocked or the bath water won't drain away and the plunger and poking-with-a-coathanger won't work, then look up the Yellow Pages and call either a drain clearing firm or your local plumber.

* For general advice on plumbing problems, contact the National Federation of Plumbers and Domestic Heating Engineers at Scottish Mutual House, North Street, Hornchurch, Essex.
* First find your drains if you want to do any repairs or clear blockages! If you don't know where they are, don't start digging, just consult your local council and ask them to help. They are required to keep plans of all buildings work including sewers and drainage systems – and indeed when a builder starts building a housing estate, he must have drainage plans passed by the local authority who will then keep a copy of those. Ask the Building Control department to show you the plans for your area and they will – unless your house was built pre-1936.

INDEX

A

B

C

D

E

F

G

H

I

J

K

L

M

Q

R

S

V

W

ACKNOWLEDGEMENTS

The publishers would like to thank the following individuals, organizations and Associations for their help:

Dr. Patricia Judd; M. E. McRae; Richard Wiles; Association of British Travel Agents; British Association of Removers; British Fur Trade Association; British Gas Corporation; British Telecom; Carpet Cleaners' Association; Consumers' Association; Council of British Ceramic Sanitaryware Manufacturers; Firth Carpets; Her Majesty's Customs and Excise; Department of Energy; Department of the Environment; Department of Health and Social Security; The Electricity Council; Greater London Council; Leather Manufacturers' Research Association; London Fire Brigade; Metropolitan Police; Ministry of Agriculture, Fisheries and Food; Passport Office; Royal Society for the Prevention of Cruelty to Animals; Timber Research and Development Association; Twyfords Bathrooms